AF482135

Theatrical Nation

Theatrical Nation

Jews and Other Outlandish Englishmen
in Georgian Britain

Michael Ragussis

PENN

UNIVERSITY OF PENNSYLVANIA PRESS

PHILADELPHIA

A volume in the Haney Foundation Series,
established in 1961 with the generous support
of Dr. John Louis Haney.

Published by
University of Pennsylvania Press
Philadelphia, Pennsylvania 19104-4112

Printed in the United States of America on acid-free paper
10 9 8 7 6 5 4 3 2 1

Library of Congress Cataloging-in-Publication Data
Ragussis, Michael.
Theatrical nation : Jews and other outlandish Englishmen in
Georgian Britain / Michael Ragussis.
    p. cm. — (Haney Foundation series)
Includes bibliographical references and index.
ISBN 978-0-8122-4220-1 (alk. paper)
    1. Theater—Great Britain—History—18th century. 2. English
drama—18th century—History and criticism. I. Title.
PN2593.R297 2010
792.0942'09033—dc22
                                                        2009029478

CONTENTS

NOTE ON PERFORMANCE HISTORIES

Brief performance histories that indicate the years in which plays were performed (at the patent theaters, unless otherwise noted) are typically given either in the body of the text or in the notes. These histories are based on, for the period through 1800, *The London Stage, 1600–1800: A Calendar of Plays, Entertainments and Afterpieces*, ed. W. Van Lennep, E. L. Avery, A. H. Scouten, G. W. Stone, and C. B. Hogan, 5 parts (Carbondale: Southern Illinois University Press, 1960–68), and for the period after 1800, Allardyce Nicoll, *A History of English Drama 1600–1900*, 6 vols. (Cambridge: Cambridge University Press, 1952–59), vols. IV (1800–1850) and V (1850–1900); *Victorian Plays: A Record of Significant Productions on the London Stage, 1837–1901*, compiled by Donald Mullin (Westport, Conn.: Greenwood Press, 1987); *Some Account of the English Stage from the Restoration in 1660 to 1830*, ed. John Genest, 10 vols. (1832; New York: Burt Franklin, 1965), vols. VII–X; and the calendar of plays printed regularly in the *Monthly Mirror* during the opening decades of the nineteenth century.

CHAPTER ONE

"Family Quarrels"

After the second Musick, some Jew Ladies and Gentlemen were
noticed in one of the Balconies, when the Cry immediately began,
No Jews, out with them, circumcise them, &c. &c. and was followed
with Showers of Apples, &c. with great Rudeness, till the Company
were obliged to leave their Seats.
  —*London Evening-Post*, December 1–4, 1753

Just before the overture began to be played, two Highland officers
came in. The mob in the upper gallery roared out, "No Scots! No
Scots! Out with them!," hissed and pelted them with apples. My
heart warmed to my countrymen, my Scotch blood boiled with
indignation. I jumped up on the benches, roared out, "Damn you,
you rascals!" . . . I hated the English; I wished from my soul that
the Union was broke and that we might give them another battle of
Bannockburn.
  —James Boswell, *London Journal, 1762–63*

PERFORMERS, PLAYWRIGHTS, AUDIENCES, theater reviewers, and the
public at large used the Georgian theater as a site of ethnic conflict and ethnic
reconciliation, making the theater the central cultural arena in which a battle
over national identity was waged. Exploring the complicated negotiations
that occurred between the theater and the culture at large, I ask why and how
ethnic identity was consistently theatricalized during this period, both on
stage and off. Concentrating on the crucial role the theater played in developing, maintaining, circulating, questioning, and subverting the ethnic stereo-

types through which the identity of the nation was defined and redefined, I draw upon a neglected corpus of popular dramatic texts and performances that focused on ethnic minorities, especially during the second half of the eighteenth century when issues of ethnic acculturation and national identity became urgent. Hence I begin by noting an especially ironic symptom of late Georgian culture, namely, the attempted ostracism of Jews and Scots from their place in the audience at the same historical moment when Jewish, Scottish, and other ethnic characters played a central role on the stage as staples of the theatrical repertoire. These cries for the ejection of ethnic minorities from the audience were an attempt to maintain them as purely theatrical, as a form of ethnic spectacle, used on the stage to locate and secure the boundary between Englishness and otherness. The same audience that saw these ethnic others presented in countless productions night after night protested their crossing the border of the stage.

The view of Georgian culture that I develop over the course of this book is based on the emergence of a cluster of significant theatrical phenomena that illuminate the central anxieties shared by the theater and the nation. Perhaps the most significant development of the Georgian stage was the multiplication of ethnic, colonial, and provincial character types: Jews, Scots, Irish, Welsh, West Indians, blacks, nabobs, and Yorkshiremen paraded on the London stage. These domestic and colonial others showcased London in particular and England in general as the center of an increasingly complex and culturally mixed nation and empire, and in this way functioned to explore the emerging and shifting identity of the recently invented Great Britain, inaugurated by the union of England and Scotland in 1707. These internal others presented an especially complex and subtle challenge to the issue of English national identity, especially since many of them were redefined and renamed as Britons in the course of the eighteenth century and sometimes even took the name of Englishman, sharing a single national identity with the English. For this reason the internal struggles over what constituted national identity during this period were seen as a series of family quarrels. In his letter "To the Printer" of the English newspaper the *Gazetteer and New Daily Advertiser* on January 15, 1766, Benjamin Franklin addressed the popular icon of England, John Bull: "Besides your rudeness to foreigners, you are far from being civil even to your own family. The Welch you have always despised for submitting to your government. . . . Why despise the Scotch, who fight and die for you all over the world? . . . Can it be discreet in you to kick up in your own house a *Family Quarrel?*"

This figure of the family quarrel was a powerful way of turning the national spotlight inward, on the kinds of internal divisions and conflicts suffered by the nation as family (as opposed, say, to external threats posed by Catholic France). In fact, a representative comedy of the period entitled *Family Quarrels*, first performed on December 18, 1802, to what several press accounts called overflowing audiences, and repeated at Covent Garden more than twenty times during the 1802–3 season, illustrates a number of the issues that lie at the heart of my project: the complex relationship between Englishness and domestic otherness, the role of the actor not simply as a general shape-changer but as an ethnic chameleon, and the role of both the audience and the press in aggressively responding to the representation of ethnic identity on the stage. The play has the kind of ethnically expansive cast of characters common at the time, even expanding before the spectator's eyes through the use of ethnic cross-dressing, while also employing a variety of dialects as markers of difference, one of the chief features of the representation of the other on the stage during this period. The cast includes a Yorkshireman, a West Indian lady, and her black maid, as well as a servant who disguises herself as a Gypsy and an actor who disguises himself as a Jew. The double use of ethnic cross-dressing signals the performance of ethnic identity as a highly significant cultural phenomenon in Georgian culture generally, realized (as I will show) in a variety of venues, including the professional stage, amateur theatricals, masquerades, and street theater.

Family Quarrels achieved a modicum of notoriety because of the vehement protests that the Jewish members of the audience made when Proteus, the protean actor cross-dressing as a Jew, sang an anti-Semitic song that disrespectfully characterized the Jewish women he has courted. The incident even became the subject of an 1806 engraving entitled *The Jew Beauties* (figure 1) that both pictured the actor John Fawcett as Proteus cowering in front of one of these "beauties" (who has learned to box from her brother) and reproduced the offending lyrics with their caricatured dialect. Such a print could manage to keep alive the controversy several years after the first production of the play and put the offensive lyrics in the hands of a wide public. The author, Thomas Dibdin, pleaded innocence mainly on the grounds of his having played as an actor and created as a playwright a number of benevolent Jews, while the press went on the attack in a way that illuminates the kind of public conflict that the theater often incited. For example, in the December 1802 issue of the *Monthly Mirror*, the aptly named "Dramatic Guardian" attempted to legitimize not only the stage's system of conventional ethnic and national marking but also the English audience's right to enjoy the satirical display of those features that underscored its own Englishness: "The *frivolity* of the Frenchman, the *effeminacy* of the Italian, the *beggarly pride* of the Spanish hidalgo, the proverbial *heaviness* of 'your swag-bellied Hollander,' the *blunders* of the Irishman, the *irascibility* of the Welch, and the *sycophancy* of the Scot, are all, in their turns, displayed in full force on the stage." The *Mirror*'s critic denigrated the protesters as "a parcel of *old cloathsmen* and *pedlars*" while upholding "the justice of an English assembly," as if the English audience were a formal legal body that would have interfered "if there had been any illiberal reflection on the Jews." This critic, pitting the English against the Jews (whom Dibdin called "the enemy" in his memoir),[1] concluded by issuing a warning, almost a threat, in which the English members of the audience represented no less than the nation: "Let them [the Jews] be careful how they proceed. It is dangerous to trifle with the English nation" (pp. 404–5). Other critics reacted in the same defensive posture against the Jewish protest, guarding the right of the London stage to caricature all those others that lived beyond the pale of London: "The natives of Yorkshire had as good right to remonstrate against the liberties taken with them. . . . If this degree of affected delicacy be justifiable, we ought soon to expect remonstrances from Scotland, Ireland, and every part of England."[2] So, not only did *Family Quarrels* use as its subject the kind of splintering of English national life that is reflected in its different ethnic, colonial, and provincial characters and dialects, it also stirred up a family quarrel that was played out first in the audience's reaction to the play and then in the press's response to the audience's reaction.

Focusing on the flood of domestic others that appeared on the London stage during the Georgian period, this book asks what kinds of ideological work such stage figures performed as well as what kinds of cultural forms were invented to accomplish this work. I concentrate on the most popular of these figures, the stage Jew, Scot, and Irishman. Insofar as such figures were caricatures, they functioned to establish the hegemony of England at that moment when the English were threatened by being diluted into Britons or, perhaps worse, diffused throughout the world in the colonies, with no geographic center, or with a center, the London metropolis, overrun by a mix of strangers who could claim to be British and even English—albeit "outlandish Englishmen," as we will see. But, while we might expect that such figures functioned on the stage solely as caricatures during this period, the theater in fact began aggressively to work toward rehabilitating a variety of minority populations, and minorities themselves made the theater a site of resistance

Figure 1: *The Jew Beauties. A Whimsical Song;—Sung by Mr. Fawcett, at Covent Garden Theatre*. Courtesy of the Library of the Jewish Theological Seminary.

by protesting plays that negatively represented them (as in the case of the Jewish protest against *Family Quarrels*). It is in this sense that I argue that the theater became quite literally a site of contestation between and among different ethnic and national groups.

From the vantage point of political history, the ethnic dimensions of the eighteenth century are framed and punctuated by the government's highly controversial attempts at merging and mixing different ethnic and national groups: the Act of Union with Scotland opened the century, the Act of Union with Ireland closed it, and the Jewish Naturalization Bill of 1753 (popularly known as the "Jew Bill") divided the century. It is within the purview of such events that a crisis of acculturation and assimilation occurred. The government's decision to fabricate through parliamentary legislation a new national identity, the (Scottish or Jewish or Irish) Briton, led to a variety of reactions. Sometimes these minorities attempted to reinvent themselves as Britons or even as Englishmen; sometimes these minorities chose to reject their new identity in favor of more local or regional identities; and sometimes these minorities were rejected by so-called true-born Englishmen, who disdained to be called Britons (alongside these ethnic others) instead of Englishmen.

Countless related historical events signal the strained and often tragic ethnic and nationalist conflicts of this period. As one scholar has noted, the Acts of Union were the sign of "an aggressive policy of an 'incorporating' rather than a 'federal' empire, . . . radiating authority from a controlling metropolitan center."[3] This meant that there were anti-Union riots in both Scotland and Ireland. The Jacobite rebellion of 1745 made the English suspicious of all Scots as crypto-Jacobites, and the slaughter of Highlanders at Culloden and after, followed by the legislation that disarmed Highlanders and forbade their wearing of the tartan and plaid (like the decades-old attempt to eradicate their language), were the signs of what various scholars have argued was "an end to Gaeldom" or even an attempt at genocide, "the formative experience of the English people" being centered on one goal, the "'Celts' forcibly or otherwise transformed."[4] Similarly, while there had been periodic riots against Irish harvest laborers in London, and "faction fights between English and Irish seem to have been common,"[5] it was the Irish Rebellion of 1798 that reinvented for the English the terror of "the wild Irish." In the Rebellion, "probably the most concentrated violence in Irish history," thirty thousand persons died, while the government's reaction altered the complexion of Ireland: "An entire generation of radical political leadership was removed from Ireland in the 1790s—by exile, hanging and transportation."[6]

Meanwhile, the public clamor against the Jewish Naturalization Bill (which sought to naturalize a small number of foreign-born Jews) forced its repeal in 1754, but not before a host of anti-Semitic speeches, pamphlets, and satirical prints led to the reemergence of a kind of medieval Judeophobia, stigmatizing and endangering the native Jewish population (with rumors that Jews would be massacred and burned).[7] Some years later, the Chelsea murder case, which ended in 1771 with the execution of four Jews, led to a popular outcry that endangered the entire Jewish population in England. According to one contemporary observer, "Every Jew was in public opinion implicated, and the prejudice, ill-will and brutal conduct this brought upon the Jews . . . did not cease for many years. . . . I have seen many Jews hooted, hunted, cuffed, pulled by the beard, spat upon, and so barbarously assaulted in the streets."[8] The *London Chronicle* reported that "a great number of Jews have left the kingdom" (December 3–5, 1771), while Horace Walpole quipped, "It is not so easy *to borrow a Jew*, now so many are hanged or run away."[9] More than half a century later in 1830, William Cobbett recollected with a kind of sadistic nostalgia, "For many years . . . we never used to see a Jew, in the country, without driving him away, with a cry of 'Chelsea' at his heels."[10]

Finally, one scholar has argued that during the virulent Scottophobia of the 1760s and 1770s the Scots were "marginally more unpopular than the Jews. To Englishmen of almost every rank the Scot was a contemptible creature."[11] The comparison between Jews and Scots in fact became popular during the Georgian period, and this Scottophobia, like the Judeophobia of the mid 1750s and after, showed that it did not require outright rebellion for intense hostilities to erupt between the English and these ethnic minorities. In the 1760s and 1770s, the popular opinion that the Scottish Lord Bute's power over the king was excessive led to a renewed hostility between the English and the Scots. Anti-Caledonian clubs were formed, and a host of satirical prints stigmatized both Bute and the German king himself, George III, as foreigners preying on the English nation. Bute was inaccurately but regularly shown as a Highlander, and he and a kind of Scottish mafia that many believed ran the government and subverted English values were typically represented as another Jacobite rebellion.

Events like those at Chelsea or Culloden regularly penetrated the permeable walls of the theater, and were used (sometimes decades after their occurrence) to frighten ethnic minorities and to inflame English audiences. In his warning to the Jews who protested against *Family Quarrels*, for example, the *Monthly Mirror*'s Dramatic Guardian invoked the "popular fury" (p. 405) directed at Jews three decades earlier after the Chelsea murder trial, while at Sadler's Wells a ballet called *Culloden* was performed nightly, celebrating the recent destruction of the Highlanders in the decisive battle of the 'Forty-Five rebellion.[12] The 1746 engraving *The Highlanders Medley, or The Duke Triumphant* (figure 2) records the theater's prominent participation in the celebration of the Duke of Cumberland's victory at Culloden by showing the text of "A Loyal Song . . . Sung by Mr. *Beard* at the *Theatre Royal* in *Covent-Garden*" that vilifies the Highlanders: "Regardless, whether wrong or right, / For Booty (not for Fame they fight). / Banditti-like, they storm they slay / They plunder rob and run away."[13] In fact, London theaters were commonly used as a site for staging and inflaming both Jacobite and Hanoverian sympathies.[14] Meanwhile, at the theater in Edinburgh in 1749 when members of the military called for the band to play the tune "Culloden," it "was regarded by the audience as ungenerously and insolently upbraiding the country with her misfortunes," and a riot ensued.[15] More generally, the kinds of tragic ethnic conflicts that mark this period contributed to an environment in which English audience members attempted to ostracize the ethnic minorities who sat beside them in London theaters, as the two epigraphs to this chapter show. I began with a quotation from the *London Evening-Post* in which Jewish members of the audience were verbally abused, while later in the century Richard Cumberland used the fictitious persona of Abraham Abrahams to complain of the way in which Jewish audience members were frequently treated: "I no sooner put my head into an obscure corner of the gallery, than some fellow or other roars out to his comrades—Smoke the Jew!—Smoke the cunning little Isaac!—Throw him over, says another, hand over the smoutch!—Out with Shylock, cries a third, out with the pound of man's flesh."[16] And my epigraph from Boswell makes clear that there were similar attempts to ostracize the Scots from the London theaters. The *Westminster Magazine* reported in December 1779 that English audience members at Covent Garden had turned "the whole force of their ridicule against the poor Scotchman, whose dialect and passion still furnished fresh fuel for the fire to roast him on; they so pestered and pelted him with ribaldry and clamorous invectives, that the poor fellow was forced to slink off" (p. 638). Such experiences at the theater brought to the surface ancient ethnic and national hostilities: notwithstanding all the ways in which Boswell attempted to anglicize himself, his trip to the theater in 1762 resurrected his Scottish ethnic pride and prodded him to call for the break up of the six-decade-old Union and a restaging of the Scots' victory at Bannockburn in 1314, suggesting the way in which ethnic

Figure 2: *The Highlanders Medley, or The Duke Triumphant*. Courtesy of the Library of Congress.

and national divisions of previous decades and even centuries could erupt in the present.

London audiences, then, could be divided and even combatively antagonized along ethnic lines, and of course audiences frequently imbibed such prejudices from the plays they watched. The name-calling that Abraham Abrahams endures, for example, descended directly from the theatrical repertoire, from *The Merchant of Venice* of course, but also from Richard Brinsley Sheridan's immensely popular comic opera of 1775, *The Duenna* (in which we find "the cunning little Isaac," an epithet that was used against Jews well into the nineteenth century).[17] A review of the second edition of Cumberland's *The Jew* in the *Monthly Review* in February 1795 explicitly confirmed Cumberland's observation on the malignant effect of anti-Semitic stage figures on the English nation: "This practice has so successfully rooted the illiberal and vulgar antipathy to the unfortunate descendents of Abraham, that few people perhaps now hear a Jew mentioned, without thinking of the *cruel Shylock*, or of *cunning little Isaac*" (p. 154). In the theater, then, the English sometimes turned on their fellow audience members by citing the same theatrical stereotypes that they had witnessed and applauded and that ethnic minorities had endured and eventually resisted.

Such episodes of ethnic conflict fly in the face of what was often the popular and quasi-official view of the theater as an arena of national unity and national reconciliation. Walter Scott, who sometimes functioned to publicize the success of the new Great Britain, summed up in 1826 the long-standing Georgian view of the theater as the great reconciler, the instrument of national unification:

> The entertainment, which is the subject of general enjoyment, is of a
> nature which tends to soften, if not to level, the distinction of ranks; it
> unites men of all conditions in those feelings of mirth or melancholy
> which belong to their common humanity, and are enhanced most
> by being shared by a multitude. The honest, hearty laugh, which
> circulates from box to gallery; the lofty sentiment, which is felt
> alike by the lord and the labourer; the sympathetic sorrow, which
> affects at once the marchioness and the milliner's apprentice;—all
> these have a conciliating and harmonizing effect, tending to make
> the various ranks pleased with themselves and with each other. The
> good-natured gaiety with which the higher orders see the fashionable
> follies which they practise treated with light satire for the amusement

of the middling and poorer classes, has not little effect in checking the rancorous feelings of envy which superior birth, wealth and station are apt enough to engender. The possessors of those obnoxious advantages are pardoned on account of the good humour and frankness with which they are worn; and a courtier, by laughing at the Beggar's Opera, like a bonny Scot applauding Sir Pertinax MacSycophant, disarms what he confronts.[18]

Scott's view makes the theater, free of riot, protest, or even disturbance, into a medium of reconciliation, almost a kind of state apparatus that minimizes class and ethnic conflict, a classic example of hegemonic control. Sir Richard Talbot made a similar claim in the December 1771 issue of *Oxford Magazine*: "As it was at Athens . . . the playhouse in London, is for all classes of the nation. The peer of the realm, the gentleman, the merchant, the citizen, the clergyman, the tradesman, and their wives, equally resort thither to take places, and the crowd is great" (p. 272). The claim stretches throughout the Georgian period. In 1830, Leigh Hunt reiterated the claim: "There high and low, rich and poor, one with another, smile at the same pleasure, and feel their eyes dimmed with the same sympathy."[19]

I read such comments as a popular cultural fiction that refused to acknowledge the kinds of ethnic and class divisions that in fact divided the nation, as if the theater were a safe refuge from such divisions. Even a recent scholar echoes the sentiments of Scott and Hunt—namely, that the theater was "one of the few urban arenas—perhaps the only one—where a variety of social orders heard and saw national virtues demonstrated, and could therefore learn together how to be English."[20] But I am arguing that learning how to be English often meant learning how to exclude Scots, Irish, and Jews. The examples of ethnic conflict among audience members that I have recorded begin to suggest the ways in which particular historical events and attitudes could bring audiences to the theater who were already ethnically divided and even hostile to one another, while in the course of this book I will explore the ways in which a significant body of plays and performances consistently, and sometimes deliberately, disrupted what Scott called the audience's "common humanity" and divided it along ethnic lines.

While most of Scott's examples focus on class reconciliation, and while theater historians (like cultural and social historians generally) have tended to view the Georgian period primarily in terms of class, Scott ends with an ethnic example that for him cuts close to the bone and for me takes us to the heart of my argument. Scott sentimentalizes (and defangs) his countryman as "the bonny Scot" who yields his applause to an extraordinarily scathing representation of Scottish identity. But Scott's example in fact defies the historical record. For decades Scottish members of the audience protested anti-Scottish characterizations such as Sir Pertinax Macsycophant in Charles Macklin's *The Man of the World* (1781), just as other ethnic minorities protested the theater's system of ethnic marking. Such a history of resistance needs as well to be placed alongside my examples of the ostracism of Jews and Scots from the English theater, so that we recognize that there was another kind of theatrical disruption, perhaps more surprising but increasingly common in the second half of the eighteenth century, in which ethnic minorities themselves caused the disturbance. Rather than being silently victimized, called to leave the theater, ethnic minorities began to reject the representations of themselves on the stage and protested what they saw. While it is well known that the Georgian theater was not infrequently the site of both small-scale disturbances and full-fledged riots,[21] there has been no study focused on the ways in which such disruptions revolved around ethnic conflict.

So, while the London theater functioned primarily as an institution that the English claimed for their own, it functioned also as a site of minority resistance, in which Scottish, Irish, and Jewish audience members protested, sometimes halting performances and even requiring playwrights to rewrite the script for the next performance. Contemporary reports record, for example, that in 1759, at the opening of Charles Macklin's *Love à la Mode*, "several Caledonians, imagining Sir Archy to have been meant as an unhandsome reflection on their nation, were very loud and turbulent during the representation, and did all in their power to cut short the run of the piece."[22] In 1767, the Irish members of the audience at George Colman the Elder's *The Oxonian in Town* threatened a riot, and half an hour of protest ensued despite the bills that had been circulated denying any anti-Irish sentiment, while on the following day the author published extracts from the play in the *Public Advertiser* in order to forestall another disturbance by Irishmen who believed their nation had been slandered.[23] In 1781 "some young Scotchmen thought [Macklin's *Man of the World*] a libel on their countrymen, and resisted it," and while the author set about to cut certain offensive passages, nonetheless "on the second night a handful of Scots in the gallery attempted to oppose it."[24] And in 1802, in the example with which I began, at the opening of *Family Quarrels* "a great disturbance arose . . . [at a remark about the Jews]. This remark threw the theatre into a flame. The *brethren* who composed a considerable part of the audience, evidently resent[ed] it as a reflection upon their whole body."[25]

Such episodes of ethnic conflict in the theater occurred at least in part because of the popular belief that managers, playwrights, and performers served at the pleasure of the audience, and that the audience was the final arbiter of all things theatrical, so it was no exaggeration to claim for the audience the role of adjudicator—representing, in the case of the disturbance at *Family Quarrels*, "the justice of an English assembly," as the *Mirror* put it. Scott's view in 1826 is a kind of summation of what had already become a truism about the function of the theater in Georgian culture: "A full audience, attending a first-rate piece, may be compared to a national convention, to which every order of the community, from the peers to the porters, send their representatives."[26] While Jürgen Habermas and others have argued that the public in general became established as a kind of "fourth estate" in the eighteenth century,[27] it was the broadly representative nature of theater audiences, and the power they exerted over managers, playwrights, and performers, that led many contemporary observers to reserve the term "fourth estate" specifically for the theater audience. At first the idea functioned as a witty figure of speech: "Noble, Gentle, or Simple, who fill the Boxes, Pit, and Galleries, . . . as K—g, L—rds, and COMMONS . . . make that great Body the Nation"; or, "Kings, Lords, and Commons, o'er the nation sit; / Pit, Box, and Gallery, rule the realms of wit."[28] The playwright Arthur Murphy, in his biography of David Garrick, further embroidered upon the idea—"the theatre engrossed the minds of men to such a degree, that it may now be said, that there existed in England a *fourth estate*, King, Lords, and Commons, and *Drury-Lane play-house*"[29]—until eventually it became a kind of truism, so that Maria Edgeworth repeated the well-known view in 1817 in *Harrington*, set during the period of the "Jew Bill."[30]

The Georgian view of the theater as a powerful fourth estate helps explain why many were so deeply invested in defining and controlling the theater itself as well as its popular and ideologically potent image as a national institution. Over the course of this book I attempt to show how the theater mirrored and reproduced the nation as a contested space, illuminating the ways in which performers, playwrights, audience members, journalists, and the public at large, motivated by competing ethnic and nationalist claims, sought to win control of the theater, and by extension, of the nation. The disagreement over the nature of the theater during this period is of such critical importance because it was essentially an argument about the nation itself. Representations of the Georgian theater functioned ideologically as a sign either of a united Great Britain, diverse but unified, or of an ethnically mixed, destabilized, and internally divided nation. John Tomlinson has claimed that "there is a 'lived reality' of national identity, but it is a reality lived in representations—not in direct communal solidarity."[31] My book is based on the twin ideas that, first, the theater had a special advantage over other forms of representation in that it provided unusually vivid (visual and aural) representations of ethnic and national identities, and second, the theater did in fact constitute a live, direct, communal environment (whether of solidarity or division) in which the community publicly inspected and responded to these representations and to one another. Peter Stallybrass and Allon White have claimed that "the history of political struggle has been the history of the attempts made to control significant sites of assembly and spaces of discourse" (such as the theater) and have complained that scholars have frequently "'dematerialize[d]'" such sites by representing them "in terms of class ideas and ideals sundered from the matrix of places, times, and habits which informed them."[32] My own attempt to return to the Georgian theater hopes to illuminate it as a specific, living site in which the public frequently felt that it experienced directly its own participation in the nation, whether divided or unified, making the theater an unusually vital testing ground for questions of national unity and ethnic division.

It is in this light that I understand the frequent contemporary remarks about Jews in the audience at the theater. When Georgian observers wanted to underscore how motley the London theater audience had become, they repeatedly recorded the increased number of Jews. The theater became par excellence the place where one could find "Dukes, Duchesses and Countesses mixt with sallow Jews and the Gentry of *Wapping* and *Rag Fair*."[33] In David Garrick's interlude *The Farmer's Return from London* (1762), the farmer reports to his family on all the sights he has seen in the metropolis, chief among them his visit to the theater: "Strange jumble together—*Turks, Christians,* and *Jews*! / At the temple of folly, all crowd to the pews."[34] The side-boxes, usually reserved for the more fashionable Londoners, had become a bewildering mix of people: "what delightful Rows! / Peers, Poets, Nabobs, Jews, and 'Prentice-Beaux."[35] Again and again, Jews in particular were noticed as members of the audience: "The Number of Jews at the Theatre is incredible," recorded the *Public Advertiser* on October 30, 1775; Horace Walpole noted at the opening of the Theatre Royal on June 19, 1789, "Our Jews and Gentiles throng it";[36] and in 1820 William Hazlitt reported for the *London Magazine* that on his trip to the minor theaters he was disappointed to find the audience composed of "Jew-boys, pickpockets, prostitutes, and mountebanks."[37] Even in cities outside London the number of Jews, especially at the theater, was noted, so that in Brighton in 1819, one observer noted, "Hook Noses, Mosaical Whiskers, and the whole tribe of Benjamin occupy every shop, every donkey-cart, and every seat in Box, Pit, and Gallery."[38]

Moreover, representations of Jews at the theater typically confirm my understanding of the theater as a site of division, antagonism, and contestation. At performances of *Family Quarrels*, for example, while Jews protested the anti-Semitic song, "The Christians . . . , bursting with laughter at its jokes, roared vociferously for its delivery, that they might enjoy the torture of the Jews."[39] An 1803 etching by Thomas Rowlandson entitled *Family Quarrels or The Jew & the Gentile* (figure 3) shows a singing competition between Jew and Gentile, with grotesquely caricatured Jews encouraging the Jewish singer ("Mine Cod, How he Shing"), while the English (non-Jewish) public cheer on the Gentile—a revision of Dibdin's *Family Quarrels* that displaces its actual content in order to focus on the audience's well-publicized and noteworthy partisan split between Jew and Gentile. In this way the etching restages the play and the notion of family quarrels by inventing a scene that did not occur in the play itself in order to focus on the kinds of divisions that marked the theater and the nation, notwithstanding the playwright's excuses that he intended no offense. This kind of partisan division was in fact the environment at the theater that observers recorded frequently. James Boaden, the playwright and journalist, recalled that "the bill at Covent Garden . . . for [the popular Jewish singer and actor] Leoni's benefit operated as an epistle to the Hebrews, and they crowded to assist a singer whom they so justly admired,"[40] while in 1830 at Covent Garden Thomas Wade's *The Jew of Aragon; or, The Hebrew Queen* was "literally howled from the stage on account of the particularity shown to the Jews."[41] Similarly demonstrating the partisan motivations of audiences, Jews boycotted the theater for the remainder of the season after the revival of Christopher Marlowe's *The Jew of Malta* in 1818.[42] The power that a Jewish audience could exert was in fact resented, as is clear in Robert Southey's account, through the persona of a Spaniard visiting England, of a similar event: "A farce was brought forward . . . called the Jew Boy; and the fraternity . . . assembled in great numbers, and actually damned the piece. This single fact is sufficient to prove that the liberty which they enjoy is unbounded."[43]

With London audience members partisan and even hostile in ethnically

Figure 3: *Family Quarrels or The Jew & the Gentile*. Courtesy of the Library of the Jewish Theological Seminary.

motivated reactions to each other, to plays, to playwrights, and to performers, an acute sensitivity to the ethnic makeup of audiences developed. Richard Cumberland recalls that at the premiere of his comedy *The West Indian* in 1771, "the gentlemen, who came under that description, went down to the theatre in great strength, very naturally disposed to chastise the author for his malignity," and that while David Garrick worried at noticing "the pit . . . more hostile than he had ever seen it" and "the tumult . . . excessive," the West Indian audience members soon realized the play was friendly to them.[44] In this light some plays were not performed in certain locales, while some were revised to have certain effects on particular ethnic groups in the audience or to serve certain nationalist goals. In the former case, Elizabeth Inchbald reported, "The tragedy of 'Oroonoko' is never acted in Liverpool, for the very reason why it ought to be acted there oftener than at any other place—The merchants of that great city acquire their riches by the slave trade."[45] In the latter case, while managers feared the incendiary potential of performing *The Merchant of Venice* during the "Jew Bill" debate, audiences deliberately requested the play—"Ye Naturalizing Bill having made some

Noise against the Jews, some people call'd out for ye Merchant of Venice, & a Letter was thrown upon ye Stage desiring that play"[46]—in order to embarrass and stigmatize their Jewish neighbors. Meanwhile the *London Evening-Post* feared the managers would remain neutral in the debate "in not obliging the Town with the *Merchant of Venice*" (September 11–13, 1753). A related but different reaction by the London playhouses occurred later in the century, when "patriotism was rampant" and productions of *The Merchant of Venice* omitted Portia's caricatures of the English and Scottish suitors (while only a few years earlier the theater had consistently skewered the Scots).[47]

Similar textual revisions, based in ethnically and nationally charged motives, occurred throughout the period. On January 20, 1794, the *Public Advertiser* reported that, at one of the many private theatricals that occurred at the time, Macklin's *Love à La Mode* (more than three decades after its first performance in 1759) carried a new, interpolated speech in which the English heroine reneges on her agreement to marry the Irish suitor by calling into question the motives of the Irish author: "Droll! to make him [Sir Callaghan] the hero of the piece! / But Romans Rome, and Grecians favour'd Greece: / Just so our Author; for the cunning elf / Was Dublin born—an Irishman himself: Who, by one stroke, his Countrymen would prove / Pure patterns of disinterested love." The heroine's new speech, after mocking Jews, Irishmen, and Scotsmen, goes on to take an increasingly popular position at the end of the century that all Britons were equal ("England, Ireland, Scotland, all are one"), castigating "the poison of false prejudice" at the same time that she rewrites the conclusion of the play from a clearly Anglocentric point of view, justifying her choice of an English husband: "Yet may not Charlotte, prejudice apart, / Be partial to an honest English heart?" In this way private individuals and groups could intervene beyond the walls of the theater to suit their own ethnically based ideological needs by critiquing and even revising what they saw in the theater.

The contradictory note that this interpolated speech sounds—on the one hand, unified in its acceptance of all Britons as equal, and on the other hand, divided along ethnic lines in its demeaning caricatures of Jews, Scots, and Irish—was in fact a dilemma the theater shared with the nation during the Georgian period. In fact, this prologue's contradictory view takes its cue from the original play itself. Already in 1759 Macklin has the heroine's guardian announce the Enlightenment lesson of tolerance at the beginning of the play when he restrains her skewering of the Scots suitor, "But we must not look upon his spleen and ill nature, my dear, as a national, but a personal vice,"[48] while the play goes on to caricature mercilessly its Scottish and Jewish characters even as it rehabilitates the character of its Irishman. So, while arguments against ethnic and national prejudice became almost a truism throughout the culture, they typically pointed not to a unified Enlightenment sensibility of tolerance, but to a divided consciousness that in fact recited the well-known text against prejudice even while indulging in it. For example, during the Gordon riots Horace Walpole exploded with ire at the role of the "monster," "the arch-incendiary," Lord George Gordon, by stigmatizing the Scots in general—"what a nation is Scotland, in every reign engendering traitors to the state"—and then half apologized on these grounds: "national prejudices I know are very vulgar—but if there are national characteristics, can one but dislike the soil and climates that concur to produce them?"[49] A similar contradiction underpinned the *Letters of Junius*, which began appearing in the *Public Advertiser* in 1768, were reproduced in other newspapers at the time, and were finally collected in book form in 1772, in which the preface claimed: "National reflections, I confess, are not justified in theory, nor upon any general principles. To know how well they are deserved, and how justly they have been applied, we must have the evidence of facts before us. We must be conversant with the *Scots* in private life, and observe their principles of acting to *us*."[50] So, both Walpole and Junius discover their loopholes: Walpole's use of the popular idea of "national characteristics" allowed his "national prejudices," while Junius argued that the Scots could be seen as an exception based on hard facts and on history.

In the theater, some playwrights built such sentiments into their plays— "National prejudices are as false as they are illiberal," one character lectures in John Tobin's *The Faro Table* (1816)[51]—while playwrights generally were quick to deny such prejudices when their works were condemned on those grounds. George Colman the Elder, for example, published an "Advertisement" in *The Oxonian in Town* that claimed, "So far from intending to cast an illiberal reflection on the Irish nation, it was evidently his main design to vindicate the gentlemen of that country from the reproach deservedly incurred by worthless adventurers and outcasts." Or, as an Irish student down from Oxford claims in criticizing a lower-class Irishman in the play itself, "National reflections are always mean and scandalous: but it is owing to such men as these that so much undeserved scandal has been thrown on our country."[52] Similarly, when Macklin's *Man of the World* was charged with anti-Scottish prejudice, he argued that his play in fact attempted "to explode the reciprocal national Prejudices that equally soured & disgraced the Minds both of English & Scotch Men."[53] And Richard Brinsley Sheridan took the "opportunity of justifying [him]self from the charge of intending any national reflection in the character of Sir *Lucius O'Trigger*" in *The Rivals* (1775).[54] So the banner against "the poison of false prejudice" was flown high, even in the midst of the most acid attacks on ethnic and national identities.

The press, having expanded with extraordinary rapidity during the eighteenth century, increasingly covered the theater and typically refereed (even while contributing to) the kinds of ethnic conflicts that occurred in the theater, through both its regular journalists and its letters from readers. In the period 1775–1800, London had at one time or another nearly sixty different newspapers, and "almost every one . . . repeatedly filled their columns with news of the theatres," testimony to the extraordinary popularity and importance of theatrical culture in Georgian England. From the 1750s on, newspapers and magazines started to run regular features on the theater, such as "The Theatre," "The Theatrical Register; or Weekly Rosciad," "The British Theatre," "A Companion to the Playhouse," "Dramatic Strictures," "Theatrical Critiques," "The Stage," and "The Playhouse Spy," while a number of periodicals were devoted almost entirely to theatrical news and analysis, so that news items about the theater—its repertoire, its performers, its successes, failures, and disturbances—were available to an extraordinarily wide public, who in turn used the press to comment on the theater (as did playwrights, as I have already suggested).[55] An ongoing topic in the press was the popularly debated role of ethnic figures on the stage. So, while the Dramatic Guardian of the *Monthly Mirror* upheld the right of the theater to display and caricature ethnic and national others (as we have seen), in April 1782 the *Westminster Magazine* ran an article, "On National Reflections," which deplored the fact that the nation "should still continue to indulge a propensity towards National Reflections," complaining that "the Scotch have long been and still are a standing jest to many in this metropolis." Such articles typically cited the theater as the central barometer of national prejudices: "I need not mention the Irish.—We are a little more cautious now with regard to them in our Dramatic Entertainments and bedaub their characters with flattery as disgusting to men of sense as their former paintings were caricatured beyond belief or probability" (p. 188). And three years later, in September 1785, the *Westminster Magazine* contained a letter from a reader, entitled "On National Prejudices," that claimed, "The galleries are sick of broad Scotchmen, blundering Irishmen, and broken tongued Frenchmen." This was of course an arguable point, but perhaps necessary to the author's attempt to unhinge the nation from its unusually strong attachment to prejudice: "National Prejudices are, perhaps, more strongly fixed in Great Britain than in any other country." The letter goes on to decry such stereotypes—"A Scotchman, hungry, full of absolute monarchy, and the itch. An Irishman, six feet in height, and a fortune hunter"—in an attempt to demystify the nature of stereotyping: "Heaven forbid that the sins of a whole nation should be laid upon the back of an individual" (pp. 491–92). Such examples suggest how the press was used to debate the legitimacy of caricaturing ethnic minorities on the stage, an issue that dominated the theater during the second half of the eighteenth century.

One of the ways in which periodicals participated in debates over the theater, in addition to printing critical essays, reviews, and letters from readers, was by reproducing translations of the major European theorists of the theater. Friedrich Schiller's essay on the benefits of a national theater, for example, appeared in translation in the *Monthly Mirror* in January 1800, in what must have been an attempt at considering whether such a national theater did or could exist in Britain. In its attack on prejudice, and in its call for the unification of the nation through tolerance, Schiller's essay represented what hardly was the reality of the theater in Britain at the time. According to "What Are the Particular Effects of the Stage?"—as Schiller entitles his essay—"Toleration and humanity" are the touchstones of a national theater, which functions to "correct the opinions of the nation" and to liberate it from "the chains of prejudice and opinion." Schiller used as his prime example Gotthold Lessing's *Nathan the Wise* (1779), a play that was imported in translation into Georgian England on more than one occasion specifically to counteract the popularity of *The Merchant of Venice*: "How general is the toleration of religions and sects become within a few years! Nathan, the Jew, and the Saracen, Saladin, have already put us to the blush." Anticipating the arguments that were espoused by Scott and Hunt, Schiller argued that the power of the theater as a national project lies in its ability to unite the nation: "It is in the power of the stage alone to produce this conformity in a high degree . . . because she alone unites in herself all classes and conditions, and possesses the directest way to the head and heart" (pp. 44–45).

Toward the end of the century the London stage did in fact begin to work toward Schiller's goal in a play like Richard Cumberland's *The Jew* (1794), which was directly compared to *Nathan the Wise* and sincerely (if not entirely successfully) attempted to fight anti-Semitism. And there were apologists for the Georgian stage who argued that it had become an important moral teacher, it had become an organ of public instruction almost as great as the pulpit, it had helped stopped the slave trade, and so on.[56] But given that Schiller's essay appeared in the same journal that was to publish only two years later an aggressive defense of the English theater's caricatures of ethnic and national others in a response to *Family Quarrels*, one must ask whether a national theater in Britain meant an English theater that represented English interests (and caricatured and antagonized its Irish, Scottish, and Jewish neighbors), or a British theater that undertook to fight ethnic prejudice in the name of all Britons. In the course of this book I will show how the theater moved in the direction of recuperating the representation of ethnic minorities even as its stereotypes were reinvented and recycled.

I now wish to explain in some detail the ways in which my double focus on theater and nation attempts to supplement, complicate, and reorient the focus of a wide range of scholarship on eighteenth- and early nineteenth-century Britain. First, while recognizing the usefulness and importance of those studies in the 1970s and 1980s that identified the general theatricality of eighteenth-century culture, my project focuses on a return to the actual theater—its repertoire, playwrights, performers, audiences, and reviewers— and on a recognition of the central importance of ethnic identity in the theatricality of Georgian culture, a topic neglected even by recent theater historians. Second, while recognizing an important debate among historians about national identity in Britain, I turn to popular culture as an unusually rich arena for the analysis of ethnic and national identity. By opening up what amounts to an entire archive of immensely popular but critically neglected plays and performances, and by understanding how they worked in tandem with other forms of popular culture (such as graphic prints, joke books, song collections, as well as the popular press of the day), I explore how and why the most popular ethnic representations in Georgian England were invented and disseminated. Such an exploration allows me, for example, to reinsert the figure of the Jew into the culture at large and into debates over national identity in particular, and to identify the consistently comparative nature with which ethnic identity was represented during the period, features of Georgian culture that have typically been neglected in recent literary and historical studies.

But in order to understand more fully how issues of ethnic difference impacted the London theater and the life of the nation generally, it is necessary to explain one additional prominent feature of the period—namely, the unprecedented demographic changes that took place in the metropolis, the nation, and the empire. Many historians have recorded the immense growth of London's population during this period. Hugh Kearney has called "the continued growth of London" to nearly one million by 1800 "the most remarkable example of social change in eighteenth-century England."[57] And it is an influx of ethnic minorities into London (and other major cities) during this period that is consistently noted, among Georgian observers as well as modern scholars. What has been commonly characterized as the general social mobility of this period was fueled, at least in part, by the frequently massive geographic mobility of ethnic minorities. The population of London almost doubled during the period 1650–1750, "with a steady stream of young Scots, Welsh, Irish."[58] London needed a large supply of immigrant workers, and a contemporary observer in 1757 estimated that "two-thirds of the grown persons at any time in London come from distant parts"; the capital was viewed as overflowing with the Irish in particular.[59] In addition, West Indian planters sent their children in large numbers to be educated in England, as did many of the wealthier Scots and Irish,[60] so the poorer classes as well as the privileged among ethnic minorities found their way to England and especially to London. These migrations were satirized in prints such as Richard Newton's *Progress of an Irishman* (1794) and *Progress of a Scotsman* (1794); the former shows an Irishman progressing from eating a potato for breakfast to entering the army (but in the end dying by "giv[ing] a Challenge while in liquor to a Brother Officer"), while the latter shows in fifteen cartoons the rise of a Scotsman who goes from being a vagrant to becoming a member of the House of Lords, and both the Irishman and Scotsman are pictured as fortune hunters, marrying rich widows. An especially large number of prints represented the exploitative ambition of the Scot, such as *The Caledonian voyage to Money-land* (1762) and *The Caledonians arrival, in Money-land* (1762).[61] In the 1761 etching *We are all a comeing or Scotch Coal for ever* (figure 4), a road sign points the way from Edinburgh to London for what looks like a veritable invasion, with coaches and carts filled with Scots expressing their expectations of becoming admirals and bishops in "the land of Plenty, that flows with Milk & Brimstone" (the latter being a cure for the so-called Scotch itch).

The magistrate John Fielding (half brother to the novelist Henry) worked to stop "the importation" of Jewish and Irish immigrants (in what became a common coupling), claiming in 1771 (in a letter to the secretary of state) that "there are certainly a much greater number of both Jews and Irish at present in England than can possibly gain a livelihood by honest means."[62] Historians have estimated that the Jewish population increased by more than

Figure 4: *We are all a comeing or Scotch Coal for ever.* Courtesy of the Library of Congress.

2,500 percent between 1700 and 1830, with a steady stream of poor Jews from Poland, Holland, and the German states, so that the Lord Mayor offered free passage to poor Jews who wished to return to their native lands.[63] Fielding also worried about the consequences of the many West Indian merchants and planters bringing their black slaves to London, and schemes were hatched to transport them to Africa.[64] Kearney concludes that during the eighteenth and nineteenth centuries "the major cities of the British isles became multi-ethnic societies in which varied ethnic groups competed for economic security, social status and political influence."[65] Finally, Paul Langford, noting that one observer in 1787 thought there were as many Scots and Irish as English inhabitants in London, has argued that during this period "national prejudice was strengthened by the sensitivity of London opinion to the sheer numbers of newcomers."[66]

In addition to the movement to England and especially to London from the peripheries and the colonies, there was a vast movement of ethnic minorities to America in what has been termed a "British diaspora." When the Irish and Scottish who poured into London could find no employment, they entered the military or went to the colonies, so that "70 per cent of all British settlers who arrived in America between 1700 and 1780 were from Ireland

and Scotland."[67] Historians have shown how, for both the Irish and the Scots, emigration to America was a way of continuing in the new world a kind of ethnic and cultural solidarity (including projects to preserve Gaelic-speaking communities) that was increasingly more difficult to maintain at home.[68] It is no surprise, then, that in his articles for English newspapers in the mid-1760s Benjamin Franklin remarked on the way in which the English typically viewed America as an ethnic dumping ground, with its *"mixed rabble of Scotch, Irish and foreign vagabonds."* These movements of ethnic and colonial populations contributed to what I have called a crisis of acculturation and national identity, because as borders were crossed and recrossed and even remapped during this period, who was English or even British became fluid and periodically shifted. So, Franklin complained that the English viewed the American colonists "as unworthy the name of Englishmen," as if they were *"Englishmen by fiction of law only,"*[69] just as the Scots or Irish or Jews were seen as reinvented by the fiction of those laws that attempted to incorporate or naturalize them as Britons.

The newly multiethnic nature of English cities, and the vast movement of ethnic populations, was the news of the day. The press recorded and disseminated the way in which a parade of ethnic, colonial, and provincial populations was occurring on the streets of major English cities, providing for the reader the kind of multiethnic spectacle that London theater audiences saw. For example, in a fairly typical week or so of the *Public Advertiser* in 1787, readers learned about (1) the multiplication of black beggars in London (and such potential solutions as putting them to hard labor, jailing them, and sending them into exile), (2) the diverse nature of the city of Bath, characterized as a mixed throng of "rich Nabobs," "broad-shouldered Irishmen," and "Jews and Gentiles," and (3) the historic mass emigration of Highlanders, "some thousands of whom are quite impatient to quit their native country, and embark for the desarts [*sic*] of North America."[70] In this way the *Public Advertiser* made readers see, in their mind's eye, the kinds of migrations I have been recording. The vast movement of ethnic immigrants and colonials to London and other major English cities, as well as beyond the boundaries of England, was reported on regularly and certainly became the most visible sign of a literal destabilization of the capital, the nation, and the empire at large.

The theater grew in direct response to the expanding city and nation. J. H. Plumb has recorded "the ever expanding passion for the theatre" in the course of the eighteenth century. Audience capacity almost doubled between 1732 and 1762 (reaching 22,182 a week at Drury Lane and Covent Garden, while in 1792 the new Drury Lane had a capacity of 3,611), the number of new plays written doubled between the first half of the century and the second, and "every town of any pretension had a well-built theatre, a regular company and often enjoyed the visits of the best London companies during the summer," so that "by 1770 England was better equipped with theatres than it is today" to meet a new demand: "the eighteenth century unleashed a great and rapid expansion of the audience."[71] Other scholars have remarked that "in 1788 the boom in theatre building started and by 1805 there were 279 theatres or recognized places of theater entertainment,"[72] giving the lie to what has been for many years an unproved commonplace—namely, that the rise of the novel spelled the death of the theater in the middle of the eighteenth century.[73]

I emphasize the vast growth of London's population, with its influx of ethnic minorities, and the reciprocal growth of London's theater audiences, not only to emphasize the newly competitive and even conflicted multiethnic nature of the city and the destabilized identities of its inhabitants but also more specifically to correct what I see as an important oversight in Richard Sennett's influential study of the eighteenth-century metropolis, *The Fall of Public Man* (1974). Sennett's major insight made a crucial link between the urban experience and the theater: "The theater shares a problem not with society in general, but with a peculiar kind of society—the great city. The problem is one of *audience*—specifically how to arouse belief in one's appearance among a milieu of strangers." But while Sennett characterized the theater as "open to a wide public," and life in the city as embracing "a relatively wide diversity of people," his narrow focus on "the bourgeois class, whose experiences will be our main concern," deliberately eschewed ethnicity. He incorrectly claimed that for eighteenth-century Londoners "the city of strangers they knew was not divisible into ethnic, economic, or racial types (save the London Irish)."[74] In the course of this book I explore the ways in which ethnic minorities stood out and were recognized in London, and I argue that even if some ethnic outsiders were not recognizable, either because they had so fully been assimilated or because they had disguised themselves in an attempt to pass as English, the stage deliberately developed both a system of ethnic marking to differentiate them from the English and a set of dramatic plots to expose their attempts at passing as English. In this way the theater defined them as outsiders even as it made them recognizable and familiar.

Sennett's book is part of an important body of scholarship from varying fields (sociology, history, literature) that established the broad theatrical nature of eighteenth-century culture. David Marshall's *The Figure of Theater: Shaftesbury, Defoe, Adam Smith and George Eliot* (1986) astutely recognized Adam Smith's view of the specular and the performative as foundations of eighteenth-century culture. Jean-Christophe Agnew's *Worlds Apart: The Market and the Theater in Anglo-American Thought, 1550–1750* (1986) comprehensively drew on what had become by the mid-1980s an illustrious genealogy, the highpoints being the seminal work of Sennett (on the theatricality of urban life) and E. P. Thompson (on the class politics of theatricality) as well as the work of Marshall (on the theatricality of the novel and other discursive forms). What emerged from such scholarly work was what Agnew characterized as "the eighteenth-century revival of the theatrical perspective in Britain," "perhaps best understood as a direct response to the overt theatricalization of social relations."[75] Typically scholars saw these social relations as organized around class relations, as in Thompson's extremely influential intervention in which he deliberately went beyond Sennett's narrow grounding of urban theatricality in the rise of the bourgeoisie: "Rulers and crowd . . . performed theater and countertheater to each other's auditorium."[76] Nonetheless, while illuminating the formalized codes and public spectacles by which different classes interacted in the eighteenth century, this useful body of scholarship had for many years the unexpected effect of deflecting attention away from the theater itself. Employing the theater as metaphor or figure (as Marshall's title makes clear), such studies rarely (if ever) took us inside the theater, and their restricted focus on class obscured the powerful ethnic conflicts that typified the theater in particular and the culture at large.

Recent interest in the issues of gender, race, and empire, under the impetus of feminist and postcolonial studies, has yielded a new and productive focus on late Georgian theater. Black stage characters, for example, have received attention in Jeffrey Cox's excellent introduction to his pioneering anthology of plays that feature black characters as well as in Felicity Nussbaum's and Virginia Mason Vaughan's fine studies of blackface on the eighteenth-century stage. These critics have worked toward what is becoming an increasingly nuanced view of race in the eighteenth century, epitomized in Roxann Wheeler's exploration of the various discourses of race that emerged, collaborated, and competed in the eighteenth century. Emphasizing Britain's imperial identity, with an eye toward romanticism's view of the East (or romantic orientalism), excellent recent studies by Betsy Bolton and Daniel O'Quinn have explored the ways in which race, gender, and class functioned theatrically in the last decades of the eighteenth century.[77] These studies are indebted to Julie Carlson's useful challenge to the "resistance by scholars to a theatricalized romanticism," and perhaps most importantly to *The Theatres of War: Performance, Politics, and Society, 1793–1815* (1995), Gillian Russell's groundbreaking study that reoriented Georgian theater history by proposing "the playhouse as a site for the articulation of social and political tensions." Russell argued for the complex intersection of theater and military culture during the Revolutionary and Napoleonic wars, analyzing not simply the stage but also the audience, as well as street theater, amateur theatricals, and provincial theaters.[78] Finally, Bolton, O'Quinn, Russell, and others have decried the continuing neglect of the theater (especially in romantic scholarship) and the naïve scholarly commonplace that Georgian theater was apolitical.[79]

Nonetheless, the topic of ethnic stage figures has remained remarkably neglected. A group of early descriptive and bibliographical book-length studies that usefully catalogued the hundreds of plays in which Jews, Scots, and Irishmen appeared curiously has not been followed up by richly analytical studies, and there is no study that tries to understand how such figures intersected, either with one another or with the host of other ethnic, colonial, and provincial figures that appeared on the stage during this period, from Welsh to black and West Indian to Yorkshire characters.[80] In this light, Wheeler's complaint that "in literary studies of the British eighteenth century, there has been, to date, little treatment of race and color"[81] is even truer of the scholarly neglect of ethnic stage figures and, more generally, the theatricalization of ethnicity in this period.

My own book situates itself within a broader time frame, and within a broader archive of plays and performances, than most of these recent theater studies, in part because the theatricalization of ethnic identity has had such a long and perpetually reinvigorated history: the production history of some of the plays I analyze encompasses more than half a century, and the history of the stage Jew and Irishman extends over centuries. It is surprising that such theatrical staples have received so little attention during their most popular and inventive tenure on the stage. Moreover, while I value the sharp historical focus of many of these recent studies, I do not think it is possible to locate transformations of theatrical culture, first, based on a handful of plays, and second, within a single decade or two.[82] Plays and performances were regularly restaged and reinvented over many decades (responding to new social and political events), and typically one theatrical phenomenon often encouraged its opposite. In my view, the mark of theatrical culture, like all cultures, is that at any given historical moment there are multiple and competing ideological discourses, as in the case at the turn of the nineteenth century when new sentimental comedies boasting a benevolent Jew encouraged the revival of decidedly anti-Semitic plays from earlier decades. So, by analyzing a large number of plays and performances over the course of the long eighteenth century (emphasizing the period from the 1750s through the opening decades of the nineteenth century, with brief looks before and after), I have charted emergent and residual theatrical trends, hegemonic and countervailing forms and strategies. And the plays that I examine cross multiple theatrical borders, suggesting that the immense popularity of these ethnic stage figures allowed them to invade an extraordinarily wide range of theaters and genres: these plays were produced at the patent as well as at the minor and provincial theaters, and they include canonical as well as obscure plays written within a wide array of genres (comedy, farce, burletta, comic opera, operatic farce, and so on).

The broad responsiveness of Georgian playwrights to their complex milieu becomes especially clear when we realize that so many of the playwrights (Hannah Cowley, Samuel Foote, George Colman the Younger, John O'Keeffe) that appear through the lens of gender, class, or empire in these recent theater studies turn up in my book as authors of a different set of plays that I read primarily through the lens of ethnic representation. But even more important, it was at the theater itself that plays about empire turned up next to plays about ethnic identity; some of the plays that are the focus of recent studies of imperial theatrical culture not only were performed on alternate nights with the plays at the heart of my book but even shared the stage with them on the same night—Philippe Jacques de Loutherbourg's and John O'Keeffe's 1785 pantomime *Omai; or, A Trip Round the World* (with its South Pacific islanders and its London Jewish usurer), for example, regularly played as an afterpiece to *The Duenna* (with its celebrated anti-Semitic portrait of Isaac Mendoza) at Covent Garden in 1786. Initially at least, what this tells us is that we have only begun to explore the rich complexity of this immense archive, and that each new study adds another dimension to our understanding of the complex engagement of late Georgian theatricality with the cultural, social, and political life of Great Britain.

One way of gaining a more comprehensive view of the many strands of late Georgian theatrical culture would be to have a full-length study of the theatrical repertory that explores how these kinds of intersections functioned—how, for example, the Jew in *The Duenna* functioned beside the Jew and South Pacific islanders in *Omai*, and how the non-English settings of both plays nonetheless functioned as interrogations of English national identity. The argument of this book depends at least in part on the fact that audiences in a single week could have seen at the patent theaters in January 1788, for example, *The Duenna* on the 22nd, *The West Indian* on the 23rd, *The Merchant of Venice* and *Love à la Mode* on the 24th, and Sheridan's *School for Scandal* on the 28th—a week of plays that featured most prominently stage Jews but also stage Irishmen, Scots, blacks, and West Indians. In a limited way, within the purview of my focus, I have tried in the course of this book to understand such intersections in repertoire at the patent theaters, as well as exploring in detail how within a single play—what I call the multiethnic spectacle— different ethnic, and even colonial and provincial, figures intersected. And one could in fact expand this notion of the multiethnic spectacle by suggesting how, within a single evening, various outsiders in entr'acte dances (such as *The Irish Lilt*, *The Highland Reel*, the *Negro Dance*, and the *German Jew, or the Pedlars*) intersected with figures in main pieces and afterpieces, or at an even larger reach, how entire weeks at the theater became a kind of massive multiethnic spectacle, so that audiences in early April 1788 could have seen at the patent theaters a Jew in *The School for Scandal* (on the 2nd); a Jew, a Scot, and an Irishman in *Love à la Mode* (on the 3rd); an Irishman in *The Rivals* (on the 4th); and a Scot in *The Man of the World* on the 8th, when *Omai*'s South Pacific natives and Jewish usurer appeared on stage in the afterpiece. What Jane Moody has usefully identified as the "monstrous generic hybridity" of "illegitimate" theater, while the mainstay of the minor theaters, had its beginnings, perhaps even more than she suggests, in the mixed entertainments of the patent (or "legitimate") theaters, and even illegitimate theater's "corporeal dramaturgy which highlighted the expressive body of the performer"[83] owes a debt, in my view, to the farcical spectacle of the ethnic body on display early on at the patent theaters, whether in a comical dance like the *German Jew* or more regularly in the popular plots and performances that caricatured, often side by side, various ethnic minorities. More research needs to be done on the ways in which repertory—the staging of main pieces, afterpieces, prologues and epilogues, and entr'acte entertainments from one theatrical season to the next—functioned in late Georgian theater, especially in order to understand how the representation of the vast and complex array of others (including such Continental figures as the Frenchman and the Italian) functioned in defining English national identity.

My view of national identity during this period has grown out of engaging an important body of historical scholarship that has focused on peripheral and minority cultures in Great Britain. By neglecting this scholarship, most recent studies of the theater miss the opportunity to analyze national identity in what many historians take to be the primary way in which it was defined in the late Georgian period—namely, in the intersecting (and often confused) categories of ethnicity and nationality. The genealogy of this body of historical scholarship begins with a series of seminal essays by J. G. A. Pocock, who claimed that "instead of histories of Britain, we have . . . histories of England, in which Welsh, Scots, Irish, and, in the reign of George III, Americans appear as peripheral peoples." Almost a decade ago I endorsed Pocock's call "to articulate the case for a pluralist and multicultural perception of British history," and began arguing that in the Georgian theater we have an extraordinarily important chapter in such a history.[84] In fact, the theater was requiring the nation to take up the questions that have been for some time at the center of academic debates by staging them in an unusually popular communal arena. If historians have regularly understood Scottish or Irish history as minor episodes (or even detours) in the continuous narrative of English history, the Georgian theater introduces us to the crisis over the categories of Scottish, Irish, English, and British identity—to their fluidity and shifting valorization—precisely at that historical moment when they were being reinvented and redefined. Similarly, if scholars working in the field of ethnic studies have typically isolated a single ethnic culture (and a single ethnic prejudice, such as anti-Semitism) for study, the Georgian theater introduces us to a complicated cultural and social world where different ethnic identities are intertwined and where toleration and prejudice collide (and where their boundaries blur). In short, the Georgian theater requires that we treat ethnicity comparatively and that we understand national identity through a variety of contradictory discourses about ethnicity—counter-discourses in conflict, residual and emergent discourses in process.

So, in response to the challenge to articulate a "pluralist and multicultural" view of British history, my book locates in Georgian culture the emergence of specific theatrical forms that interrogate directly the kinds of historiographical and multicultural issues scholars in a variety of fields are currently attempting to address. While the history I write in this book is largely limited to London, London theatrical culture in fact gives us unusual access to the wide varieties of Britishness at the time in a broad diversity of playwrights, performers, character types, and audiences. Precisely insofar as London was the point of intersection for so many ethnic, provincial, and colonial populations, it became the central testing ground of identity. London, the overflowing metropolis, was the place of unknown identity, of hidden and new identities, as the theater demonstrated in its widely diverse ethnic characters and its plots of ethnic passing. London city, at once the heart of England and the center of immigration, and London theater, with its mixed audiences and its repertory of various ethnic performances, posed the central dilemmas of ethnic and national identity. At the same time, while the activities of theaters in the provinces as well as in major "peripheral" cities such as Dublin and Edinburgh began to be regularly reported on in the Georgian press, our knowledge about these theaters remains limited, and further research will be needed to explore how such theaters, as well as theaters in the colonies, participated in defining ethnic, religious, provincial, national, and colonial identities during this period and beyond.[85]

While a number of historical studies, in response to Pocock, eventually attempted to expand the parameters of "English" historiography by using a "four-nations" (rather than an Anglocentric) paradigm, these studies nonetheless neglected the figure of the Jew in the construction of national identity. This is especially remarkable given that the Jew began to function as integral to newly emergent definitions of England as a commercial nation early in the eighteenth century. In part this neglect has occurred because of the ways in which historiography, even when it attempted to challenge dominant nationalist historiographical traditions, nonetheless used the nation as the model by which to proceed (and thus overlooked a variety of ethnic, regional, and religious minority populations). More recently, some scholars have usefully attempted a "new British history" that supersedes the four-nations model by grounding their analyses in narrower (local and regional) or broader (imperial) categories, or by challenging the ascendancy of political over other forms of history (social, economic, demographic, and so on).[86] But even these studies typically neglect the ways in which the figure of the Jew in particular and the theatricalization of ethnicity in general negotiated ethnic conflict and the construction of national identity at this time. In Georgian England, Jewish identity typically functioned at a highly symbolic level to set the farthest limits of the question of the internal other within Britain, both entirely opposite to, and yet increasingly a double of, the English. Hence the prominence I give to the figure of the Jew in the pages ahead.

At the same time, I also claim that Jewish identity was used comparatively, as a focal point in a variety of ethnic comparisons. My cue here, as elsewhere in this book, was taken from the plays themselves. While my initial research focused on the stage Jew as an important but neglected phenomenon of Georgian culture, I soon realized that this staple of the eighteenth-century stage was regularly located in relation to such other stages figures as the Scot, the Irishman, the black, the Yorkshireman, and so on. Such figures were typically either drawn into comparison with Jews or even collapsed into Jews, demonstrating the highly symbolic valence of the figure of the Jew as well as the comparative way in which the culture generally mixed, compared, and confused ethnic identities. Ethnic and regional populations were quick to distinguish themselves from Jews—the Yorkshireman in Thomas Dibdin's *School for Prejudice* (1801) insists, for example, "We munna be look'd on like Jews"[87]—precisely because such comparisons were common, and often quite elaborate. For example, in a one-shilling pamphlet entitled *The true-born Scot* (1764), Lord Bute is compared to a black (in a tangled simile about changing color), and then the Scots and the English anathematize each other as Jews: "Tho' *we* the *gen'rous* SCOTS as JEWS despise, / Yet *us* the SCOTS as JEWS shall *nat'ralize*." The (in)famous attempt to naturalize the Jews in 1753 becomes the paradigm for the kind of incorporation in the 1760s that the English fear at the hands of the Scots, resulting in a clear Scottish ascendancy: "The Royal Robe shall to the *Plaid* transform."[88] Such a text suggests how the government's attempts at incorporation and naturalization signaled a threat to English national identity, constructing a world in which transformations of identity could lead to an interchangeability of Scottish and Jewish and English identities. In a similar vein, a graphic print overlaid its attack on the "Jew Bill" with a clear citation of the Jacobite rebellion, suggesting that both events—and both groups, Highland Scots and Jews—threatened to transform the English nation, to overtake it.[89]

Georgian culture also made ethnic comparisons by representing a competition among different minorities. In the theater's comic plots, for example, different ethnic outsiders competed against one another for the English heroine's hand. The most patent version of this form of competition occurred in boxing matches in which different ethnic groups were pitted against each other (the Irish lad versus the Jewish champion, or the Jew beating the tartaned Scot), pictured in graphic prints[90] and staged at the theater in entr'acte interludes in which boxers were typically drawn from immigrant (especially Jewish, Irish, and black) populations.[91] But Georgian culture could also show a threatening collaboration among minorities against the English, as in Edward Long's highly influential *History of Jamaica* (1774), in which a black makes the following proposal to a Jew: "You Jews, said he, and our nation (meaning the Coromorantins), ought to consider ourselves as one people. . . . You differ from the rest of the Whites, and they hate you. Surely then it is best for us to join in one common interest, drive them out of the country, and hold possession of it to ourselves."[92] In short, English nationalist fantasies ran the gamut, from the self-gratifying image that saw ethnic minorities engaged in quarrels and competitions among themselves, to the anxious paranoia that saw them conspiring to threaten Englishness and the English Empire. Either way, ethnic minorities and foreigners were grouped together, on the other side of Englishness, however they might be strung together—"A *Scot* hath no more right to preferment in *England* than a *Hanoverian* or a *Hottentot*."[93]

In reviewing the kind of work that has been produced since his initial essays of the 1970s, Pocock himself has recently underscored how a "relative" historiography can usefully explore a "politics of identity formation,"[94] and both he and Kathleen Wilson have underscored the idea that Englishness itself functioned as the hegemonic ethnic position. Pocock writes of "the ethnocentricity and conceptual imperialism of English national consciousness," and Wilson recognizes that the name "Englishman" functioned as an "ethnocentric noun," persuasively arguing that certain minorities were excluded from definitions of Englishness: "The exclusive nature of definitions of 'Englishness' . . . were always at play and in tension with the broader categories of 'Britishness.'"[95] Such ideas engage what has become a heated debate, largely initiated by Linda Colley's highly influential but increasingly controversial *Britons: Forging the Nation, 1707–1837* (1992). In her push toward the unified Briton and united Britain, Colley has complained that historians are "in thrall" to Pocock and "this new scholarly fashion" of the four-nations paradigm.[96] My project suggests that such a debate (on the relative importance of British national unity versus ethnic difference) reflects an opposition that was current in the period and central to its theatrical culture, and attempts to understand the ways in which the theater reflected, negotiated, reoriented, and generally intervened in this debate. I see my work as contributing one of the many varieties of British history now being written rather than as resolving or closing a debate that inhered in the culture itself. And until now there has been virtually no extended attention to the ways in which the theater participated in and shaped this debate, even though theatrical culture was at its center. Moreover, while Colley argues that British national identity and solidarity functioned primarily through contrasts with Catholic France, a study of the Georgian theater makes a powerful case for the ways in which a large and mixed group of internal others (Jews, Scots, Irish, blacks, West Indians, Yorkshiremen, and so on) negotiated, questioned, and often splintered notions of a single, coherent, and unified national identity.

In an important and ambitious summation entitled "Ethnicity in the British Atlantic World, 1688–1830," Colin Kidd downplays the significance of ethnic identity in the eighteenth century by focusing on what I see as a narrow set of discourses. He argues that "respect for the ethnically undifferentiated polities of classical antiquity pushed ethnic factors to the margins of political culture, while sacred history reminded Britons of the aboriginal interconnectedness of 'Self' and 'Other.'" But I must ask the question that Thompson has asked of Colley's united and unified Britons: "*Which* Britons?"[97] Did "Britons" in general (as a unified group) really live, think, and behave within the highly intellectualized context that Kidd ascribes to them? And while Kidd has persuasively shown that anglicization was the articulated goal within certain fields of discourse (such as Scottish Whig intellectual history),[98] it is too simple to conclude by declaring "the easy Anglicization of the eighteenth-century British Atlantic world" and by downplaying the significance of the annihilation of entire cultures: "Although improvement was closely linked to cultural extinction, the intended goal, as in the case of late eighteenth-century attitudes to the Native American, was the absorption of the ethnic other into civilization." Kidd wants to locate a boundary between eighteenth-century attitudes, based on "a universalist language of philanthropy and improvement," and "the more overtly racialist climate of the early nineteenth century,"[99] but like the argument that chooses sides on whether Britain was a unified or divided nation, the attempt to fix a temporal boundary between eighteenth-century views of ethnicity and nineteenth-century racism is doomed to oversimplification. In my view, there is an elastic continuum between the kinds of ethnic markings at work everywhere in eighteenth-century popular culture and the more scientifically articulated racism of the nineteenth century.[100] Finally, the relative importance of ethnic difference and division in the long eighteenth century depends on the kinds of discourses and public arenas within which it is represented. So, while recognizing that the representations on the stage were inventions and simplifications of ethnicity (a view the theater itself came to realize, articulate, and work against), my focus is on the nonetheless profound pragmatic and ideological power such representations exerted in the culture. My emphasis on the importance of ethnicity as a foundational category for understanding Georgian culture derives primarily from the theater, and thereby underscores that this book is a study of the politics of representation, and of how individuals and groups fought to control the power of ethnic representation and the communal site that was seen as the central cultural battleground in this fight. Finally, then, while Kidd is persuasive about certain elite and intellectualized religious and philosophical discourses (though Wheeler argues that racial ideologies were inherent even in some of these), in my focus on the theater and popular culture in general I ask that we understand a wide range of discursive, performative, and visual representations that tell a different story.

In this light, I wish to conclude this introduction by underscoring the preeminence of the idea of ethnic identity in Georgian popular culture by briefly outlining the broad range of representations that articulated ethnic difference during this period. Popular songbooks and joke books, for example, were frequently organized around the same ethnic and provincial figures represented on the stage. *The Universal Songster; or, Museum of Mirth* lists its songs according to such categories as "Irish," "Jews' Songs," "Scotch," "Welsh," and "Yorkshire and Provincial," demonstrating the ways in which ethnic and provincial groups were highly recognizable categories that organized the culture in a basic way. The frontispiece features images of a Scot in Highland dress, a Jew selling his wares, and an Irishman dancing a jig. Moreover, some of the so-called songs are really short skits in which several ethnic minorities interact in dialect just as they do on the stage.[101] Similarly, *The new British universal jester* is replete with a cast of characters who are not given proper or family names because they function generically; these figures are named either simply with their ethnic names ("Irishman," "Welchman," "Scotchman") or with the nicknames that popularly served to identify (and condescend to) their ethnicity, such as Sawney, Teague, Paddy, and so on.[102] As on the stage, such figures are marked through dialect and through specific linguistic blunders and ethnic associations. The jokes especially theatricalize such figures by often bringing two different ethnic figures into comical dialogue with each other, much as the stage did. Many of the jokes were well known, and some (like some of the songs in the songbooks) were borrowed from the stage. In such ways the English public was offered conventional and well-known ways of mimicking, or performing, ethnic difference—that is, reproducing, in the generic form of the joke, the dialects and blunders that caricatured the Scot or the Jew. Similarly, individuals at masquerades regularly dressed as Scots, Irish, Jews, Welshmen, and blacks. These were, after all, the figures the public saw on the stage and in graphic prints and heard about in popular jokes, and thereby learned to imitate, in what I see as a broad, fundamental cultural form essential to the period—namely, cross-ethnic performance. So, just as the theater frequently staged the ethnic outsider attempting (and failing) to pass as English, the English in particular and Britons in general frequently participated in ethnic performance, in staging ethnic minority difference as a specular event. In this way the government's attempts at incorporating the ethnic other were literally enacted when individuals in performance incorporated ethnic minorities in a form of masquerade—that is, took control of ethnic bodies as their own.[103]

But such forms of cross-ethnic performance could be overtly violent and in fact demonstrate the darkest side of the theatricalization of ethnic identity. Street theater, whether orchestrated by a boisterous crowd or a repressive government, regularly made use of the ethnic body in violent performances. English crowds constructed, hung, and burned effigies of the Irish, the Jews, and Bute.[104] Such crowds performed a pageant in which Bute, dressed in Scottish plaid, led the king by the nose. A mock execution in London in 1771 took the effigies of Bute and the Princess Dowager to Tower Hall, where they were decapitated and burned.[105] The symbolic violence of such popular performances of ethnic identity grew out of the kinds of literal violence that the populace witnessed as part of their daily lives in a theatrical culture where ethnic minorities functioned as a typical site of spectacle. For example, the public medical examination of the executed Jews in the Chelsea murder case drew huge crowds of spectators, making it a kind of theatrical event. Similarly, the hanging and disemboweling of Highland rebels was a public spectacle that concluded with the heads of the rebels being placed on spikes at Temple Bar for all to see daily.[106] The popular graphic prints of the day in their turn drew on such public spectacles and invented acts of symbolic violence based on them. The 1763 engraving entitled *The Glorious Minority in 1763, With the Head of the Majority Blason'd* (figure 5), published almost twenty years after the Jacobite rebellion, shows a group of audience-like spectators (the Minority, represented by John Wilkes, William Pitt the Elder, and others) approvingly looking out from behind the king's tapestry, a kind of theatrical curtain, at Bute's head stuck on a pole for all to see and appreciate. The print suggests that Bute's influence over the king was tantamount to the 'Forty-Five rebellion and that he should be executed and exhibited in public like a Highland rebel, which of course the print itself achieved in symbolic form, especially since such prints were regularly exhibited in print shop windows for all passers-by to see. Other graphic prints showed Bute in tartan kilt, strung up on a gallows, his effigy being burned.[107]

So, the representation of ethnic identity found a wide variety of outlets

Figure 5: *The Glorious Minority in 1763, With the Head of the Majority Blason'd.*
Courtesy of the Library of Congress.

in Georgian culture, and different arenas and media often cooperated and
borrowed from one another in standardizing a set of visual and aural clues
by which to mark ethnic identity, making the ethnic other available for
symbolic construction, mutilation, and destruction. Ethnic minorities were
marked by costume, by body, and by dialect (especially as an extension of
the body), and were frequently represented by the culture's misapplication of
such markers—a Lowland Scot like Bute, for example, was regularly shown
dressed as a Highlander. The tartan and plaid, the kilt, and the bonnet of the
Highland Scot, like the broad-brimmed hat and long coat of the Jew, were
highly popular and readable signs in Georgian culture. Not just skin color (a
marker for blacks, Jews, and Creoles) but certain body parts and bodily in-
firmities became conventional (if frequently fantasized) markers, such as the
Jewish nose and beard, the contagious itch of the Scots, and the leprosy and

venereal disease of the Jews. These conventional markers became so popular and so fully disseminated that Frank Felsenstein has argued that circumcision, for example, functioned as a popular metonymy for Jews (as in "the unforeskinn'd race" or "the circumcis'd"), and I want to suggest that this kind of metonymy became part of a widely understood semiotic system that included a host of metonymic figures that referred not only to Jews but to various ethnic minorities. So, the public recognized immediately that a slogan like "No long beards nor whiskers" referred to Jews,[108] while Herbert M. Atherton has shown that "the bonnet," "the thistle," and "the bagpipe" were used in the satiric prints of the day to stigmatize Bute's (and other Scots') "ethnic origins"—thistles, for example, surround Bute's "blason'd" head in figure 5.[109] Such metonymic figures became a short-hand naming system, a covert and specialized code of images and words that the English used but that was in fact understood by all Britons. At once cryptic and legible, such markers were a specialized language invented to classify and stigmatize the ethnic other by stereotyping entire populations through a small but well-known group of features.

The generalized threat of the foreign body was regularly sharpened to represent the Scots, Irish, and Jews as potent threats to English womanhood. All three ethnic minorities were typically characterized in Georgian popular culture as fortune hunters, and sometimes as sexual transgressors and even rapists. Graphic prints showed Highlanders during the 'Forty-Five marauding quiet English villages (including raping English women) and Scots in general ravishing English women,[110] while Bute was regularly revealed in a variety of sexual transgressions, both with the king's mother and with the icon Britannia. For example, by flogging the naked Britannia with a thistle in *The Whipping Post* (1762), Bute "makes poor Britannia shew her Breech," and in so doing exposes how both the English nation and English womanhood are vulnerable to Scottish penetration, while in another print Bute helps Spain sodomize Britannia with a sword.[111] Similarly, in an odd rewriting of Genesis, the *London Evening-Post* imagined the Jews circumcising and then murdering the English male population, while "all their Little-ones, and their Wives, took they Captive" (October 18–20, 1753). Such examples suggest how the marking of the ethnic outsider was regularly associated with protecting (and maintaining English control over) English womanhood: the *London Evening-Post* (September 11–13, 1753), in an advertisement for a historical book on the Jews in England, claimed "that a Jew has no Right to appear in England without a yellow Badge fix'd on the upper Garment, nor co-habit with a

Christian Woman." English control of the ethnic female body could function as a necessary corollary, so a Jacobite journalist made a modest proposal that responded sardonically to the Hanoverian government's excessively brutal reaction to the 'Forty-Five by calling for the sterilization of all Jacobite women of child-breeding age and the starvation of the Highlanders generally (as a cost-cutting effort in lieu of transporting them to the colonies).[112] Finally, the fear of foreign contamination was so pervasive that the importation of German mercenaries to assist in defending England against France led to an ironic commentary that reflected on the (Hanoverian) royal family itself as a threat to Englishness: "Bringing so much *German* Blood into *English* veins . . . may put an End to all national Distinction . . . [and] raise up a Race, properly germanized, without one home-spun *Englishman* to disgrace the Breed."[113] So, ethnic difference was represented through the threatening foreign body, and figures of ethnic conquest, genocide, and extinction regularly bled into representations of ethnic difference. The ethnic outsider was not simply an abstraction but rather a fully embodied presence that threatened the English physically, especially when the ethnic body endangered the pure propagation of the English.

This kind of paranoiac fear led to the culture's claim that ethnic minorities were marked by inherent characteristics at the same time that it sought to mark them (publicly and unambiguously) for all to see and recognize. So, the Jewish body was at once seen as visibly marked by nature as well as requiring a yellow badge, while the mark of circumcision was obsessively cited in defining and locating Jews, even as a kind of inherent or natural bodily mark. This idea of particular groups bearing a natural mark that set them apart was common, even when it took the form of a kind of national fantasy. Horace Walpole reports a "conversation [that] soon fell on Lord George Gordon's Mosaic beard—on which one of the company said, it was lucky when *converts* wore distinguishing marks by which they might be reconnoitred."[114] Similarly, in the famous letter that Junius addressed to the king on December 19, 1769, the author denounced the king's special predilection toward the Scots, and in what had become a common practice compared them to the Jews, claiming that both groups were marked for all to see: "Like another chosen people, they have been conducted into the land of plenty, where they find themselves effectually marked, and divided from mankind."[115] And in his *History of Jamaica*, Long claimed of Jamaican planters, "Although descended from British ancestors, they are stamped with these characteristic deviations."[116] Finally, the culture contemplated and sometimes practiced the most violent forms of marking. The Society for the Propagation of the Gospel in Foreign Parts branded slaves on the chest with "Society,"[117] while the Crown Solicitor recommended that Highland rebels who were exiled should be branded on the face with a hot iron to prevent them from returning to England from the colonies, and a law passed the House of Commons (but failed in the Lords) decreeing that unregistered priests found in Ireland should be branded with a hot iron on the face to make them easily detected if they returned after banishment.[118]

Identifying the inherent (natural) marks of otherness and fixing the constructed (social) marks of difference on minorities for all to see were practices that had their echo in the ways in which ethnic difference was marked on the London stage. The theater (re)presented and pretended to exhibit the living body of the other, but this body carried a violent history of oppression. For this reason, the history of various penal and sumptuary laws haunted the marking of ethnic minorities on the stage, even while the stage's comic entertainments typically attempted to gloss over or trivialize a history of oppressing cultural and religious differences in scenes of intended humor. Jewish characters, for example, were force-fed pork (poking fun at their dietary laws) or kicked and expelled from the stage (recalling their expulsion in 1290), and Scottish, Welsh, and Irish characters spoke broken English (recalling the suppression of their native languages). So, while at the beginning of this chapter I noted the *Monthly Mirror*'s defense of what it saw as the stage's harmless, comical system of marking ethnic and national others for an English audience, I have concluded by contextualizing some of the more serious ways in which the marking of ethnic difference functioned in this culture and reverberated on the stage.

The chief difficulty in attempting to reconstruct theater history arises from the ways that it typically redoubles back on itself, offering no simple or single chronological thread: plays resurface, sometimes decades or longer after a first run, sometimes adapted or even significantly revised, with different performers, performance strategies, and audiences, and with a renewed or altered purpose that depends on a new social or political context. Moreover, with the kind of broad canvas of plays and ethnic figures that I discuss, there are at any one moment competing discursive and performative forms and goals, not simply across the culture but even within individual plays. So, over the course of this book I do not attempt to construct a single chronological development. Instead, my chapters focus on particular theatrical forms and strategies that were invented to negotiate questions of ethnic difference, especially from

the 1750s through the opening decades of the nineteenth century, when issues
of ethnic conflict and reconciliation were especially prominent.[119]

In Chapter 2 I analyze the development of the multiethnic spectacle and
the ethnic passing plot, explaining how the traditional comedic marriage plot
was refashioned to respond to an ethnically diverse and competitive nation
by imagining a wide cast of ethnic minorities in pursuit of a rich English
heiress. I explain how the multiethnic spectacle was used both to denigrate
and to recuperate ethnic identity, how dialect functioned as a central marker
of otherness at a time when a widespread debate about the standardization of
the English language was under way and minorities fought to establish the legitimacy of their own voice, and how the professional actor functioned in the
culture at large as a carrier of the idea and practice of ethnic passing. In Chapter 3 I analyze the centrality of the figure of the Jew to definitions of English
national identity in the eighteenth century and the deliberate confusion of
the identities of Jew and Englishman on the stage. I also explore how, toward
the end of the century, playwrights attempted to recuperate Jewish identity
on the stage through the construction of a new character type, the benevolent, sentimental stage Jew, and how this initiated a national debate about
the staging of Jewish identity and anti-Semitism in the history of England.
In Chapter 4 I explore another new theatrical form, the cross-dressing Gentile, in an attempt to elaborate what was at stake in the doubling of Jew and
Englishman on stage and off in Georgian England. I analyze the trope of the
cross-dressing Gentile, which exposed to audiences the means by which actors performed Jewish identity, as a radical strategy in the theater's attempt to
uncover its own system of ethnic marking and to deconstruct what it and the
culture at large had invented—namely, the theatricalization of Jewish identity. In order to suggest how influential and fully disseminated the theater's
construction of ethnic types was, and to continue my analysis of the different
ways in which minorities themselves attempted to reclaim their identities, I
move beyond the London stage in Chapters 5 and 6 to follow the geographical trajectory of this project, explaining how novelists based in Ireland and
Scotland (Maria Edgeworth, Sydney Owenson, and Walter Scott) in the early
decades of the nineteenth century made a special detour through the theater to reconstruct minority ethnic identities, and even in so doing revealed
theatricality at the heart of the interactions between the English and ethnic
minorities. I explain how, in order to displace the caricatured male figures of
the stage, novelists invented the beautiful female ethnic other as the object of
the English hero's desire in what became the popular cross-ethnic love plot,

and I explore the benefits and dangers of cross-ethnic identification. In the epilogue I outline briefly the afterlife of the Georgian stage (and its relationship to the novel) over the course of the nineteenth century, focusing on the kinds of traditions and innovations that mediated the perennial significance of staging Jewish identity in England. Throughout this book my emphasis remains on the invention and development of cultural forms at a time when the theatricalization of ethnic identity lay at the center of the nation's life—that is, when questions about national identity and the incorporation of the ethnic other were preeminent.

CHAPTER TWO

"Cutting Off Tongues"

Multiethnic Spectacle and Ethnic Passing

We have the characters of an Irishman, a Jew, and a musical black
servant. . . . The Jew is made benevolent, and yet he is to be turned
into ridicule; the Irishman has no bulls to make, and *Dingy*, the
black, no jokes to crack—Yes I beg his pardon—one. To conceal
himself he gets into a boiler, but before he puts the lid down, he
exclaims, *"Ah, me go in black, suppose me come out red, like a lobster."*
—Review of Andrew Cherry's *In and Out of Tune, Monthly
Mirror*, March 1808

THE MULTIETHNIC SPECTACLE was a new cultural form that engineered
the intersection of several different ethnic figures on the stage in the course
of a single entertainment, whether a brief farce or a full-fledged comedy, typically putting these ethnicities on display at the same time that it brought them
into conflict and competition. While most often fused onto the traditional
comedic marriage plot—we see here the way in which a conventional literary
form accommodates a new cultural anxiety—the multiethnic spectacle was
centrally concerned with two other issues: how to mark ethnic difference,
and the logical corollary of such an idea, how to pass, how to cross-dress, how
to impersonate. The *Monthly Mirror*'s reviewer of *In and Out of Tune* (1808),
after listing the three ethnic characters on whom the comedy depends, seizes
on a joke based precisely on these two aspects of the multiethnic spectacle—
namely, the black man, marked by the color of his skin, imagines turning red
by falling into a boiler, a comical way of imagining passing. But the black

43

man in the farce has already argued, in a more serious way, for his transformation. When stigmatized with a series of racist epithets—one character calls him "an ebony faced Baboon" and "a sooty faced slave"—the black man responds: "No more slave now, good Englishman." Like this example of the black slave transformed into a red lobster or a white Englishman, destabilizing and fantasized transformations of ethnic identity became a common trope during this period, exploring what constituted Englishness and what strategies ethnic minorities used in their attempt to pass. In a similar vein, *In and Out of Tune*'s Jew, frightened by the black man and calling out for rescue in dialect ("Shave me, shave me"), is farcically converted into a Gentile when a barber answers his call and (instead of saving him) shaves off the Jew's beard.[1] In such ways the multiethnic spectacle staged the spectacle of ethnic difference, located the markers of otherness, and caricatured and exposed the ethnic outsider's attempts at passing. At the same time, in Cherry's farce these ethnic markers are seen as extravagantly comical, unusually fluid, and even purely theatrical—a suggestion that the theater itself had begun to question the very nature of ethnic difference instead of merely reproducing it.

The theater played a special role in articulating the issues of ethnic marking and ethnic passing for two reasons. First, unlike other popular media (such as graphic prints or novels or pamphlets), the theater brought directly and immediately before the public's senses the visual and aural cues of ethnic identity, including its preeminent marker in this culture, dialect. In part my focus in this chapter is directed at understanding why and how dialect began to function as it did, both on the stage and in the culture at large. Second, the theater explored such issues through a special brand of illusion. Through the use of metatheater—that is, through the self-conscious exploration of role playing, impersonation, and spectatorship—the theater became the primary vehicle for exploring the theatrical construction of ethnic identity in the culture at large. In short, the stage both produced ethnic spectacle and interrogated it by asking in what ways ethnic identity was merely performative. For these reasons, the theater, with its mixed, multiethnic audience, became the central arena in which the important cultural sign systems of ethnic difference were inspected and regulated, popularly and publicly, daily and communally.

Just a few days after the production of *In and Out of Tune*, the *Monthly Mirror* recorded a performance of the double bill that will be the center of my discussion here—namely, *The Merchant of Venice* and Charles Macklin's afterpiece, *Love à la Mode*, produced a half century after the double bill's first production in 1759. One contemporary observer noted that by the 1780s "Mr. Macklin . . . was more generally talked and written about than any other member of his Profession,"[2] and in my view, Macklin is the actor and playwright who takes us most directly to the center of the politics of ethnic identity in the Georgian theater and Georgian culture generally. An Irish actor, he was nonetheless famous for his portrayal of both Jews and Scots in a feat of ethnic (re)invention that at once epitomized the culture and appalled it, so much so that he was mocked as a kind of monstrous hybrid, a one-man multiethnic spectacle: after Macklin's controversial performance as the title character in *Macbeth* in the early 1770s, one observer quipped, "I learned tonight what ne'er before I knew, / That a Scotch monarch's like an Irish Jew."[3] This idea found its way into a 1773 satirical engraving entitled *Shylock turnd Macbeth* (figure 6) that depicted Macklin's celebrated Jewish persona suddenly transformed into a Scot wearing a Balmoral bonnet and tartan stockings (with the hint of Shylock's threatening knife lingering in Macbeth's deadly weapon), suggesting Macklin as a kind of ethnic shape-changer. Meanwhile, even as a playwright Macklin was famous for penning important Jewish, Irish, and Scottish characters—not the least of which included the Scottish caricatures Sir Archy Macsarcasm and Sir Pertinax Macsycophant, both the objects of repeated Scottish protest.

Love à la Mode, which was performed at the patent theaters every year but one from 1759 through the mid-1790s and continued to be performed in the opening decades of the nineteenth century, can serve as a paradigm of this new kind of comedy, the multiethnic spectacle, especially since it was staged in such a way as to make clear its revisionary status. When *Love à la Mode* debuted in 1759, it looked like not simply an afterpiece to *The Merchant of Venice* but rather a reprise of the apparently minor scene in the first act of Shakespeare's play in which Portia satirically reviews the (ethnic) failings of her suitors. But Shakespeare's foreign settings (Venice and Belmont) and Portia's foreign suitors (Neapolitan, French, German) were replaced in *Love à la Mode* with an English setting and a Georgian roll call of decidedly British ethnic types, each battling for the wealthy heroine and for his own place in the newly emerging Great Britain: the Scottish Sir Archy Macsarcasm, the Irish Sir Callaghan O'Brallaghan, the English Squire Groom, and the Jewish Beau Mordecai. By staging his contest at home on English soil, with local ethnic types, Macklin was putting on display the new world of mid-eighteenth-century Britain, socially mobile and ethnically diverse and fractious—that is, the world of the multiethnic spectacle. Macklin's revisionist pen lifted this

Figure 6: *Shylock turnd Macbeth*. The Harvard Theatre Collection, Houghton Library. TS 941.5F., vol. 2.

brief scene from Shakespeare's play and expanded it into a farce that focused entirely on ethnic spectacle and conflict.

Moreover, Macklin moved the Jew directly into the love plot as one of the suitors. Such a move was a significant event in the history of the theater. Macklin had been playing a number of Jewish roles from as early as 1738, but it was not until 1741 that he made his mark in an astonishing performance as Shylock, in what every stage history then and now records as a theatrical watershed. Macklin restored Shakespeare's *Merchant of Venice* to the stage and thereby displaced the ridiculous version of the play that had been popular since 1701, George Granville's *Jew of Venice*, in which Shylock was little more than a clown. Macklin's reinventions of Jewish identity on the English stage, in his role first as actor in 1741 and then as playwright in 1759, therefore made him a profoundly influential figure in eighteenth-century Jewish portraiture. It was a historic theatrical event at Drury Lane on the evening of December 12, 1759, because this was no ordinary double bill but rather one that was invented to make the spectator see double: the restored Shylock (played, of course, by Macklin), fierce, vengeful, the eternal outsider, and the new Beau Mordecai, the product of the new commercial age, a fawning interloper insidiously bent on becoming an insider in England. The audience saw two competing Jews on the stage: one legendary and one contemporary, one almost mythic and one newly satiric, as if Macklin were asking the audience to rethink Jewish identity once again (as he had done in 1741). This doubling of Jews on the stage perhaps even functioned as a kind of destabilization of Jewish identity, especially insofar as it challenged the long-standing character of Shylock; at the very least the appearance of Beau Mordecai on the same evening as Shylock announced an expansion of the possibilities of Jewish representation in the theater.

If this double viewing potentially ironized the figure of the Jew on the stage, at the same time it established the Jew as spectacle for the less thoughtful theatergoer, who could simply sit back and relish this double dishing up of the Jewish character. Twice in the course of the play the beau Jew is "turned about,"[4] once by the Irishman and once by the Scot, who function as audience models by staring at, ogling, and mocking the Jew. By being turned about the Jew is made to display himself to the mocking eyes of his fellow characters and the audience at large: "tricked oot in aw the colours of the rainbow," he is the product of the new commercial age, a fop and a fool (*LM*, p. 50). The supertheatricality of the Jew suggests the Jew as actor, as dissembler; he is the outsider trying to pass himself off as an insider, a gentleman. Before we even meet him we hear the limits within which we are to view him; the heroine describes him as "a beau Jew, who, in spite of nature and education, sets up for a wit, a gentleman, and a man of taste." His "chocolate coloured phiz" and his overadorned dress expose his laughable attempt at passing (*LM*, pp. 45, 67). Hence Beau Mordecai's theatrical excess is viewed as the obvious foolishness of his performance.

But this deliberate display of the beau Jew, what we might expect to be the standard trope of the Georgian theater—the satiric construction of a particular ethnic type—needs to be placed beside an emerging strategy of the theater, namely, the deconstruction of certain ethnic types. As an Irishman himself, Macklin aimed to fight anti-Irish prejudice, particularly as it had become crystallized in the blundering, fortune-hunting stage Irishman. The chief method of fighting anti-Irish prejudice in the play came from its attempt to detheatricalize the Irish character. In a pivotal scene in *Love à la Mode* Sir Archy and Charlotte, the heroine, plan a little scheme: she will allow the Irishman to court her—that is, to make a fool of himself, to "make love in Irish" (*LM*, p. 69)—while the other suitors watch from behind a screen. We have, then, a play within a play in which the audience is reproduced on the stage through a mock audience, the other suitors. But the results are anticlimactic, antitheatrical: the Irishman on exhibit fails to make a fool of himself, in a metatheatrical scene of failed spectacle. The discrepancy between his actual behavior and the expected blunders of the stereotypical Irishman exposes the stage Irishman as a theatrical construct and invites the audience to reflect on the very conditions of spectatorship and spectacle that engross it. So, in *Love à la Mode* we see the Irishman detheatricalized and the Jew supertheatricalized. And therefore we see how the Georgian theater could use ethnic spectacle in opposing ways—demystifying it through metatheater, exploiting it through caricature.

In both its maintenance and its subversion of ethnic prejudices, *Love à la Mode* reveals the double and often contradictory motives of the multiethnic spectacle in particular and Enlightenment discourse about ethnicity generally. *Love à la Mode* reveals from the beginning this double attitude, opening on a defensive note, with the heroine justifying the play's mirth—namely, making fun of the different ethnic types—while her guardian quickly sets certain limits to the game of ethnic ridicule. At one level, the guardian's warning—to view the Scot's ill nature "not as a national, but a personal vice" (*LM*, p. 46)—is nothing more than self-defensive and self-allowing, placed at the beginning to defend the play from its critics and to give full allowance to the ethnic slurs that follow. This sort of disclaimer appears to uphold (but actually puts to rest) the Enlightenment value of liberal toleration, and probably succeeded in satisfying those who wanted to believe that the play did not present ethnic stereotypes, only individual fops and fools. At another level, however, the play can be seen to rehearse this Enlightenment sentiment only to expose its bankruptcy in actuality—that is, in the ethnic strife and prejudice that lie just below the surface of the nationalist project of "Great Britain." In this view the play exposes the way in which the Enlightenment ideology of liberal toleration simply does not hold up in the face of the everyday anxieties and conflicts in a nation as socially mobile and ethnically diverse as Great Britain.

Many multiethnic spectacles included this double movement—both maintaining and subverting ethnic prejudice—while others existed simply to caricature all its minority ethnic characters. For example, *Mordecai's Beard*, an interlude performed at Drury Lane in 1790 and 1792, brings together a Jewish old-clothes man and an Irish chairman who immediately get involved in an altercation in comical dialect. The Jew is consistently stigmatized, with a series of jokes based on his differentiating marks of otherness. When the Irishman tries to "make a good Christian" of the Jew by trying to force-feed him bacon and fails, he decides, "If I can't convert your whole Body, I will at least Christen your Beard" and proceeds to grease the Jew's beard with bacon in a symbolic defilement. This is the kind of mock conversion or transformation of otherness that these plays comically rehearse time and again, fooling with the boundaries of otherness. When both appear before a justice to complain of each other, the scene revolves around the Jew's (ethnic) marking: the justice sees no marks of violence, the Jew offers to show them, the justice quickly intercedes ("Don't pull off your cloaths") as if the Jew were going to show him the mark of circumcision. And even when the Jew claims "de marks are in my Face," he inadvertently supports the popular notion that the Jewish physiognomy was marked and readable as other. All the marks of Jewish religious and ethnic difference are mocked in the scene, from the mark of circumcision, to the dietary laws (the Jew secretly licks the bacon off his beard with relish), to the beard (the shaving of which the Jew announces is a defilement, while in an aside he confesses that the beard is no more than an attempt to "disguise" the fact that he is a criminal who has just returned from having been transported). The interlude in this way manages to devalue the Jew's genuine religious difference while upholding his otherness, his foreignness. *Mordecai's Beard* ends with the kind of double gesture I have been noting, stigmatizing both characters but apparently protecting them too, in what is not so much an embrace of toleration as a puff for English national identity. The justice tells the Jew and the Irishman, "You are both notorious Characters, and not to be trusted," but in England "Men of all Countrys [*sic*] and Religions are equally protected in the pursuits of their lawful Avocations with the native Englishman."[5]

Another multiethnic spectacle that caricatures its two foreigners is by a Jewish playwright, Moses Mendez. When members of an ethnic minority (like Macklin) wrote such plays, it was assumed that they would be partial to their own ethnicity, but Mendez's play has no Jewish character and therefore does not attempt the rehabilitation of Jewish identity, though it is quick to mark others as outsiders. *The Double Disappointment*, which played on the stage regularly from 1746 to 1773 and was "the most profitable success that Garrick inherited on his arrival [at Drury Lane],"[6] follows the multiethnic formula, with a Frenchman and an Irishman in competition for the hand (or wealth) of the rich English heroine. Both are mocked as suitors: "The Frenchman is all Feather, the Irishman all Lead." The Frenchman speaks with a heavy accent, the Irishman with many bulls, or blunders. The plot revolves around the eventual exposure of both characters' attempt at passing, and both are eventually exposed as adventurers and thieves. The play visibly demonstrates (and deconstructs) the mechanics of passing, emphasizing it as a failed theatrical feat, when the exposed Irishman finally confesses, "So I will pull off my Wig and my Sword, and be a Gentleman no more, because I verily believe it does not become me."[7] In the end, English marriage, threatened by ethnic and national outsiders, finally succeeds. The central irony here is extratextual: in a real-life comedic plot that supported (rather than exposed and prevented) the ability of the outsider to pass, Mendez was baptized at birth and married an Englishwoman, and "his descendants rejoiced in time in the possession of a baronetcy and the Anglo-Saxon surname of Head."[8] Such a real-life story was of course a primary reason behind the theater's system of ethnic marking: to prevent such incursions into English national life, the theater had to expose the attempts by outsiders to pass by keeping them marked.

While many of these plays simply pandered to the English audience's desire to see such outsiders caricatured, nonetheless some also performed the work of liberal toleration, even as they often maintained certain prejudices. Thomas Sheridan's *Captain O'Blunder: or, The Brave Irishman*, performed (with slight variations in title) in Dublin in 1737 and in various London venues (including the patent theaters) in 1746, 1755, 1770, and 1779, featured an Irish captain newly arrived in London, where the English stare and laugh at him. He competes with a Frenchman for the hand of the English heroine. The two outsiders exchange insults, and the Frenchman seems to know all the barbs that are typically aimed at the Irish in England—"you be de Teague, de vile Irishman—de potato face"—and in an attempt to dismiss the Irishman, the Frenchman orders what many English felt: "Go to your own hotontot contre," your "outlandish contre."⁹ When the father of the heroine appears to have lost all his money, the Frenchman relinquishes his suit, but the Irishman remains true to the heroine. A clear precursor to Macklin's *Love à la Mode*, Sheridan's play was an early attempt by another Irish actor-playwright to recuperate Irish identity by exposing the stereotype of the Irish fortune hunter.

The multiethnic spectacle, precisely because it brought together different ethnic minorities, also became a vehicle for rehabilitating several ethnic identities at once and exposing the breadth of English prejudice. In Joseph Reed's farce *The Register-Office* (1761), the Englishman Gulwell runs a London register office, and a series of outsiders—all the usual suspects—come to him to look for work: a Frenchman, an Irishman, a Scot, and a servant woman from Yorkshire, all of whom misspeak standard English and most of whom tell stories of how they have been stigmatized by Londoners in particular and Englishmen in general. The Yorkshire woman, for example, explains how Londoners giggle at her, while the Scot complains of his treatment, "It was a downright *National* Reflection!" The play ends with a rout of Gulwell, literally forcing him off the stage: Irishman and Scot join forces, physically beating Gulwell, having found out that he has gulled their countrymen and has sent many of them to be transported to the plantations in the West Indies, "to be turn'd into a black negro." And when the Frenchman tries to get his licks, the Irishman says, "For no Foreigners, but the *Irish*, must pretend to kick an *Englishman*." So, the play comically makes fun of the outsiders, especially their failure at pronouncing London English and their general gullibility in the urban metropolis, at the same time that in the end it takes their side against English prejudice and English chicanery. And as if to make the multiethnic spectacle complete, the figure of the Jew exists in the shadows of the plot: in a caricature of the hypocrisy of outsider religions, a Methodist bawd comes to the register office in search of a young girl because "I have promised a young Virgin to Mr. *Zorobabel Habakuk* to Night."¹⁰ The rich Jew (named after another predator Jew in an earlier play, by Henry Fielding, which I discuss in my next chapter) is not one of the gulled outsiders but is, like the Englishman Gulwell, feeding off the young provincial women who find themselves in poverty in London.

Finally, the multiethnic spectacle sometimes functioned as the perfect medium for constituting the union of the three kingdoms in the kind of ideological work that Linda Colley's *Britons: Forging the Nation, 1707–1837* sees as standing behind the construction of the Briton. *The South Briton*, performed at Covent Garden in 1774, assembles its cast deliberately from the three nations whose solidarity is essential to combat French influence (and the regular threat of French invasion) and to complete the work of the empire. These characters work deliberately toward such a union by first acknowledging the kinds of differences that have often divided them in the past. So, initially there is the kind of Irish/Scottish argument that we see represented in a variety of late Georgian texts: the Irishman and the Scot have a debate, "Your country is not as ancient as ours."[11] But in fact both Irishman and Scotsman work to reconcile the three kingdoms, even to see the kingdoms' descendents as part of the same family and its disagreements as simply another manifestation of those family quarrels that disturbed simple family union. While the Scot declares, "We are all children of the same empire, and to disparage a part, is some reflection on the whole" (18), Mowbray the Englishman nonetheless maintains his prejudices against the peripheries and even London in favor of the Continent. But by act IV, he copies the Scot's words: "Nobody more detests national distinctions. . . . We are all children of the same empire" (57). And by the fifth act, the Englishman who has brought home a group of foreign servants from his travels abroad (in a conventional trope of the period) finally decides to get rid of all his "foreign mercenaries" (72), not one of whom "speaks a plain syllable of English" (8). And with that decision he is told, "Now you speak like a Briton" (72). The Irishman applauds the decision: "Here is an Englishman, an Irishman, and a Scotchman, agreed upon one point together; and if they'd take my advice now, they'd always endeavour to do so; for we have enemies enough abroad, and not to be disputing among ourselves at home" (72). Tellingly, once again the Jewish character fails to be assimilated in the union, and the Irishman is his punisher, getting him locked up in jail, and declaring: "'Tis well for our poor country, that she does not produce milk and honey enough to invite these eastern locusts amongst us! . . . The devil a plain word can he speak of the language of a country he has been so long plundering!" (43–44). The "dirty reptile" (55), a Portuguese Jew who has emigrated to England, is shut out of the union, shown to be attempting to prey upon the Englishman, and thereby revealed to be a true outsider, unlike the Irishman and Scot. In such a case the multi-ethnic spectacle functions to forge alliances between some ethnic minorities and to equalize Scot, Irishman, and Englishman as Britons, while identifying the Jew as the genuine outsider. At the same time, the effort the characters must exert to supersede their prejudices in order to forge an alliance exposes the deep rifts in the nation.

In the Georgian theater's comedic plots based on ethnic marking and passing, there was no stronger ethnic marker than dialect. Skin color of course played a central role in such plots—the "chocolate coloured phiz" of Beau Mordecai set him apart, just as the black woman, practicing the convention of the bed-trick,[12] attempts to pass for white in Samuel Foote's *The Cozeners* (1774) but is discovered when the darkened room is brightened and her skin color is revealed. Nonetheless, the most consistent sign that marked all outsiders and that became the center of the stage's passing plots was dialect. Ethnic cross-speaking became the primary means by which the other sought and failed to pass in England, and English audiences delighted in plots that showed the ethnic passer being detected on the basis of dialect. So, the first telltale sign of the black woman's identity in *The Cozeners* occurs when she speaks: the man she tries to dupe exclaims, "One may find out by her tongue she is a foreigner."[13] In other words, skin color in this play only later confirms and supplements what her tongue has already revealed. Dialect functioned as the marker of otherness for black, Scottish, Irish, Welsh, Jewish, and provincial characters in a culture that began to be obsessed with the correct pronunciation of the English language. So, in George Farquhar's popular *Beaux Stratagem* (1707), where the same apothegm rules ("You may know him, as the saying is, to be a Foreigner by his Accent"), when an Irishman attempts to pass as a Frenchman, he is found out by his tongue, and comically asks if there is "a Brogue upon my Faash, too?"[14] inadvertently underscoring the way in which dialect works as a kind of bodily marker, the aural clue that in many ways supersedes the visual clues to otherness.

So, while much of the banter between Sir Archy and Sir Callaghan in *Love à la Mode* is predictably in defense and celebration of their native cultures, they nonetheless argue over who speaks better English, as if they were eager to divest themselves of the linguistic marker of their native countries. Macklin catches them at a critical historical moment, when they are neither fully assimilated as Englishmen nor fully at home in their native cultures—that is, the moment when they maintain a kind of double identity, when for many new Britons passing became a requirement:

> *Sir Archy*: Ye hai gotten sic a wecked, awkward, cursed jargon upon
>   yeer tongue, that ye are never intelligible in yeer language.
> *Sir Callaghan*: I beg your pardon, Sir Archy, it is you that have got
>   such a cursed twist of a fat scotch brogue about the middle of
>   your tongue, that you can't understand good English when I
>   speak it to you.
> *Sir Archy*: Aw the world kens I speak the Sooth Country so well, that
>   whereever I gang, I am awways taken for an Englishman.
>   (*LM*, 61–62)

Sir Archy and Sir Callaghan finally turn to the heroine and ask her to decide who has the brogue and who speaks proper English, as if she will choose her husband on that basis, in strict conformity to English (pronunciation) standards. In this light the plot to win the English heroine becomes confused with the plot to pass as an Englishman—after all, the reward is not simply the heroine but also the sizable English fortune she represents. In the competition to win the hand of the rich heroine, then, Macklin reconfigures Shakespeare's test of the caskets as the test of the brogue.

In Georgian culture, the central trial or test centered on passing—that is, on who could perform Englishness and escape the linguistic marker of difference—and the theater functioned as the model for staging this trial or test. For example, in *Essay on Irish Bulls* (1802), a pioneering sociolinguistic experiment in which Maria Edgeworth and her father attempted to record and explore what were seen as the peculiarities of Irish speech, there is a chapter modeled on the kind of multiethnic stage play I am describing. The "Bath Coach Conversation" brings together three ethnic types, an Irishman, a Scot, and an Englishman, to discuss the recent Act of Union with Ireland. This chapter is cast in the form of a kind of drama—there is virtually no narrative, only dialogue—though here (as opposed to the typical stage comedy) the conversation is entirely free of the differentiating dialects typical of the stage. The didactic purpose is to demonstrate the three ethnic types on par with one another—in other words, all speaking English without dialect. In this utopia of an entirely homogenized culture, all educated gentlemen speak perfect English. But within this conversation the Irishman eventually tells a "Hibernian Tale," called "The Irish Incognito," that is really an allegory of

Ireland. An Irishman insists he can pass as an Englishman because he has lost the brogue, but, while successful at that, he is found out repeatedly because of another form of Irish linguistic error, the Irish bull. In the end he finds that the only way he can avoid these linguistic blunders is through self-enforced silence, with his hands literally covering his mouth, and so he returns to Ireland. The Hibernian tale reveals the Irish fear of always being found out by one's tongue: even without the brogue, there is always the bull.

It is this plot of ethnic difference and passing that I am attempting to locate, both on the Georgian stage and in the mixed culture of Great Britain generally. Perhaps the most famous attempt and failure at ethnic passing in Georgian England occurs when James Boswell is first introduced to Samuel Johnson. Boswell's attempt to pass is appropriately represented as entirely theatrical: it is overseen, regulated, and finally undone by an actor. Boswell records in his *Life of Johnson* (1791) that it was "Mr. Thomas Davies the actor," who, at the approach of his friend Johnson, "announced his aweful approach to me, somewhat in the manner of an actor in the part of Horatio, when he addresses Hamlet on the appearance of his father's ghost."[15] With the father figure in place to chastise the son, Boswell asks Davies not to tell Johnson he is a Scot, but the actor, a man who makes his living though theatrical disguise, unmasks him. When Boswell finds his identity discovered, he implores Johnson's forgiveness: "Mr. Johnson, (said I) I do indeed come from Scotland, but I cannot help it." Boswell is met with a taunt meant to establish his illegitimacy—"That, Sir, I find, is what a very great many of your countrymen cannot help" (*LJ*, 277). Johnson functions as a special paternal figure able to rewrite Boswell's genealogy: if by nature Boswell is a Scot, by culture he is an Englishman—or at least will become so, under Johnson's guardianship. Boswell goes on to survive Johnson's anti-Scottish prejudices by becoming what Johnson calls, in an intended compliment to Boswell, "the most *unscottified* of your countrymen" (*LJ*, 531), or "a very unnatural Scotchman" (*LJ*, 1021)—in other words, saved by his new paternity, his new (af)filiation with the lexicographer of the English language.

The "unscottified" Boswell is one of many portraits we have inherited of the Scots' attempt at learning English and being English. After all, like so many ambitious Scots of the second half of the eighteenth century, Boswell represents a new and complicated cultural hybridity, caught between a former Scottish and a new British (really English) identity: they are the children of an ambiguous and "unnatural" union—the Union of 1707. And Boswell's linguistic experiences suggest this double identity, cross-speaking in both his native and his adopted lands: a friend told him, "When you was in London you spoke Scotch to Englishmen and English to Scotchmen."[16] Boswell's *Life of Johnson* is filled with examples of the Scots' attempts at speaking English, all placed beside Boswell's portrait of Johnson, whom he calls on several occasions "the true-born Englishman." For example, as part of his own attempts to master English, Boswell recorded that the man who was tutoring him in English pronunciation remarked to Johnson, "I doubt, Sir, if any Scotchman ever attains to a perfect English pronunciation" (*LJ*, 468)—an example of the English paranoiac self-assurance that the tongue will always expose the Scot, so that passing becomes impossible. At another point Boswell gives advice to his fellow Scots about mastering English, warning them "not to speak *High English*, as we are apt to call what is far removed from the *Scotch*, but which is by no means *good English*, and makes 'the fools who use it,' truly ridiculous." Boswell also records that one Scot was told by an English shopkeeper: "I suppose, Sir, you are an American. . . . Because . . . you speak neither English nor Scotch, but something different from both" (*LJ*, 469, 470). Such anecdotes reflect on the difficulties and dangers involved when the Scot tries to reconstruct himself as English: in an attempt to claim his new British identity, the Scot may wind up alienated from both his native identity and his new national identity. Each of these anecdotes could be called a Caledonian tale, like the Hibernian tale "The Irish Incognito." They are fables of the ethnic tongue.

With such examples we begin to see that the verbal competition between Irishman and Scotsman in *Love à la Mode* lays bare a much wider cultural and political problem. During the eighteenth century, with the relocation of many Scottish and Irish immigrants to England, and with the geographical extension of the empire into different parts of the globe, there was an acute recognition of the lack of a standardized common language. This was of course clearest when it came to the spoken word. We already begin to hear this in the examples from Boswell, as we realize that at mid-century the British identified a number of varieties of spoken English: High English, Scotch English, American English, Irish English, cockney English, court English, London English, and the different provincial dialects of English. Michael Hechter has argued that England's, and especially London's, relationship not only to Ireland but also to Wales and Scotland was that of colonizer to colonized. A system of "internal colonialism" depended on devaluing and sometimes prohibiting the native languages of these nations and on using the English language to ensure colonial control and national unification.[17]

And it was in the eighteenth century that, more and more, London became identified as the metropolitan center around which all else functioned as the periphery—everything from Yorkshire to the Highlands, Ireland, and the West Indies. London became the standard of English culture, and set the standard of the English language. Christopher Hill has written of "this imposition of London standards and London speech on the rest of the country," and of how, in the interests of national unification, "the struggle of pious protestants to extend English religion and English civilization, first to the 'dark corners' of England and Wales, then to Ireland and the Highlands of Scotland, was a struggle to extend the values of London."[18]

The London stage became the most popular cultural expression of London's hegemony. Audiences were treated to a host of dialects, and the Yorkshire country clown, a kind of native exotic, was frequently placed beside the Jew or the Scot as if to underscore that even a native-born Englishman could fail to meet London standards. For example, in one multiethnic spectacle, when we hear the conventional remark, "We shall no doubt know him by his dialect," the characters are referring not to a Frenchman or a Scot but to a Yorkshireman.[19] In a play like Henry Carey's popular *Honest Yorkshire-man* (frequently performed between 1735 and the 1770s), the rich but unsophisticated Yorkshireman is chosen by a wealthy guardian to marry his ward, but his clownish blunders on his arrival in London, especially his dialect and his gullibility, disqualify him for marrying her, and instead he mistakenly marries a man who is posing as his intended bride. In the end the London/English hero (who wins the girl) offers the kind of patronizingly benevolent guardianship of the infantilized Yorkshireman that we have seen offered to the Jews and the Irish (after the skewering of the outsider has been completed): "For the honour of Yorkshire, I'll see you shan't be abused here."[20] Eventually, over the course of the eighteenth century, the arrival in London and the attendant culture shock of the Yorkshireman, or the Irishman, or the West Indian and his black slaves became a popular trope of the London stage. A play like *The Cozeners*, which Reed's *Register-Office* copies, is in fact based on the idea of a pair of London sharps taking advantage of such recent London arrivals as a gullible Irishman and a wealthy family from the country. And the conflation of such different (non-London) identities, and their exaggeration as "foreign" upon their arrival in the great English metropolis, was sounded in a title like William Macready's popular farce *The Irishman in London; or, The Happy African* (performed frequently between 1792 and 1800, and well into the nineteenth century), in which both Irish and African servants are dialect figures who, on their arrival in London, are comically compared. In short, London was the metropolitan center, and all else was peripheral, even foreign (not to mention fair game for every form of chicanery).

It was precisely this increasing importance and centrality of London that led different ethnic groups to reinvent themselves as English, more specifically as Londoners, and this in turn began to make clear to the culture at large the instability and artificiality of the new "British" identity. In the rush to reinvent themselves, these ethnic groups called into question all ethnic and national categories, and exposed the ways in which Britishness was in the process of being manufactured, invented, performed. Ethnic reinvention took several forms: the Scots and the Irish not only attempted to remove the burr and the brogue from their tongues, they anglicized their names, and Irish Catholics converted, as did English Jews, who frequently also changed their names (Jewish husbands, for example, took the names of their Protestant wives). This is why the figure of the ethnic incognito is so important, and why the theater played such a critical role in examining this phenomenon of the (re)construction of ethnic and national identity. The identity of the new Briton was performative, if nothing else. Focused on the "true-born Englishman" (Boswell's term for Johnson), with "his prejudices . . . not only against foreign countries, but against Ireland and Scotland" (*LJ*, 93), the outsider Britons anxiously reinvented themselves. This explains why actors seemed to be in charge of both the different minority ethnic identities and the one homogenous national identity. I do not mean simply that it was the job of actors to represent these different identities on the stage, replete with dialect. I mean that actors were enlisted, off stage, to reinvent the Scots and the Irish as English. Boswell notes that he took "some pains to improve my pronunciation, by the aid of the late Mr. Love, of Drury-Lane theatre; when he was a player at Edinburgh, and also of old Mr. Sheridan" (*LJ*, 469). Thus, two actors (James Love and Thomas Sheridan) make Boswell English, while another actor (Davies), in introducing him to Johnson, exposes him as Scottish.

And it was two actors, Macklin and Sheridan, who were in charge of what was taken to be a classic example of ethnic reinvention in this culture. Alexander Wedderburn was a Scot who had been educated at the University of Edinburgh and who believed that his accent would prevent him from realizing his dream of becoming the first Scot to be named Lord Chancellor (which he accomplished in 1793). Boswell describes the awkwardness of Wedderburn's bookish High English, and then recounts a success story that he advertises for all Scots—namely, how Wedderburn "got rid of the coarse part of his Scotch accent": "When I look back on this noble person at Edinburgh, in situations so unworthy of his brilliant powers, and behold LORD LOUGH-BOROUGH at London, the change seems almost like one of the metamorphoses in *Ovid*; and as his two preceptors, by refining his utterance, gave currency to his talents, we may say in the words of the poet, '*Nam vos mutastis*' [You transformed him]" (*LJ*, 274). Two (Irish) actors, Macklin and Sheridan, work the godlike power of transformation by teaching the Scotsman to speak English, in what amounts to another Georgian fable of the ethnic tongue.

Boswell recounts the story of Wedderburn's transformation because "it affords animating encouragement to other gentlemen of North-Britain to try their fortunes in the southern part of the Island, where they may hope to gratify their utmost ambition" (*LJ*, 274). With this kind of advice, it is no wonder that the art of public speaking—or English speaking—flourished. Horace Walpole exclaimed in 1754: "The new madness is Oratorys."[21] Macklin, Sheridan, and another actor-playwright, Samuel Foote, all set up "oratories," but it was Thomas Sheridan (the father of Richard Brinsley) who popularized the idea of the social and political functions of a standard pronunciation of English through a series of well-attended lectures and influential publications. As an Irishman, an actor, and a playwright, Sheridan understood directly the advantages of a plan to standardize the pronunciation of English: "It cannot be denied that an uniformity of pronunciation throughout Scotland, Wales, and Ireland, as well as through the several counties of England, would . . . contribute to destroy those odious distinctions between subjects of the same king, and members of the same community . . . which are chiefly kept alive by difference of pronunciation." According to Sheridan, dialect was the critically divisive marker of difference in the new nationalist and imperial project, Great Britain, and all dialects had "some degree of disgrace annexed to them."[22] It was through hearing Sheridan's lectures on elocution in Edinburgh in 1761, for example, that members of the Edinburgh Select Society (which boasted such figures as David Hume, William Robertson, and Adam Smith) formulated a plan for promoting the reading and speaking of the English language in Scotland. And while it was Sheridan who first noticed the importance of training Irish and Scottish children in English, he insisted on doing so in their native lands. Sheridan predicted nothing less than "the Ruin of *Ireland*" because he understood that an education in England was a form of assimilation that would alienate Irish children from Ireland.[23] Both Boswell and Hume similarly understood "the advantage of an English education" (*LJ*, 1167) while warning of the consequences; Hume noted, "Few Scotsmen, that have had an English Education, have ever settled cordially in their own Country,"[24] and Boswell warned about English-educated Scots "being totally estranged from their native country" (*LJ*, 1167). Johnson joked with Boswell but in fact portrayed a grim reality: "As an Englishman, I should wish all the Scotch gentlemen to be educated in England; Scotland would become a province; they would spend all their rents in England" (*LJ*, 1167). Johnson well understood—and boasted of—the power of English assimilation: "Much (said he,) may be made of a Scotchman, if he be *caught* young" (*LJ*, 494).

The theater responded aggressively to the ambitions of ethnic minorities as speakers and especially as masters of English. In Samuel Foote's *The Minor* (1760), for example, the prologue has two characters asking Foote what kind of play he is currently rehearsing; illustrating the taste of the Georgian English audience, they implore him, "Give us then a national portrait: a Scotchman or an Irishman." Foote answers in what at first seems a critique of all the plays that make fun of the Scot's and the Irishman's attempts at spoken English: "If you mean merely the dialect of the two countries, I cannot think it either a subject of satire or of humour." He then goes on, however, to direct a blow at the Scot who thinks he has mastered English: "If indeed a North Briton, struck with a scheme of reformation, should advance from the banks of the Tweed to teach the English the true pronunciation of their own language, he would, I think merit your laughter."[25]

The theater proceeded to stage the competition over the mastery of the English language in what became a formulaic plot that demonstrated how ethnic minorities misspoke even as they claimed absolute authority over the English language. So the competition between the Scot and the Irishman in *Love à la Mode* became, only a few years later, reprised in Richard Cumberland's popular *Fashionable Lover* (1772), a multiethnic spectacle intended to recuperate Scottish identity (at the same time that it ridiculed all the other ethnic minorities as foolish or malicious, or both). In Cumberland's play all four outsiders—Scot, Frenchman, Welshman, and Jew—were marked by dialect. More specifically, we see how central the English language became in the competition between different ethnic figures in this culture when the Scot and the Welshman argue (in dialect) about speaking English properly. Dr. Druid, the Welshman, exclaims, "Pray, Gentlemens, bear witness: is Master Colins here a proper teacher of the dialects, d'ye see, and pronunciations of the English tongue?" while Macleod, the Scot, replies: "Why not? Is there not Duncan Ross of Aberdeen that lactures twice a week in oratory at the Seven

Dials? And does not Sawney Ferguson, a cousin of mine awn, administer the English language in its utmost elegance at Amsterdam?"[26] So, by the early 1770s the stage was explicitly recording that administering the English language (whether at home or abroad) had became a significant profession that ethnic minorities competed to master. In fact, the competition among ethnic minorities over the mastery of language generally became so popular that it was staged as a comedy in various discourses. For example, a little farce in *The Universal Songster* entitled "Life of a Collegian" functions as a kind of multi-ethnic spectacle based on language use in which different characters interact and implicitly compete in dialect. A young collegian arrives at Oxford, where a money-lending Jew (Smouchey Solomon) is presented to the student's tutor as a rabbi (who instructs him in Hebrew). Meanwhile, the "Scotch Proctor" (Dr. McJargon) examines both a Welsh and an Irish student in the Greek language, and all three recite Greek and speak English with strong native accents, with the Scot providing the following verdicts: about Mr. Shenkin ap Watkins, "We must e'en send him back to his native goats again," and about Mr. Terence O'Terry, "He mun gang back to the bogs again."[27]

The stage relentlessly tested its ethnic characters in speaking proper English and in cross-ethnic speaking. In John O'Keeffe's *The Irish Mimic; or, Blunders at Brighton* (1795), for example, the only ethnic or national identity the Irish mimic Mr. Parrots declares he is incapable of performing (with a comical lack of self-knowledge) is that of the Irishman. He claims that he produces different speech patterns "second-hand," and that in a theater, appropriately enough, he has caught the dialects of a Scot, a Frenchman, and an Irishman, but only the latter has been too difficult for him to mimic: "He has such a devil of a brogue, that he's the only person there I cannot mimick neatly." But another character of course disputes this by exclaiming that Mr. Parrots "attempts to imitate every character and dialect the most opposite; yet, with such an invincible brogue, that when he fancies he speaks or sings a variety of voices, you can only think yourself in a debating society at Tipperary."[28]

Every Scot or Irishman or Welshman attempting to speak English is in some sense a "Mr. Parrots," for in such plays the idea of passing is exposed as the act of an ethnic outsider performing at "second-hand" a language that is not his own. Even off the stage the ethnic other was consistently shown as nothing more than a mimic, a kind of parrot, as Hume's characterization of Francis Williams, the Cambridge-trained mathematician, made clear. In his well-known essay "Of National Characters," after admitting "I am apt to suspect the negroes . . . to be naturally inferior to the whites," Hume adds:

"In JAMAICA indeed they talk of one negroe as a man of parts and learning; but 'tis likely he is admired for very slender accomplishments, like a parrot, who speaks a few words plainly."[29] Once again, the test of the tongue is the ultimate test in Georgian England. Edward Long, in his *History of Jamaica*, devotes an entire chapter to Williams, a native Jamaican who was sent to England to be educated as "the subject of an experiment," to see if "a negroe might not be found as capable of literature as a white person." Long opens his chapter with a theatrical metaphor—"to introduce [Williams] upon the stage"—and measures his literary accomplishment (a Latin poem) as a "performance," as if Williams were only an actor pretending to be white, wearing "in common a huge wig, which made a very venerable figure" at the same time that it seems to underscore his impersonation. Long quotes Williams— "He defined himself 'a white man acting under a black skin'"—but what Long gives us is a portrait of a black man acting like, impersonating, a white man. Long approvingly quotes Hume on Williams, and simply gives us a more extensive portrait of the parrot, in a series of performative imitations, in which, for example, Williams's pupil is no more than a copy of Williams's copy of whiteness: "The chief pride of this disciple consists in imitating the garb and deportment of his tutor."[30]

Stage comedies and farces began to focus on the competition among ethnic minorities within a deliberately theatrical setting, as if to underscore the performative nature of the Scot or the Irishman speaking proper English and the critical role the theater played in judging and demonstrating who could speak English and who could not. In Arthur Murphy's immensely popular *The Apprentice* (1756), for example, an Irishman and a Scot (generic names are the only names they are given) both aspire to careers on the stage: the Scot contends, "I should have *sheened* in *Macbeeth*," while the Irishman, blacking his face, declares, "I should have *boddered* 'em in *Othollo*," where speaking the lines of the English bard is the ultimate test of Englishness. The Scot declares his superiority—"For the elocution you will see that we have the preference"[31]—in what became a standard comic gesture on the stage (in *The Register-Office*, for example, the Scot boasts, "Ye may ken by my Elocution, A'm a Man o' nae sma' Lair").[32] George Colman the Elder's *New Brooms!*, a prelude performed on opening night at Drury Lane Theatre in 1776 (and for several weeks thereafter), anticipates the entire theatrical season and encapsulates the central ideological battle over the English theater by representing a Frenchman who in broken English argues for introducing a ballet for the new season, an Irishman who blunders in his brogue while aspiring to be an actor on the English stage, and an Englishman who implicitly argues for the enshrinement of the English language by arguing for the importance of Shakespeare on the English stage. The Irishman who travels to London (in the conventional trope of the outsider arriving in the English metropolis) to be an actor declares, when asked if his brogue will stand in his way, "It's very will known that nobody spakes English so will as your Irishmen—except the Scotch, indeed."[33] The argument over who speaks proper English in these texts engages directly the issue of a national theater, with the English theater represented in need of protection against foreign invasion. Attacks on foreign performers typically focused on their failure to speak English properly: for example, Madame Catalani, an Italian opera singer who appeared on the English stage in the early nineteenth century, was said to be "murdering our native tongue with broken English," while Leigh Hunt argued, "Such a person has not quite the least pretense for appearing on an English stage, if it is only for one reason—that one *great* object of the drama is, or at least ought to be, *the improvement and ornament of the* ENGLISH LANGUAGE."[34]

So, the battle lines in the contest over the English language were drawn quite starkly along ethnic and national lines, both in the theater and beyond. Johnson had made metropolitan English the standard by which all other forms of the language fell short, and he was consistently on his guard against the intrusion of outsiders. We see this in Johnson's reaction to Thomas Sheridan's plan to publish a dictionary that would standardize English pronunciation: "What entitles Sheridan to fix the pronunciation of English? He has, in the first place, the disadvantage of being an Irishman" (*LJ*, 470). We see it again in Johnson's reaction to Hume's project to make a collection of Scotticisms: "I wonder, (said Johnson,) that *he* should find them" (*LJ*, 404). It is not surprising, then, that one of the many popular prints satirizing the Scottish Lord Bute represents Johnson offering to teach him English: "I'll teach his Lordship to speak English."[35] So, while the theater was representing ethnic minorities in competition over the English language, Johnson saw himself (and was seen by others) as the master pedagogue, the master Englishman. Johnson, the chief lexicographer of English, guarded the English language, while Irishmen threatened to become masters of spoken English and Scotsmen threatened to become masters of written English. On this last point, Hume gloated with the pride of the underdog (even while admitting that the Scots had lost the battle of the tongue): "Is it not strange that, at a time when we have lost our Princes, our Parliaments, our independent Government, even the Presence of our chief Nobility, are unhappy, in our Accent &

Pronunciation, speak a very corrupt Dialect of the Tongue which we make use of; is it not strange, I say, that, in these Circumstances, we shou'd really be the People most distinguish'd for Literature in Europe?" But he remained painfully self-conscious about his spoken English: "As to my Tongue, you have seen, that I regard it as totally desperate and irreclaimable." And even changing the spelling of his name to conform to the rules of English pronunciation failed to settle Home/Hume comfortably in England, with an English identity: "Can you seriously talk of my continuing an Englishman? Am I, or are you, an Englishman? Will they allow us to be so? Do they not treat with Derision our Pretensions to that Name?" Finally, Hume even growled about "my Misfortune to write in the language of the most stupid and factious Barbarians in the World"—as if he wrote in the language of a foreign people.[36]

While Hume growled at the English and bemoaned his accent, the Irishman Sheridan saw correct English pronunciation as the central component of a dream of lost and reclaimed legitimacy, based on a family romance in which the sons that have been cast out are finally reclaimed and restored to power. It was the dream of a common language that would mean the end of family quarrels. For Sheridan, correct pronunciation became the central component of this dream: "Thus might the rising generation, born and bred in different countries, and counties, no longer have a variety of dialects, but as subjects of one king, like sons of one father, have one common tongue."[37] This is the dream of the Briton, the peripheral outsider who through language reaches the center. But this "one common tongue" was a fiction on a number of counts, most clearly because it inevitably meant leaving behind one's native language for English as it was spoken in London. The dream of restoration was in fact a mask for the dream of reinvention.

Moreover, the kinds of ethnic anxieties I am exploring in Georgian culture actually reached into the royal chambers, for the national father figure himself, the king, was not the paternal fount of English but an outsider marked by a foreign accent. After the Hanoverian succession in 1714 even the royal family had trouble defining itself as English. Foreign by birth and tongue, born and brought up in Germany, the first two Georges were unpopular at least in part because of their failure to define themselves as distinctly English monarchs. Walpole noted about the third George, "Being the first of his line born in England, the prejudice against his family as foreigners ceased in his person."[38] The view of the foreignness of the Georges included everything from the criticism of George II's slighting of England for Germany, to George III's slighting of England for Scotland.[39] In a variety of ways, then, the House of Hanover was pictured as un-English, even anti-English. Sheridan in fact marks the fall from a common language with the Hanoverian succession: "There was a time, . . . during the reign of Queen Anne, when English was the language spoken at court. . . . This produced a uniformity in that article in all the polite circles. . . . But on the accession of a foreign family to the throne, . . . the English language suffered much by being banished the court, to make room for the French. From that time the regard formerly paid to pronunciation has been gradually declining."[40]

By focusing on multiethnic spectacle as a specific cultural form invented during the reign of the Georges, I mean to signal the way in which even the ruling Hanoverian dynasty itself represented the kinds of ethnic diversity, division, and reinvention that marked the age. This intersection between the foreign Georges and the multiethnic spectacle in fact occurred when George II, rarely attending the theater at seventy-three years of age, sent for a copy of *Love à la Mode* and ordered that it be read to him. He revealed his discomfort at the notion of acculturated foreigners unsuccessfully posing as English:

Sir Archy: Whereever I gang, I am awways taken for an Englishman.
Sir Callaghan: O be, bo, bo boo! An Englishman! Ha! Ha! Upon my
    honour, it must be such an Englishman as I am then.
Sir Archy: What mean ye by sik an Englishman as ye are then?
Sir Callaghan: Why an outlandish Englishman, Sir Archy.
Sir Archy: I do not understand you, Sir.
Sir Callaghan: Why I am an Irish-englishman, and you are a Scotch-
    englishman, and so by the rule you know Sir Archy we are both
    outlandish Englishmen.[41]

This passage, eventually cut from the play (perhaps at royal suggestion), must have reminded the king that he himself was seen by his subjects as a kind of outlandish Englishman.

The specific picture we have of George II listening to *Love à la Mode* only confirms why he would not have been able to forget his own foreignness: "An old Hanoverian gentleman was commanded to read it to him. Eleven weeks were spent by this person in misrepresenting the Author's meaning. He was totally void of humour, and unacquainted with the English language."[42] This reading of the play presented quite a mixture of "brogues," Scottish, Irish, and German, extending our notion of how ethnically hybrid England in fact was, and how many levels of impersonation constituted the project of

Great Britain. The king heard the Scot and the Irishman compete over who spoke better English through the heavily accented impersonation of the old Hanoverian, who must have reminded the king of his own unsuccessful attempt to pass as an Englishman.

I am arguing that a play like *Love à la Mode* divided its audience along ethnic lines—including the discomfort of the old king at his own foreignness, the disturbances caused by the Scots who attended the opening performances of the play, and the attempt by the Scottish Lord Bute to have the play prohibited.[43] In addition, contemporary reports explain that the English enjoyed the play all the more for the Scottish protests it caused: "The petulance of these North Britons . . . served only to increase its popularity, and they had the mortification to witness its success."[44] Finally, English reviewers noted that the author was Irish and that Sir Callaghan's triumph in the courtship contest was in part owing to Macklin's "national partiality" to his own countrymen (*Monthly Mirror*, June 1800, p. 372). *Love à la Mode*, then, demonstrates the way in which a play could invite viewing not from the position of what we saw in my previous chapter Walter Scott called our "common humanity" but rather from a particular subject position that is partial, ethnic. Jewish, Scottish, German, Irish, and English audience members would have had varying experiences, and the multiethnic spectacle as a new cultural form was constitutive of this kind of multiple, ethnically based response.

Sir Callaghan's realistic skepticism about the likely success of a Scot or Irishman passing as English illuminates not only the anxieties of the king but also those of the Irish author. We hear in this passage Macklin's own first-hand knowledge of the Irishman who never felt accepted as an Englishman, and who at once both escaped and compounded the dilemma of his own outlandish Irishness by making a career out of impersonating different ethnic types, most notably Jews and Scotsmen. In his early days as an actor Macklin's Irishness especially dogged him, for while he changed his name from MacLaughlin, his tongue still marked him as Irish, and it is not too much to say, in the words of an early biographer, "He . . . made the English language the object of his pursuit." "Though he took much pains to get rid of the natural brogue, it stuck to him a long time, and was certainly a great bar to his advancement" because "this defect . . . [was] so gross to an English audience." So he began to study with an accomplished Englishwoman who undertook "to cure him of his brogue." All of his earlier attempts, over the years, "to get rid of his natural accent" paled beside the new regime instituted by this Englishwoman: "Every word he spoke with the Irish tone, every provincial phrase, every singularity, she noted, and interrupted him in." Finally he presented himself to a theater manager who hired him on probation, and after seeing Macklin perform, told him that "if he could cut three or four inches more of the brogue from his tongue, he would speak the part well. Macklin replied, he wished he could; but observed, that cutting off tongues was a dangerous experiment."[45] This picture of Macklin's attempts at acculturation suggests how the birth of the Englishman meant the silencing, even the mutilation, of the Irishman—a more sober view of sharing "the common tongue" than another Irishman, Thomas Sheridan, imagined.

Macklin did in fact learn to pass as an Englishman, and it is in this guise that he actually created the Irish hero of *Love à la Mode*. At a Covent Garden tavern Macklin and another celebrated Irish actor, Spranger Barry, met an Irish soldier who became the model for Sir Callaghan and the impetus for the play in general. With Macklin passing as an Englishman, Barry told Irish stories and "brought [the Irishman] out in the full blow of self-exhibition." *Love à la Mode*, then, is born in a moment of ethnic spying and passing that casts Macklin in the role of the English spectator observing the spectacle of Irishness. Under (acculturated) English eyes, the native Irishman is at once simple and comical, pure and provincial—in this case, one's former self that one views with a mixture of nostalgia and critique. "When Macklin (who passed himself off for an Englishman all the while) attributed [the soldier's] successes with the ladies from having a *tail behind*, as common to all Irishmen, he instantly pulled off his coat and waistcoat, to convince him of his mistake, assuring him 'that no Irishman, in *that respect*, was better than another man.'" Here the Irishman's self-exhibition sets off his sexual prowess. After all, "In his person he was near six feet high, finely formed, of a handsome manly face," and he related "a long list of his amours both in France and Prussia."[46] Macklin, the Irishman masked as English, is the spectator with his tongue cut off, watching the Irishman exhibit himself as Irish, that is, as the speaker who blunders but who is nonetheless physically intact, in tongue as well as elsewhere—the unemasculated Irishman showing off his parts. In short, the actor, the reconstructed man, is contrasted with the native, the original man.

This scene of the genesis of *Love à la Mode*, with its picture of two Irishmen, one hiding behind the mask of Englishness and the other fully self-exhibiting his Irishness, suggests the two alternatives for ethnic minorities in Georgian culture. In the Georgian theater ethnic identity is frequently doubled, whether this means simply that two or more different ethnic types appear on the stage at the same time (as in the multiethnic spectacle in general), or that two different versions of the same ethnicity appear on the stage at the same time—as in my example of the two Jews in the double bill of *Merchant* and *Love à la Mode*, or as in *The Oxonian in Town*, where the refined Irishman disparages his dark double, "too gross to pass" because of "the rank brogue in his mouth."[47] We have a significant example of the doubling of Irish identity between the unreconstructed native and the acculturated impersonator in a play written by Macklin a few years later. In *The True-born Irishman* (which premiered in Dublin in 1761 and in London in 1767 with the new title *The Irish Fine Lady*), Irish identity is split between a husband, the true-born Irishman (played by Macklin himself), and his wife, the Irishwoman who has pretensions to be something other than Irish. This gender split is typical of Macklin's working out of the differences between the native (the male) and the acculturated (the female or the emasculated). The wife, after a visit to London, changes her name from the Irish Mrs. O'Dogherty to the English Mrs. Diggerty, and brings back to Ireland "a new kind of a London English" as opposed to "our Irish English"—though her pretentious mispronunciations ("veestly," "imminsely," "compirison," "neem") expose her failed mastery of London English.[48] The husband fears his wife has brought back from England a "distemper" that he names "the Irish Fine Lady's delirium, or the London vertigo," and the play becomes an attack on the Irish "phrenzy of admiration for every thing in England" (*TBI*, 85). The portrait of the Irish fine lady suggests the foolish lengths to which minority ethnic populations will go in order to appear English, and the stage appropriately becomes the vehicle for the exposure of such performative reinventions.

While the first act of this two-act comedy focuses on the follies of the anglicized Irish woman, the second act focuses on the designs of the Englishman who plots to seduce her. In this way the anglicization of the Irish woman is configured as her seduction by an Englishman: acculturation, seduction, and dishonor are one and the same. The charge of "an infectious stain upon [her] chastity" (*TBI*, 109) becomes in effect the charge of her submission to English charms—that is, the loss of her innocence, her pure, natural state, her Irishness. But the play ultimately engineers the undoing not of the Irishwoman, but of the English seducer, in a metatheatrical scene in which the women whom he has charmed hide themselves in the next room so they can watch unnoticed as the audience of the Englishman's fall. In a comical scene the Englishman tries to pass—as a woman—when he dresses in Mrs. O'Dogherty's clothes to avoid detection by her husband, thus highlighting the difference between the masculine Irish husband and the feminine English seducer. So, this scene turns upside down the topos of the Irishman (or the Scotsman) trying to pass and being found out. While in the first act an Irishwoman tries to pass as English, and fails, in the second act an Englishman tries to pass as a woman, and succeeds. The Englishman's "passion for himself" (*TBI*, 107) indicates an English self-absorption that is represented as a kind of narcissistic perversion, a confusion in gender and in sexual object choice. The Englishman in drag, "ten times fonder of himself—if possible—as a woman . . . than he was as a man" (*TBI*, 107), on the point of being penetrated—"run through the body" (*TBI*, 118)—by the Irish husband, calls for a closet in which to hide himself, but instead is forcibly installed in a large trunk, which becomes at once his prison and his display box. So the gendered splitting of Irish identity in the first act, between the masculine Irish husband and the feminine anglicized wife, becomes reconfigured in the second act as the ethnic difference between the masculine Irish husband and the feminine English seducer/transgressor. In a ritualized unmanning of the Englishman, amid his cries of "don't expose me" (*TBI*, 120), the Irish women approach him, laugh at him, throw snuff in his face, and ridicule him. The Englishman exposed and displayed in public: it is the triumph of the true-born Irishman (played by Macklin) to have produced at last this spectacle of Englishness.[49]

So, for all the pressures to assimilate, to succumb to "the London vertigo," to speak London English, there were in fact acts of resistance on the stage. I have explored the ways in which in *Love à la Mode* the Irish suitor triumphs over the Englishman in the competition of courtship, and in *The True-born Irishman* the Irish husband mortifies the feminized English seducer; in the course of this book I explore other such acts of resistance, especially the attempt to recuperate Jewish identity on the stage. Moreover, I have shown that in both plays the act of passing as English is caricatured, and I have been suggesting that the Georgian theater was replete with ethnic imposters who tried to pass but failed. While at first this may have expressed the hegemonic culture's refusal to allow any outsider to pass as English, the trope of the failed pass also began to critique the imposter's devaluation of his or her own native culture. Especially in the hands of an author drawn from an ethnic minority, as in the case of Macklin, the trope of the failed ethnic imposter became a way of authenticating minority cultures.

A number of scholars have demonstrated the different ideological debates regarding the English language that emerged in the second half of the eighteenth century, and I am attempting to reinsert the theater's role into these debates, especially as the culture's premier arena of the spoken word. John Barrell and Olivia Smith have shown how Johnson's privileging of the language of books over the language of the living voice came under radical attack, from Thomas Paine and Joseph Priestley through William Wordsworth and William Hazlitt.[50] Barrell suggests the wide divergence of opinion about the English language, on the one hand showing that for Johnson the "current metropolitan language" was the standard by which everything else was to be judged and that "whatever is in London, is right for everywhere else," while on the other hand showing that for Priestley "dialects . . . have flourished most in conditions of political freedom."[51] Because Johnson (seeing himself in the role of Caesar) contemplated the invasion and conquest of English, Barrell rightly insists on "the political nature of the task—in settling and subduing the language, Johnson will also be settling and subduing the inhabitants of England, the speakers of English"—the latter of which included, I would add, the Scots, the Irish, men and women from the provinces, and essentially all members of the growing empire of Great Britain. In addition, scholars have recorded the emergence of the Scots and Gaelic literary revivals and a widespread Celtomania, stimulated through the prominent success in the early 1760s of James Macpherson's *Oisin* poems (which fused an oral tradition of poetry to a Scottish ethnic and nationalist identity) and institutionalized through the establishment of societies to protect the Irish language (such as the Hibernian Antiquarian Society in 1779, the Royal Irish Academy in 1782, the Gaelic Society in 1808). Both Katie Trumpener and Janet Sorensen have persuasively demonstrated the ways in which the Scots in particular fought against Johnson's standardization of English and his valorization of the written word over the spoken.[52] J. C. D. Clark has written of the symbolic timing of Johnson's decision to undertake the project of his *Dictionary* (1755) "in spring of 1746, as the Stuart cause was going down to final and crushing defeat."[53] In this context, the *Dictionary* looks as if it functioned as the final defeat of the Scots, a linguistic Culloden. When one recent scholar remarks, "The eighteenth century was the age of the triumphant march of English,"[54] his figure of speech suggests the inherent militancy of the anglicization of the peripheries as a form of cultural conquest. And Linda Colley has suggested the length and breadth of that triumphant march in estimating that "At least three hundred guides to the English language were published between 1750 and 1800: six times more than had been available in the previous half-century."[55]

While scholars have shown how the English language became an object of scrutiny and ideological contest for everyone from linguists and radical reformers and poets to Scottish and Irish nationalists and antiquaries, the central arena of the theater, in which language in general and speech in particular were negotiated before a live audience and open to public review and the commentary of a wide diversity of people, has been neglected. Increasingly in the second half of the eighteenth century the entire theatrical community, from actors and playwrights to audiences and reviewers, acutely examined the representation of the speech of the regional and the peripheral outsider on the stage. In what I wish to call the emergence of the ethnic or native voice, I recognize a new effort at legitimately reproducing the various dialects of Great Britain, both within the theater and without. In such a context, the rustics of Wordsworth's "preface" to *Lyrical Ballads* (1800), who speak a pure and even philosophical language, function as a critique not simply of Johnson's attack on the speech of those whom he names "the ignorant" and "the vulgar" in the "preface" to his *Dictionary*, but perhaps even more pointedly of the rustics who speak a jumbled regional jargon on the stage, like the Yorkshire clown. And I take the true-born Irishman's demand, in Macklin's play, for a return to Irish English as a representation of a much larger movement toward the legitimization of the ethnic and provincial voice in the culture at large.

In addition to the many guides to English, Georgian culture produced (increasingly in the second half of the century) a host of guides and glossaries to the various dialects across England, sometimes to entertain an English audience by caricaturing these dialects and their practitioners, but sometimes to preserve these dialects and even to argue for their authenticity and ancientness (along the lines that were argued by antiquarians for Gaelic). Such works attempted to reproduce the Cornish, Lancashire, Manchester, Somersetshire, and other regional dialects, and while many aim at humor and perhaps even caricature, in sum they aim at the accurate documentation of the vast array of dialects that were still spoken (but that were slowly declining) throughout Britain: "Hence every County has its peculiar Dialect, at least in respect to the vulgar *Language* of their Rustics, insomuch that those of different Counties cannot easily understand each other." Precisely as the standardization of (written, London) English was advancing, the growing disappearance of these many dialects became recognized, so that works began to appear that represented the extraordinary diversity of dialects and inspected them in a new attempt at accuracy and preservation. The theatricality of these works is plain in their attempt to reproduce a spoken language through inscribed dialogue, but they were also aimed against the sloppy and inaccurate stage dialect that typically assimilated all regional dialects into one entirely invented comic dialect. Authors insist, for example, that the language they have recorded is "not an arbitrary Collection of ill-connected clownish Words, like those introduced into the journals of some late Sentimental Travellers as well as the productions of some Dramatic Writers, whose Clowns no more speak in their own proper Dialects, than a dull School-boy makes elegant and classical *Latin*; their supposed *Language* being such as would be no less unintelligible to the Rustics themselves, than to those politer Pretenders to Criticism who thereby mean to make them ridiculous."[56] And theater reviewers began to be consistently on guard against such inaccuracy when performers attempted to reproduce regional dialects. A reviewer in the *Monthly Mirror*, for example, complained of the collapsing of all rural dialects into the Yorkshire dialect: an actor was criticized as "reprehensible for not acquiring thoroughly the Somersetshire dialect. . . . I am aware your great Covent Garden actor makes almost every county in England *Yorkshire*" (July 1805, p. 62).

Guides to provincial dialects typically used a variety of scholarly apparatuses that looked forward to Maria Edgeworth's glossary in *Castle Rackrent* (1800) and to the Edgeworths' documentary attitude toward Irish speech in *Irish Bulls.* So, for all its humor, different editions in the 1780s and 1790s of *An Exmoor scolding, in the propriety and decency of Exmoor language, between two sisters* contained either a glossary or a pair of columns reproducing the dialect version and a standardized English translation. Even a primarily comic text like Tim Bobbin's *A View of the Lancashire dialect* (published in Manchester and London in various editions from the 1740s through the 1790s), which contained "the adventures and misfortunes of a Lancashire clown," offered a serious explanation of the pronunciation of the Lancashire dialect. At the more scholarly end of the spectrum, William Pryce's *Archaeologia Cornu-Britannica; or, an essay to preserve the ancient Cornish language; containing the rudiments of that dialect, in a Cornish grammar and Cornish-English vocabulary* (Sherborne, 1790) carried as subtitle, "An essay to preserve the ancient Cornish language," and attempted to explain how the "old British language," superseded by the "Saxon tongue," "was driven to the borders and extremities, such as Scotland, Wales, and Cornwall, where it still maintains a reverence and footing among the respective inhabitants, in the dress of differing dialects." Pryce, with full antiquarian melancholy, "lament[s] the loss of our native language" (the editor's preface, n.p.).

The same kind of critical attention was directed at Scottish and Irish dialects, both on stage and off. Boswell the Scot, for all his attempts at self-anglicization, told Irishman Edmund Burke "that it was better for a Scotsman and an Irishman to preserve so much of their native accent and not to be quite perfect in English, because it was unnatural. . . . I said it was unnatural to hear a Scotsman speaking perfect English. He appeared a machine. I instanced Wedderburn," and told Lord Lisburne that "it put me in a passion to hear a Scotsman speaking in a perfect English tone. It was a false voice."[57] So, here in Boswell's remarks, as well as in Macklin's caricature of Mrs. Diggerty's mincing metropolitan English, the ethnic critique of the "false voice" begins to emerge in what amounts to an ideological backlash against the imperative to pass, to speak London English, to denature oneself, to become a mechanical parrot. In fact, the resistance to the standardization of English began to include a strong note of rebellion, suggesting the way in which peripheral and colonial cultures could form an alliance against England, so while a Scot like James Beattie complained, "We are slaves to the language," Benjamin Franklin in the *Gazetteer* suggested a form of liberation by chastising England for critiquing its fellow countrymen "because they cannot yet speak 'Plain English'" and issuing a threat that reinterpreted the notion of "plain English": "It is my opinion, Master BULL, that the Scotch and Irish, as well as the colonists, are capable of speaking much *plainer English* than they have ever yet spoke, but which I hope they will never be provoked to speak."[58]

More and more, ethnic minorities asserted the value of their own languages, as is clear in the following anecdote about an encounter between the two titans Johnson and Macklin, who compete over the question of linguistic competency as if they were characters in one of the plays that I am analyzing, even Macklin's own *Love à la Mode*. Because Macklin was proficient in a number of classical and modern languages, Johnson's attempts to stump and even embarrass the Irishman finally settled on addressing him

with a string of sounds perfectly unintelligible. "What's that, Sir?" inquired Macklin. "Hebrew!" answered Johnson. "And what do I know of Hebrew?"—"But a man of your understanding, Mr. Macklin, ought to be acquainted with every language!" the Doctor's face glowed with a smile of triumph.—"*Och neil en deigen vonsht hom boge vaureen!*" exclaimed Macklin. Johnson was now dumb-founded, and inquired the name of the lingua? "Irish, Sir!"—"Irish!" exclaimed the Doctor. "Do you think I ever studied that?"—"But a man of your understanding, Doctor Johnson, ought to be acquainted with every language."[59]

By displacing the conventional competition over speaking English between an Irishman and an Englishman (both of whom, in this case, saw themselves as experts in English) onto a field of different languages, this anecdote suggests how Irish had commonly been seen as a primitive language and hints at the increasing recognition of Irish as an ancient language worthy of being taught and learned. In this encounter Macklin brilliantly manages to make Irish, not English, the insider language, the language of the learned. A similar point is made on the stage in *The Oxonian in Town* when the English-educated Irish student Knowell, down from Oxford, meets an uneducated Irishman in London, whom he tells that at the university the scholars "study the languages." When McShuffle asks, "Do they understand Irish, honey?" and the student answers, "No," McShuffle responds: "Oh, then the devil burn me, if mine ownshelf, or Paddy the chairman in the Pee-a-ches, is not a grater scholar than any of them. (*Gabbles Irish*.) Can they talk so, my dear?"[60] Such an episode both makes fun of McShuffle's gabbling and questions Oxford as a seat of learning where the ancient language of Irish is untaught.

Speaking ethnic dialects with accuracy on the stage began to do battle with speaking a kind of uniform ethnic jargon meant only as caricature, and in this way the voices of a genuinely multiethnic society began to emerge. The legitimization of the ethnic voice on the stage occurred at several levels: it began to put ethnic minorities themselves in charge of speaking native dialects (as actors), authoring ethnic characters (as playwrights), and judging ethnic representations (as critics and audience members). In the *Monthly Mirror* in 1808, for example, an actress was chastised because "her Scottish dialect was so imperfect as to be . . . little better than broken English" (March, pp. 268–69), while another actor was praised for "speak[ing] the dialect in its '*ancient purity*'" (May, p. 401). And part of the almost universal protest against the caricature of Irish identity in the original version of Sheridan's *The Rivals* focused on an actor's unsuccessful attempt at the Irish dialect; he was criticized for speaking a "horrid medley of discordant brogues," "gabbling in an uncouth dialect, neither Welch, English, nor Irish." This criticism was part of a larger complaint about the representation of Irish identity in the play: "Sir Lucius O'Trigger was so ungenerous an attack upon a nation . . . it is the first time I ever remember to have seen so villainous a portrait of an Irish Gentleman, permitted so openly to insult that country upon the boards of an English theatre." This final critique, which appeared in the *Morning Chronicle*, came from a writer who signed himself "A Briton" in an obvious attempt at national solidarity and unity.[61] This kind of public pressure forced the play to close, and it did not reopen until Sheridan had revised the role of Sir Lucius, which was played with great success by a new actor—an Irishman well known for having begun his career in Dublin and for having, in his debut year on the London stage, a "Voice a Little too much upon the Brogue."[62]

But the ethnic voice was rescued not simply by Britons who came to the aid of ethnic minorities to save their speech from sloppy (mis)representation or cutting caricature. Ethnic minorities began to see themselves as the proper judges of dialect, and ethnic voices were raised in approval or disapproval of those actors who attempted to represent them. In a pamphlet in which the author names himself solely in ethnic terms—*A Scotsman's Remarks on the Farce of "Love à la Mode"* (1760)—we have not simply an attack on the anti-Scottish prejudice of the play ("Why then impose all the scoundrelism of the piece upon Scots shoulders?") but a critique of Macklin's "execrable imitation of the Scots accent, through which breaks out ever and anon the *Irish brogue*."[63] By signing himself "A Scotsman," the writer authorized himself simply by his ethnic identity, which he used as the basis of a critique of the play's anti-Scottish prejudice in two ways: he is an authority on the Scottish dialect in particular and on the Scottish character in general. His position begins to raise important theatrical questions: Can an Irishman play a Scot, and is a Scot's view of Sir Archy Macsarcasm especially valid, authorized in some particular way? The question of an Irishman playing a Scot was another way of raising the issue of the multiple viewing that occurred in the Georgian theater, where the ideological positions represented in the theater as a whole could be determined in multiple and competing ways. For example, writing in 1805 about Macklin's attempt at a Scots accent, an early biographer of Macklin claimed "he was never considered by the natives as a good Scotchman; though what he had substituted for Scotch, was not only always accepted, but always applauded as such by an English audience."[64] On the one hand, the performance of ethnic identities functioned as a kind of game or sport (look at the Irishman playing the Jew or the Scot!). On the other hand, we see emerging an unusually modern approach to identity politics—namely, the idea that one sees and speaks from a specific ethnic position and is thereby authorized to challenge the authenticity of another's representation of one's own ethnic group.

The growing recognition and acceptance of ethnic differences in audiences was typically pitted against the idea of a homogenized Great Britain where all different identities were supposed to be subsumed in the single identity of the Briton, or more likely, the Englishman. So, when another Scotsman complained about the character of Sir Pertinax in the name of "A Scotsman"—"I am in heart, in soul, A Scotsman"—he was chastised by a reader of the *Monthly Mirror*: "You a Scotsman? Not you, indeed, Mr. Pamphleteer. No man is either a true Scotsman, or a true Englishman, who is not a true Briton, as the *worthy* natives of both countries well know. National prejudices . . . have long been out of fashion in England" (August 1806, p. 136). This is the voice of an increasingly popular ideology at the turn of the century, the voice of the new Briton, beyond all ethnic and national distinctions. But I have been articulating the ways in which the theater illuminated and often provoked the experiential truth that an Irish or Scottish audience might see a play differently from an English audience: how could a Scot not respond as a Scot to such a patently anti-Scottish portrait in a play that always provoked "*John Bull's* perpetual roar of enjoyment" at the expense of the Scots (as another Briton recorded about Macklin's *The Man of the World* in the same pages of the *Monthly Mirror* [March 1808, p. 268])?

As an Irishman, Macklin was acutely aware of these divisions in audiences, so he was not surprised when *The True-born Irishman*, with its lively success in Ireland, failed in London (under its revised title, *The Irish Fine Lady*). Macklin probably understood that, with its attack on the anglicization of Irish culture, the comedy was bound to fail in England, and he explained: "There's a *geography* in *humour* as well as in *morals*, which I had not previously considered."[65] In another example of this geography, an Irish Catholic wrote to the editor of the *Irish magazine* in 1809 to wonder how "the Catholic part of the audience," "a Dublin Catholic audience," could sit through Sheridan's popular English comedy *The Duenna*, a play filled with "sarcasms on their religion."[66] The theater world increasingly began to acknowledge this geography (as I suggested in the previous chapter): reviewers understood, for example, that a play that succeeded in London might have "too coarse a portrait of an Irishman to please *here* [in Dublin]"—this from an Irish reviewer who complained that Dublin's theatrical news was listed under "Provincial Drama," "*coupled* with the lowest *clod-hopping village* in Great Britain" (*Monthly Mirror*, March 1807, p. 217; hereafter abbreviated *MM* in this chapter). Meanwhile, English audiences were instructed in how to respond to the so-called speech defects of minority characters, so that the prologue to Cumberland's *The West Indian* tells the audience about the Irish character, "Laugh, but despise him not, for on his lip / His errors lie; his heart can never trip."[67] Plays could even directly reach out to specific ethnic groups in a diverse audience. An epilogue to *Love à la Mode*, for example, acknowledges (as part of the recuperation of Irish identity) that "*Hibernia* . . . / Has long been only laugh'd at on the stage": "Her very *accent* swell'd the comic song, / And every phrase was nationally wrong, / As if *Britannia* could herself conceal, / Her thoughtless slips of *winegar* and *weal*." (Thomas Sheridan made the same point about cockney pronunciation: "They call veal weal, vinegar winegar.")[68] The epilogue not only points out that the English themselves suffer from imperfect pronunciation but actually goes on to address the Irish members of the audience directly, in a kind of call to arms: "Ye sons of Ireland, wheresoe'er ye sit / For once take off the manacles from wit; / And let these lords of beef and pudding know, / That merit springs in *every* soil below."[69] At the same time, ethnic audiences did not like to be patronized, or talked down to. John O'Keeffe, the Irish playwright, tells the story of "a regular Dublin performer [who] told a young English novice to please an *Irish* audience he should say [in one of his speeches, not *saucy* but] *cobbaugh* . . . which produced hisses and uproar among the audience, as an intended disrespect to them, although the word in the Irish language has much the same meaning as *saucy*."[70] Such an anecdote reveals that actors on the Georgian stage were keenly aware of these differences—of their own ethnicity, of the ethnic makeup of their audiences, of the place of dialect in the roles they played. The anecdote also reveals that it was one thing to acknowledge respectfully the Irish members of an audience; to talk down to them, to act as if they could not understand English, was quite another. And minorities were increasingly acknowledged as the best judges of their own speech, so that an English reviewer could admit that the attempt by English actors to speak the brogue was a failure, confessing that one actor in an Irish role had pleased English audiences "by his rich *English brogue*, for so we may call it, since the Irish tell us that it is not perfect to their ear" (*MM*, December 1807, p. 446).

Finally, the emergence of the ethnic voice can be seen in the idea of the valorization of the ethnic author—namely, the idea that authors might in fact write not from a universal but rather from a particular ethnic position. In 1800, for example, a reviewer explained that Macklin "has been blamed for indulging too great national partiality in the construction of this piece [*Love à la Mode*], for that, of the four lovers, . . . he has made the [Irishman] the only man who is disinterested in his addresses to the young; but perhaps the author was more desirous of rescuing the character of his countrymen from the odium of being considered, indiscriminately, as *fortune-hunters*" (*MM*, June 1800, pp. 372–72). In a similar vein, O'Keeffe argued that "an Irishman, and none else, can play [Irish characters]; and I will venture to say, that none but an Irishman can write an Irish character."[71] Finally, recognizing that the original story on which *The Merchant of Venice* might have been based on a vengeful Christian who threatens to take a pound of flesh from a Jew, a reviewer remarked: "Had a Jew been the dramatist, it [the play] would have been otherwise" (*MM*, March 1808, p. 269). Even Shakespeare, then, wrote not from a universal but rather from a specifically Christian and anti-Judaic position—an argument that the Spanish Jew, Mr. Montenero, makes when he too cites a Christian as the model for the vengeful moneylender, in a deconstructive, materialist reading of *The Merchant of Venice* in Maria Edgeworth's *Harrington*.[72] Written in 1817, this novel in many ways functions as a summation of the kinds of theatrical developments I have been describing, in its representation not only of a Jewish critique of *The Merchant of Venice* but also of theatergoing in the late 1770s and early 1780s, when the Protestant protagonist begins to see Macklin's performance of Shylock under Jewish eyes—that is, by watching and sympathizing with a Jewish woman in the theater (as I discuss in chapter 5). These examples suggest the ways in which both ethnic minorities and the hegemonic community began to acknowledge and legitimize the complex cultures and mixed ethnic composition of Great Britain.

Because the multiethnic spectacle typically brought together in competition different ethnic character types, reviewers often tried to unravel audiences' responses to the representation of different ethnic figures. A reviewer of a Jewish performer in the role of Sheva in Cumberland's *The Jew* cautioned:

> The individual who comes forward in a character of this description, subjects himself to difficulties which do not attach to the representatives of Scotch or Irish characters. We laugh at their brogue rather than detest it, and are willing to sympathize with all their feelings, peculiarities, and distresses. But the very idea of Judaism, and very aspect of a Jewish countenance, are associated in the minds of the English multitude, with roguery, insensibility, and cunning . . . with malignant villainy, or contemptible meanness. . . . The operation of these feelings injured the effect of Mr. Sherenbeck's performance;

and the only plaudits proceeded from his own brethren. (*Theatrical Inquisitor*, May 7, 1814, p. 311)

We need to recognize that the reviewer's opinion here was one among many, because audience members and reviewers frequently sympathized with Sheva, and Cumberland's play did in fact represent a revolution in the representation of Jewish identity on the English stage. But this reviewer at least reminds us that the different ethnic minorities of Great Britain were not simply collapsible into one single other, and the figure of the Jew was generally the odd man out (as is evident in so many multiethnic spectacles). And I wish to explain that the invention of the Jewish dialect became an obstacle to the full recuperation of Jewish identity on the stage, and made much more difficult for the Jews the kind of authorization of ethnic voice that occurred for the Scots and the Irish. In fact, it is startling that in the midst of the liberal revisions of Jewish identity that took place in the late Georgian theater starting with Cumberland's Sheva, the Jewish dialect remained a comic marker that uniformly tended to reduce Jewish portraits (including Sheva) to caricature.

We can see some of the distinctions in the representation of different ethnic identities on the stage when we return to the trope of doubled ethnic identity. I have argued that in a play like *The True-born Irishman* the doubling or splitting of Irish identity critiqued the flight from native integrity in two ways—by caricaturing the imposter, the anglicized self-hating Irishwoman, and by dignifying the native, the true-born Irishman. But the doubling of Jewish identity typically ran the risk of producing only double spectacle, as in the double bill that presented Shylock and Beau Mordecai, or even more tellingly in *The Fair Refugee or The Rival Jews* (1785), a multiethnic spectacle whose cast of characters included an American heroine (the fair refugee of the title), an Irish servant, and the bonus of not just one but two Jews. At first the splitting of Jewish identity here functions to signal the culture's growing awareness of the historical moment when the size of an ethnic population and its social mobility begin to outstrip a single, conventional type. In this way we see the potential undermining of the single Jewish stereotype. But the two Jewish cousins in this play are made to function in a binary opposition that allows no genuine variation; in fact, one Jew is simply a masked version of the other. So, when the splitting of Jewish identity occurs in *The Rival Jews*, it produces not (as in the case of *The True-born Irishman*) the imposter and the dignified native but rather the imposter and the degenerate native, or, as the dramatis personae list describes them, a beau Jew (Solomons) and a Change Alley Jew (Levi).

The use of dialect within this trope of Jewish doubling remains the marker of degeneracy, so that we hear about the stockbroking Jew, "by his English, one would swear he was born in the Jew's Quarter in Amsterdam."[73] The beau Jew, the Jew who masks himself as a gentleman in order to pass, explains to his counterego, his unreconstructed self, that he has learned to sing and dance and fence, but what he has learned best is how to speak; he berates the stockbroking Jew, whom he attempts to reinvent in his own image, "We'll begin with your Language. You have a damned Jew's dialect" (*FR*, 35). The beau Jew, like the Scot and the Irishman in this culture, confesses that he has been learning oratory; after all, he hopes to become a member of Parliament (*FR*, 35–36).

In a highly suggestive scene of spectacle and spectatorship, the beau Jew places the stockbroking Jew by his side before a mirror for a scene of epistemological demonstration: "Look in the glass. . . . Now you see the difference between a *Jew* and a *Gentleman*" (*FR*, 32). But this ocular demonstration fails to convince either the Change Alley Jew or the audience. What both see revealed is the work of ethnic reinvention, where the end result of the passer's imposture is reflected in the mirror—the mere superficiality of image, the Jew as actor. Such a scene of metatheatrical inspection, like the scene in which Beau Mordecai is turned about to display his artificial finery in *Love à la Mode*, shows us the act of imposture being inspected: "Make yourself look a little more like a Gentleman" (*FR*, 32). At the same time, while the mirror reflects the beau Jew as an actor, it reflects the unreconstructed Jew as a primitive, "a piece of Antiquity. Why you look as if you was preserved in the Ark" (*FR*, 40). The autochthonous Levi is the Caliban of Jewish identity—inarticulate, ugly, rapacious. The play in this way exposes the strategies used to fabricate the un-Judaized Jew, like the "unscottified" Scot. And I have been arguing that this culture is at every moment inspecting these reinventions of ethnic identity: during the controversy over the "Jew Bill," for example, the *London Evening-Post* satirically represented the Jew's attempt to pass, portraying Jews as looking for "any Secret that will help *Complexions*, remove *Antipathies*, and give the true *Saxon Bloom* to a HEBREW Carcase" (September 11–13, 1753). In any case, the so-called rival Jews prove a dead end in the representation of Jewish identity on the stage, a fruitless binary in which the imposter labors to reproduce himself through his cousin, in a kind of "no exit" in the dilemma of the Georgian stage Jew.

Quick to unmask all attempts at Jewish passing, the stage used Jewish dialect as the surest safeguard against imposters trying to pass. It functioned like a lisp or a stutter, a special kind of speech impediment that only rarely could be hidden, a kind of bodily imperfection. Moreover, Jewish dialect on the stage became regulated and even required by reviewers and audiences. One reviewer complained about an actor, "When he personates Jews, it would add much to the effect of those characters, if he endeavoured to speak the dialect" (*MM*, March 1801, p. 202). The following year a reviewer in the same magazine came back with satisfaction to report about the same performer: "I could not perceive that Mr. Ward, in the Jew, was at all guilty of neglecting the dialect" (April 1802, p. 286). This insistence on the use of the accepted, conventional dialect stands in contrast to what was happening with respect to Irish and Scottish characters on the stage: it was a matter not of authenticity but of caricature and more specifically of marking—that is, identifying Jewish identity under whatever English guise it might try to appear. After all, Sampson Gideon, perhaps the most famous Jew of late eighteenth-century England, an important financier who had extraordinary influence (especially after he helped the ministry squelch the 'Forty-Five rebellion), was frequently represented as having the foreign speech of an Ashkenazi pedlar or old-clothes man, even though he was a Sephardi who had been born in London.[74] The Jew's dialect could even function to give the lie to the recuperation of Jewish identity, to the benevolence of the good stage Jew, as in the following comments by a reviewer of Cumberland's *The Jew* (fifteen years after its first performance): "The mongrel dialect, used by Mr. Dowton, sometimes Duke's Place gibberish, but more commonly articulate English, was very bad indeed.—Perhaps Mr. D. thought by this cross of Jew and Christian, the latter preponderating, to account for the preposterous *benevolence* exhibited in his character" (*MM*, May 1808, p. 396). According to this reviewer, there is an easily recognizable moral gulf between two different forms of speech— Jewish "gibberish" and "articulate English." In such a view, the unnatural invention of the dramatist, the benevolent (or Christian) Jew, could at least be undermined and exposed by the mongrel dialect.

Since Jewish roles were of course typically played by non-Jews, it was a significant event when, all too infrequently, a Jewish actor stepped forward to play a Jewish role. A reviewer at a production of *The Jew* at Covent Garden in 1814 remarks, "The only novelty was the first appearance of a Mr. *Sherenbeck*, in the character of *Sheva*," and goes on to suggest the way in which the Jewish performer divided the audience: "The house indeed, contained no small proportion of circumcised auditors, who were inordinately clamorous in supporting their representative, and seemed exceedingly supercilious towards a few Christian critics who happened to differ in their estimate of Mr. Sherenbeck's talents."[75] The first notices of Sherenbeck began to appear in 1805 when he played Shylock and then Sheva in the provinces, signaling a new cultural phenomenon that aroused a great deal of public interest. In 1805, at the Theatre Rochester, it was reported that "a Mr. Sherenbeck . . . of the Jewish persuasion, attempted the part of Shylock in the Jewish dialect. . . . Its effect was wonderful in the hands of this gentleman. . . . So great was the public curiosity, the house overflowed at an early hour, and hundreds could not obtain admittance" (*MM*, February 1805, p. 134). A few months later a report of his continuing success followed: "Mr. Sherenbeck, who so ably performed the character of Shylock, in the Jewish dialect, has again made his appearance on the boards, in the character of Sheva, to an overflowing audience." Because of these successes, "it is expected that he will visit the London theatres in the ensuing season" (*MM*, April 1805, p. 274). But when Sherenbeck left the provinces and played Shylock in dialect in London, a reviewer protested its use in Shakespeare's play: "The equipment of this Jew in the dialect of his tribe seemed equally absurd and ineffective." Was it threatening to have a Jew—"the Rochester Israelite" as he is named by the reviewer—playing a Jew (*Theatrical Inquisitor*, July 1817, p. 71)? Or is it possible that the Jewish dialect (or "gibberish"), in the case of Shakespeare, was seen as polluting the pure wells of English?

In any case, Jewish dialect did begin to be seen as infecting Christian discourse, and reviewers began to argue against Jewish performers in Christian roles. In this way we see that the notion of the authentic could be used not only to empower ethnic minorities to represent themselves but also to bar them from playing anyone but themselves. The most famous Jewish performer of the time, who changed his name from John Abraham to John Braham and claimed he had converted to Christianity, was nonetheless regularly marked as Jewish, and a variety of reviewers could not separate Braham the Jew from the roles he was playing and the music he was singing. In the well-known essay "Imperfect Sympathies" in which Charles Lamb compares his prejudices against Scots, blacks, Quakers, and Jews, he remarks about Braham: "There is a fine scorn in his face, which nature meant to be of—Christians. The Hebrew spirit is strong in him, in spite of his proselytism. He cannot conquer the Shibboleth. How it breaks out, when he sings, 'The Children of Israel passed through the Red Sea!' The auditors, for the moment, are as

Egyptians to him, and he rides over our necks in triumph."[76] This comparison between the Jews in Egypt and the Jews in England was a frequent frame of reference for the Jewish invasion and spoliation of England, as was the trope of the converted Jew always remaining a Jew at heart ("in spite of his proselytism"), secretly undermining English culture. But if Lamb felt the power of Braham as Jew, scornful of his Egyptian/English hosts, other reviewers objected to Braham in the opposite role—the Jew as Christian: "It is impossible always to divest oneself of particular circumstances, relating to the private character and *persuasion* of persons. Who can hear *Mr. Braham* . . . sing in the *Messiah*, '*They that have seen him have scorned him*,' . . . without sensations of a ludicrous kind, or something worse?" (*MM*, February 1808, pp. 136–37). Similarly, a reviewer in *John Bull* complained that "to hear MR. BRAHAM at any time, seriously telling twelve or fifteen hundred people 'that he knows his Redeemer lives,' when if he have any religion at all, he believes no such thing, is a little disgusting, and to find puffs disseminated all over the town upon his opening the 'MESSIAH,' in which he has no faith, is carrying the thing quite as far as is decent, considering the words to be uttered and the book whence they are extracted" (February 13, 1826). One could additionally ask what it was like for a Jewish performer to sing in the person of a Christian, or even more important, to act in the anti-Semitic plays of the time, and one member of the public did in fact wonder about Braham's performance in Sheridan's *The Duenna*, "How must Mr. Braham, who is himself a Jew, have been tortured by the overcharged and disgusting representation of the foolish (though knavishly inclined) Israelite, Isaac Mendoza?" Unfortunately, this writer goes on to worry more about the anti-Catholic slanders in the play, and links Braham to them: "And on the other hand, how delighted must he not have been at the mockery of the cross!"[77]

Reviewers repeatedly attempted to unmask the Jew passing as Christian (in Handel's music) in the kind of paradigmatic plot of passing and unmasking that I have been identifying on stage and off. And, typically, the ultimate mark of Braham's otherness, his un-Englishness, was found in "his acting and pronunciation of our language": "Surely Mr. Braham might, amongst his acquaintance, find some one christian enough to tell him that moment should not be pronounced *momunt*, nor principle, *principal*, nor indeed, *inteet*, &c." But it was not only his pronunciation, it was his voice itself, which was characterized as inherently Jewish and dimly associated with the archetypal Jew, Shylock, as the same reviewer noted "Mr. Braham's nasal voice" and complained that "Mr. B. like Shakspeare's [*sic*] bagpipe '*sings i' the nose*'"

(*MM*, November 1807, p. 347). When Braham tried to move from singing to acting, he was met with the following criticism: "To say nothing of his face and figure, his 'Babylonish dialect,' made up of French, Italian, *old cloaths*, &c. wholly disqualifies him for an actor" (*MM*, March 1807, p. 207). Finally, Braham's unduly ornamented dress was criticized in a catalogue of sartorial mistakes summed up in this way: "Next to the savages, the Jews most delight in dress and ornament" (*MM*, May 1808, p. 397). Like the Scottish/Jewish/Irish Macklin, Braham is French, Italian, and savage but not English, and while he sang at the great opera houses of Europe and was the preeminent English tenor of his day, his critics claimed they could still detect in him the dialect of the Jewish old-clothes man.

In an anecdote that portrays the ultimate unmasking of Braham, we see the way in which his so-called real identity as a Jew continually breaks through his performance, exposing to the audience his Jewish roots. In a play in which Braham in character asks the question, "Who, tell me, WHO IS MY FATHER?" the following event occurred: "Scarcely had Braham put this question when a little Jew stood up in an excited manner in the midst of a densely crowded pit and exclaimed, 'I knowed yer farder well. His name was Abey Punch!' The performance was suspended for some minutes in the roars of laughter that followed this revelation."[78] Whatever the play on stage, the scene in the audience becomes its own comical farce in an unmasking similar to those we have seen on the stage itself. The anecdote, like the Hibernian and Caledonian fables I have explored, becomes a fable of the inescapability of one's ethnic origins, a fable of passing and unmasking. Braham meets his double in the audience, who recognizes and exposes him: "the little Jew" in the audience, Braham's double, speaking in dialect, reaches out from the pit onto the stage to claim him. The Jewish actor on stage, who masks himself in Christian parts, is like the Jewish imposter offstage, who tries to pass as an English gentleman.

With a heavy dialect laid on the tongue of the stage Jew, and with the most famous Jewish performer of the day, a brilliant singer of international renown, stigmatized in his person, his dress, and most sharply, his tongue, the Jewish voice was the ultimate marker of the Jew's otherness. Moreover, this system of marking Jewish difference was never far from resorting to the mark of circumcision. For example, in a depiction of Jews coming to the defense of Braham, the singer's anglicization of his name was caricatured as a kind of (re)circumcision, an unsuccessful attempt at (re)marking himself as a Briton: "From the depths of Rag-fair to the very centre of Duke's-place, they are all in arms to defend Mr. Braham, . . . as if his name still retained its due proportion, and had not suffered from the cutting off of its *fore*-letter *A*" (*MM*, January 1808, p. 47). Reinventing oneself as English, then, meant not only the cutting off of tongues but also the cutting off of names—in both cases, a kind of self-mutilation. And this mutilation remains the sign of the Jew, for Braham's use of a Judaic procedure to Christianize himself betrays what we already know: he remains a Jew, "in spite of his proselytism." The circumcision of name cannot erase (and in some sense only repeats) the indelible mark of Jewish identity.

The Gentile community frequently used the act of circumcision as a violent figure of representation, to stigmatize Jews and to hold them to their identity of difference, as in the taunt that I quoted at the head of my previous chapter, when the public cried at the appearance of Jews at the theater, "*No Jews, out with them, circumcise them.*" Here the figure of (re)circumcision insists on both marking them and ostracizing them as other in a single gesture. But I am especially interested in the symbolic relocation of the act of circumcision to the name and even to the tongue as a way of understanding the politics of ethnic reinvention in Georgian culture. For example, in one of the reports on masquerades that appeared regularly in the *Westminster Magazine*, we find the following account of a masquerade at the Pantheon: "Mr. Franks the Jew, in a Domino, was importunated greatly by a Lady to converse, or to answer her questions; but he being dully silent, she observed, *That the Fathers of the Synagogue had certainly made a mistake, and had unhappily circumcised him in the tongue*" (May 1773, p. 166). The relocation of the mark of Jewish identity onto the tongue functions as a paradigm for the way in which Georgian culture represented the tongue as the site of difference, both for Jews and for other ethnic minorities. Especially in an empirical culture that prized demonstration and proof, dialect was a way of making ethnic difference available to the senses—that is, of displacing the hidden mark of Jewish difference onto the tongue, where it could be easily detected. Before the lady's questions the Jew stands silent, powerless, the object of her taunts, for in this culture the tongue cut off or circumcised functions as a figure for ethnic disempowerment—for the loss of sexual potency and the loss of voice.

At the same time, I have explored the ways in which the theater functioned as a crucial vehicle to destabilize and to rewrite the caricatured stereotypes of ethnic difference. This included, as I have shown, the metatheatrical uses of spectacle to undermine the hegemonic community's theatrical constructions of ethnic identity, the erasure of derogatory markers of difference (though this sometimes could simply reduce these minorities to the homogenized Briton), and perhaps the most radical development—the authentication and legitimization of ethnic difference, especially through the empowerment of the ethnic voice. But while such strategies functioned to begin the recuperation of the Irishman and the Scot, the Jew remained unredeemed, unrehabilitated, in *Love à la Mode, The Fashionable Lover, The Cozeners, The Fair Refugee or the Rival Jews,* and countless other plays. In these multiethnic spectacles the unredeemable Jew functioned as the limit to the idea of the recuperation and empowerment of ethnic minorities. Nonetheless, the attempt to recuperate Jewish identity was a notable, and in many ways the most noticed (because the most controversial), of the stage's work in the service of liberal toleration at the end of the eighteenth century. So, while the Jew shared with other ethnic minorities the problem of being reduced to a theatrical stereotype, in some ways the Jew suffered "difficulties which do not attach to the representatives of Scotch or Irish characters," and it therefore remains to be seen what special means the theater developed to liberate the stage Jew from the conventions of prejudice. This means understanding, first, why the Jew in the eighteenth century became such an immensely popular figure on the stage, and second, how the stage Jew was demonized as well as demythologized and deconstructed, the topics of my next two chapters.

CHAPTER THREE

"Cheeld o' Commerce"
Merchants, Jews, and Fathers in a Commercial Nation

Take a view of the *Royal-Exchange* in *London*, a place more
venerable than many courts of justice, where the representatives
of all nations meet for the benefit of mankind. There the Jew, the
Mahometan, and the Christian transact together as tho' they all
profess'd the same religion, and give the name of Infidel to none
but bankrupts. . . . At the breaking up of this pacific and free
assembly, some withdraw to the synagogue, and others to take a
glass. This man goes and is baptiz'd in a great tub, in the name of
the Father, Son, and Holy Ghost: That man has his son's foreskin
cut off, whilst a sett of *Hebrew* words (quite unintelligible to him)
are mumbled over his child.
—Voltaire, *Letters Concerning the English Nation*, 1733

AS A FOREIGN observer living in England in the late 1720s, Voltaire recognized commerce as one of the chief distinguishing features of his host
nation, and he located the figure of the Jew at the symbolic center of commercial England. During Voltaire's two-and-a-half-year stay in England, he
immersed himself in the English language, eventually claiming, "I think and
write like a free Englishman,"[1] and in the passage I have quoted he writes remarkably in the vein of Joseph Addison, one of his favorite writers: "There is
no Place in the Town which I so much love to frequent as the *Royal-Exchange.*
It gives me a secret Satisfaction, and, in some measure, gratifies my Vanity, as
I am an *Englishman*, to see so rich an Assembly of Country-men and Foreign-

ers consulting together upon the private Business of Mankind, and making this Metropolis a kind of *Emporium* for the whole Earth."[2] Moving among the various representatives at the exchange, Addison loses his own identity in theirs in a kind of performative embrace of different religious and national identities that signals the epitome of English tolerance: "Sometimes I am lost in a Crowd of *Jews*, and sometimes make one in a Groupe of *Dutch-men*. I am a *Dane, Swede,* or *French-man* at different times."[3] In Voltaire's and Addison's version of an ideally secular culture, the Royal Exchange is the symbolic center of enlightened tolerance, more powerful even than the courts of justice, because it is a place so supremely beyond religious conflict and national prejudice. Here men of every religion and every nationality meet as equals; here the strange customs that divide men—the archaic rituals of different religions—are offset by what brings men together, the modern enterprise of commerce, and the Royal Exchange, a uniquely English institution, represents the kind of religious tolerance and political liberty that characterized the English nation—and that Voltaire, in self-imposed exile from the restrictions of *ancien régime* France, celebrated in his *Letters*.

Addison was one of the most influential apologists for "the Benefits and Advantages of Commerce"[4] in early eighteenth-century England. He was a central participant in an important cultural debate that J. G. A. Pocock has brilliantly analyzed as a major key to eighteenth-century social thought. According to Pocock, consequent to the Financial Revolution of the 1690s (which saw the founding of the Bank of England and the creation of a system of public credit), there arose in the eighteenth century "an ideology and a perception of history which depicted political society and social personality as founded upon commerce."[5] While Pocock has shown how, during the first half of the century, this debate questioned the status of money and land, and even the foundations of social personality, I wish to show how, in the second half of the century, this debate found its most notable and popular expression on the stage, through the characters of the merchant and the Jew, and through an exploration of England's national reputation for both commerce and tolerance.

In the opening decades of the eighteenth century, "commerce, it was argued, was the sole agency capable of refining the passions and polishing the manners."[6] Social relations, while based on the master-slave, lord-serf model in precommercial society, broadened and deepened in commercial society, especially because commerce staged encounters among a variety of human beings in a variety of exchange situations. For this reason, both inside and outside England the commercial identity of England in the eighteenth century became a central constituent of its reputation for liberty and tolerance. Voltaire claimed, in his newly beloved English language, "Where there is not liberty of conscience, there is seldom liberty of trade, the same tyranny encroaching upon the commerce as upon Relligion." He went on to argue that in England "jews, mahometans, heathens, catholiques, quackers, anabaptistes," while holding different religious beliefs, in commerce "deal together freely and with trust and peace; like good players who after having humour'd their parts and fought one against another upon the stage, spend the rest of their time in drinking together."[7] So, the kind of Anglomania that characterized the French (and other Europeans) in the early eighteenth century depended on England's commercial identity. Montesquieu made England's commercial and legal systems a centerpiece of his *Spirit of the Laws* (1748), arguing that "they [the English] know better than any other people upon earth how to value, at the same time, these three great advantages—religion, commerce, and liberty." And he claimed that "commerce is a cure for the most destructive prejudices."[8] The issue that haunts this entire picture, and that lies at the heart of this chapter, is whether or not commerce became a cure for the anti-Jewish prejudice that had marked English history for centuries.

In this chapter I claim that the new commercial age in England was launched with a rehabilitation of two stock figures central to the popular imagination in England, the merchant and the Jew. In *The Spectator* Addison claimed, "Merchants . . . knit Mankind together in a mutual Intercourse of good Offices,"[9] while Voltaire gave this idea an especially ironic French twist: "I cannot say which is most useful to a Nation; a Lord, powder'd in the tip of the Mode, who knows exactly at what a Clock the King rises and goes to bed; . . . or a Merchant, who enriches his Country, dispatches Orders from his Compting-House to *Surat* and *Grand Cairo*, and contributes to the Felicity of the World."[10] But, while contemporary Englishmen and foreign observers thought of England as a nation characterized not simply by the achievements of its merchants but also by its tolerance for Jews, modern scholars (including Pocock) have omitted the crucial role Jews played in the ideology of commerce in eighteenth-century England. Jews were located as an important feature in the English national landscape according to more foreign observers than just Voltaire. Another foreign visitor put it bluntly in 1729: "Commerce is considered England's strength, and care has been taken not to drive away anyone who contributes to build it up. Jews are therefore protected by laws, and even granted certain privileges."[11] Meanwhile, Montesquieu showed the commercial and social benefits of the Jews' invention of bills of exchange in a chapter entitled "How Commerce broke through the barbarism of Europe."[12] And Addison went so far as to rewrite his remark about merchants knitting together the wide world by giving this role to the Jews in particular: "They are, indeed, so disseminated through all the trading Parts of the World, that they are become the Instruments by which the most distant Nations converse with one another, and by which Mankind are knit together in a general Correspondence."[13] The traditional figure of the Wandering Jew, isolated and outcast for his crime against Christ, doomed to wander until the Second Coming, is reinvented in a secular vision of the Jewish merchant of land and sea, uniting the farthest reaches of the globe and mediating among a wide variety of peoples. Finally, in the ultimate underwriting of both merchant and Jew, Addison took the theatrical step of dissolving his own identity to play the roles of both: "I have been taken for a Merchant upon the *Exchange* for above these ten Years, and sometimes pass for a *Jew* in the Assembly of Stock-Jobbers at *Jonathan*'s."[14] In such ways, the propagandistic program in favor of commerce in early eighteenth-century England found its farthest reaches in the reinvention of the Jew, the conventional figure of hard bargains, extortion, and usury, thereby undoing the traditional binary division between the charitable Christian merchant and the usurious Jew, especially as it was popularized on the stage in *The Merchant of Venice*.

But while a new, secular, sanitized image of the Jew was installed at the heart of a specific ideology about Englishness and commerce early in the eighteenth century, by the middle of the century the Jew as the hard-hearted economic man reemerged as the popular view, especially during and after the public outcry against the Jewish Naturalization Act (1753)—that is, once the symbolic value of the Jew (as part of the apology for commerce) was superseded by a legislative act that would have made it easier for foreign-born Jews residing in England to become naturalized. London's merchants feared the economic competition of the Jews, and soon a variety of different constituencies, both in the city of London and beyond, became inflamed at the thought of being overwhelmed by Jewish influence in every sphere of life. During the clamor over the "Jew Bill" a reactionary picture of the Jew took hold, noticeably different from Addison's and Voltaire's. For example, in the first issue of the weekly periodical *The Connoisseur*, a survey of London clearly revised *The Spectator*'s view in the opening decades of the century: while both place the commercial center at the symbolic heart of London and locate Jews prominently in this picture, the figure of the Jew in 1754 has returned to its function of earlier centuries, which is made especially clear by a quotation from *The Merchant of Venice*, concluding that "one might almost doubt, where money is out of the case, whether a Jew 'has eyes, hands, organs, dimensions, senses, affections, passions.'"[15] In 1754 the tour of London begins ominously with a kind of hunt after Jews, an attempt at unmasking them, finding them out in their secret haunts, "penetrating into the most secret springs of action in these people." They are the mysterious other, and yet at the same time they inhabit the very center of English life. Another periodical at the same time printed a letter that reported a Jew on the Royal Exchange saying, "I hope to live now to see the day not to meet a Christian in this place or an Englishman in the kingdom."[16] The exchange, once the symbol of the humane and polite intercourse among men of different religions and nationalities, has become the point of infiltration by which Jews hope to take over English culture.

The national hysteria over the "Jew Bill" produced numerous pamphlets, leaflets, broadsides, songs, newspaper articles, periodical essays, and satirical graphic prints on the topic of the Jews. Some pamphlets went through several editions in a period of weeks, while works on the Jewish religion were published or reissued. While recent scholarly debate about this bill has focused on whether or not the public outcry represented a deep-seated strain of anti-Semitism in English culture,[17] I see the passage and repeal of the bill as a critical moment in Anglo-Jewish history less because of the traditional stereotypes it recycled and more because it was the entrance of the Jew into public discourse in England as never before. It was during the popular excitement generated by the bill that the Jew became a popular subject of representation. Jews had become the talk of the town, as announced at Drury Lane Theatre in 1753, when David Garrick's prologue was recited by Samuel Foote: "The many various objects that amuse / These busy curious times, by way of news, / Are, plays, elections, murders, lott'ries, *Jews*."[18] And the author of *A Scotsman's Remarks On "Love à la Mode,"* who complained in 1760 of Beau Mordecai as a slur on the Jews ("to be abused, insulted, and have jokes cracked about him"), found Macklin's Jewish caricature especially insulting, "since the Jew-act has not taken place."[19] Meanwhile, almost three decades after the debacle of the "Jew Bill," we hear in Miles Peter Andrews's comedy *Dissipation* (1781): "Some things, indeed, one can't help being familiar with, such as the national debt, or the ruin of one's country, or naturalizing a Jew."[20] The "Jew Bill" became a point of reference for representing Jewish identity, for locating the Jew within English culture, and, according to this last quotation, for signaling the ruin of England. The popular excitement over the "Jew Bill" placed the Jewish question on England's national agenda, making it available to a much wider public and locating it in a far greater range of representations than ever before.

After the public clamor over the "Jew Bill," there was a slow but steady increase in the number of new plays with Jewish characters, especially in the 1770s, 1780s, and 1790s, and the repertory at the patent theaters (as I have already suggested) gave the public the opportunity to see several different stage Jews on different nights, sometimes within a single week. So, once the uproar over the bill had established the Jew as a central figure in the English national landscape, the stage Jew became an indispensable symbolic figure in the way in which England worked out conceptions of Englishness, and especially those features of national identity that dealt with English commerce and English tolerance, reactivating what had already been an ongoing debate about England's commercial identity. My focus in this chapter will be on the emergence, especially from mid-century onward, of a complicated, multivalenced, contradictory group of representations of Jewish identity on the London stage. During this period the stage Jew was a fop, a lover, a sexual predator, a guardian, a father figure, a gull, an extortionist, and a philanthropist. At the simplest level, some of these representations took the form of decidedly anti-Semitic or philo-Semitic portraits competing for public approval, and in this way mirrored the oppositional form of debate generated by the parliamentary debates over the "Jew Bill." I see the theater's opposing views, which were produced between the bill and the parliamentary debates on Jewish emancipation that began in 1830, as underscoring the way in which the theater functioned as a fourth estate, at first supporting the repeal of the bill with its money-mad stage Jews but eventually, in certain radical reinventions of the stage Jew at the end of the century, helping the nation to recover from the debacle of the bill and in fact preparing the way for the long journey toward Jewish emancipation. It was the public that forced the repeal of the "Jew Bill," and it would be the public once again, this time in the theater, that would review and adjudicate the question of the Jews in late eighteenth-century England. For according to Richard Cumberland it was the public that allowed and even encouraged his radical portrait of a benevolent Jew in *The Jew*: "The benevolence of the audience assisted me in rescuing a forlorn and persecuted character, which till then had only been brought upon the stage for the unmanly purpose of being made a spectacle of contempt, and a butt for ridicule."[21] Moreover, as I will show, the popularity of *The Jew* touched off nothing short of a national debate in the press about the representation of the Jew on the stage in England and the history of the Jews in defining English national identity.

In the course of this chapter I explore how the eighteenth-century stage began to show the Jew as mirroring the upwardly mobile middle class, and how the simple act of blaming the Jew as other, scapegoating him for the corruption of England, began to dissolve in the more complicated exposure of the way in which England had turned itself over to Jewish money, or even hidden its own greed behind the mask of Jewish avarice, in an increasingly Judaized English nation. In fact, the stage began to show the Jew specifically as the double of the English merchant, in what became a subversive attack on England as a commercial nation. With its indictment increasingly aimed squarely at English merchants, the stage eventually disconnected the Jew from the English merchant to produce a benevolent Jew who in fact became not the violator but rather the purveyor of ethical values, the model and guardian of tolerance and generosity, even the teacher of the English merchant. In this way the stage pointed to the ways in which commerce—even, or especially, commerce with Jews—could broaden the sympathy and tolerance of the English people.

In commercial England of the eighteenth century, the traditional comedic marriage plot typically became a thinly disguised economic plot, consistently focused on a few staples: the courtship competition for the rich heiress, the sale of the young heroine to the highest bidder, the test of the suitors' financial suitability, the trial and exposure of the fortune hunter. This plot demonstrated the inextricability of marriage and commerce, with the woman as an object of exchange in a plot that explored the marriage of sex and money. The marriage market was dimly shadowed by the prostitution market, or, as the heroine of Cumberland's *The Fashionable Lover* points out, "There may be a legal prostitute as well as a licentious one."[22] The Jew, in a surprising variety of roles, became indispensable to this plot.

The economic foundation of the marriage plot during this period was apparent even in the stage's consistent return to the plot of *The Merchant of Venice*, both literally, in the innumerable performances of what became one of the most popular of Shakespeare's plays,[23] and figuratively, in the kinds of rewritings of it that were produced during the period, from Granville's *The Jew of Venice*, whose title moved the figure of the Jew into the foreground, to Macklin's *Love à la Mode* and beyond. What was especially new in these plays was the role of the Jew: the Jew's financial success made the English heroine available to him for the first time, so typically the stage showed the Jew as a lover, either the beau Jew (the foppish suitor) or the threatening Jew (the lecherous seducer and even potential rapist) in a newly commercialized, socially mobile England. Moreover, the plot that tested the suitors' greedy motives in *Love à la Mode* and in eighteenth-century comedy in general, while inherited from the casket plot of Shakespeare's play, had a new urgency because it reflected and shaped the debate on money, commerce, and the new role of the Jew in English life that informed the century. Macklin's Sir Archy Macsarcasm offered a scathing critique of commercial England, formulated through the main terms of this debate: the landed man versus the moneyed man, the value of trade and commerce, and the question of Jewish identity and English national identity. Even Sir Archy's claims about his Highland ancestry were taken over directly from this debate, in which the feudal, pre-commercial Highlands were often set against the moneyed, commercial society of England.

Perhaps most important of all, Sir Archy's critique of commercial England argued for a profound connection between England and the Jews. From the beginning Sir Archy characterizes the English heroine and her fellow citizens in the following terms: "Ye are a composeetion of Jews, Turks, and refugees, and of aw the commercial vagrants of the land and sea—a sort of ampheebious breed ye are. . . . As ye yeersel are na weel propagated, as ye hai the misfortune till be a cheeld o' commerce, ye should endeavour till mak yeer espousals intill yean of oor auncient noble families of the North; for ye mun ken, madam, that sic an alliance wull purify yeer blood."[24] This is not a very successful way of courting, but Sir Archy's speech nonetheless expresses an increasingly popular view of the English in the eighteenth century, strategically allowing the Irish author to critique England safely behind the mask of a sharp-tongued Scot. Sir Archy closely echoes Daniel Defoe, who at the beginning of the century gave the lie to the idea of "the true-born Englishman" by arguing that "From this Amphibious Ill-born mob began / *That vain ill-natur'd thing, an* Englishman."[25] Moreover, Sir Archy also echoes those who used the idea of the hybridity of the English as an argument to support the "Jew Bill": "*England* is a Composition of Foreigners, whose Forefathers were as much Strangers as the Jews can possibly be."[26] In such ways Macklin ties Sir Archy's apparently personal rant to the precise terms of the ongoing national debate about England's commercial identity.

By positing English identity on commercial grounds, Sir Archy argues that the new English man or woman is "a cheeld o' commerce." Instead of the genealogy of land and aristocratic families, the English are given a genealogy of money. And once Sir Archy thinks that Charlotte has lost all her money, after canceling his own suit he argues that she will find an appropriate mate in the Jew: the English heroine, "sprung frai . . . a coonting hoose," can find her match in "a wandering Eesrelite, a casualty—a mere casualty, sprung frai annuites, bulls, bubbles, bears, and lottery tickets" (*LM*, 73). In the secular world of commercial England the Jew quickly moves from being the "cheeld of circumcision" (*LM*, 49) to "this offspring of accident and mammon" (*LM*, 73). In eighteenth-century commercial England, a startlingly new family tree appears: English woman and Jewish man are, so to speak, blood relatives, sharing the same genealogy of money.

The eighteenth century was obsessed with the Jew whose money was his ticket with English women. In 1704, Thomas Baker's comedy *An Act at Oxford* announced the arrival of the beau Jew for the entire century: "A parcel of fluttering Fop Jews . . . of late disperse themselves in all publick Places, but of most forbidding Aspect Nature ever fram'd; and yet these Beaus, thro' Treats, Balls, and raffling away a world o' Mony, were the Ladies only Favourites."[27] Periodicals printed variations on this theme; in fact, *The Spectator* and *The Connoisseur* on this point seemed to agree in their anti-Jewish propaganda. Early in the century, in a purported letter to Mr. Spectator, Betty Lemon reports, "Coming last Week into a Coffee-house not far from the *Exchange* . . . a *Jew* of considerable Note, as I am informed, takes half a Dozen Oranges of me; . . . he give me the Guinea with no other Intent but to purchase my Person for an Hour."[28] And at mid-century *The Connoisseur* reported, "A very pretty Young Woman, but a good deal in debt—would be glad to marry a Member of Parliament, or a Jew"[29] (where the joke suggests that all members of Parliament who supported the "Jew Bill" are Jews). In Thomas Brown's "A Letter to Madam ——, kept by a *Jew* in *Covent-Garden*," the author is at first "surpriz'd . . . that Mrs. Lucy had thrown off her old Christian acquaintance, and revolted to the *Jews*," but then he realizes "that you were wholly directed by your interest in this choice, and troth I can't blame you. Our statesmen and senators, our divines, merchants, and lawyers, all act upon that principle. . . . So then, I find, 'tis neither circumcision nor uncircumcision that avails any thing with you, but money."[30] Woman's susceptibility to Jewish money is in fact a sign of the entire nation's susceptibility, and the letter to Mrs. Lucy becomes a vehicle for a critique of commercial England: all of England prostitutes itself to Jewish money. As Levi explains in *The Fair

Refugee or The Rival Jews, "I have de moneysh, dat make de Shentlemans in dish conetree, and everywere elshe."[31]

The first major Georgian representation of a Jew financing his sexual adventures with an Englishwoman occurs in a cluster of works (including several theatrical texts) originating with William Hogarth's *Harlot's Progress* (1732). Hogarth's celebrated graphic series and an afterpiece by Theophilus Cibber using the same title (performed at Drury Lane and various fairs in 1733–34) pictured the rich, foppish beau Jew (named Beau Mordecai by Cibber, and later adopted by Macklin for *Love à la Mode*) as the keeper of a country girl who has recently arrived in town: London, money, and Jewish cunning are a corrupting complex of factors to which the young English country girl falls prey. Henry Fielding's farce *Miss Lucy in Town* (1742) is the most interesting of the early variations on this theme because of the way its nationalist ideology works out the Jew's role in the new class economy of England. Here the country girl who arrives in town is a young, recently married woman, the wife of a footman who aspires to become a country squire. A Jew (Zorobabel) and a lord (Lord Bawble), a significant pairing that recurs later in the century, attempt to seduce her. Both the immensely rich Jewish upstart and the morally corrupt aristocrat represent a threat to the values of the newly emergent middle class. This threat is signified as nothing short of a threat to the English nation, represented here by the vulnerability of the domestic sphere, figured in the innocent wife from the country.

The Jew, who was played by Macklin, is seen as a new source of power in commercially driven England, an idea that the actor would incorporate in *Love à la Mode* a decade later. Here in Fielding's play the Jew is more powerful even than the effete landed aristocracy: Zorobabel chastises the procuress, "How . . . promise her to a Lord without offering her to me first? . . . Who is it can support you? Who have any money besides us?"[32] He delights in the economic system he has worked out, which simultaneously cheats Christian men of their money and Christian women of their virtue: "Soh! the Money of Christian Men pays for the Beauty of Christian Women. A good Exchange!" (*MLT*, 17–18). And the procuress confirms the economics of sex in commercial England: "Foolish Slut, to prefer a rakish Lord to a sober *Jew*: But Women never know how to make their Market 'till they are so old, no one will give any thing for them" (*MLT*, 32–33).

The comic denouement requires the husband to deal with both the rich Jew and the beau lord, different versions of the corruptions of London. The husband literally kicks the Jew off the stage and addresses to the lord a proud speech about class and national identity: "Fortune, which made me poor, made me a Servant; but Nature, which made me an *Englishman*, preserv'd me from being a Slave. I have as good a Right to the Little I claim, as the proudest Peer hath to his great Possessions" (*MLT,* 41). When the lord asks what property he is accused of trespassing, the husband declares, "The Property of an *English* Husband"—namely, his wife (*MLT,* 40). Woman functions as the legitimate property of her husband and as the illegitimate or criminal property—"a Piece of Goods" (*MLT,* 14) auctioned to the highest bidder—of the lord or the Jew. Zorobabel offers the husband, "If you intend to part with your Wife, I will give you as much for her as any Man" (*MLT,* 39). The moral order is finally restored when the husband expels the Jew and calls for those English laws that protect even a common man by restoring his property to him.

The satire is aimed not only at the rich Jew and the dissolute lord but also at the socially ambitious, newly emergent middle class—mainly at the wife, who wants to set herself up as a lady of fashion, but also at the husband, who is excessively proud of his new status and rushes out to buy himself a fine suit of clothes so "that I might appear like a Gentleman" (*MLT,* 35). The Jew is the double of these middle-class upstarts. Like the newly emergent middle class, the Jew apes the world of English high fashion, so brilliantly shown in plate 2 of Hogarth's *Harlot's Progress,* where the Jew is pictured as a dandy in the middle of taking tea, surrounded by the various toys of his newfound wealth—a monkey on a chain, a black boy in waiting, and the country girl turned harlot, all three versions of each other. In such a view, the Jew is not simply the outsider, a kind of foreign influence that invades and preys upon the innocence of English men and women, using his money to defeat the former in public life and the latter in the domestic sphere; the Jew also inhabits the very core of Englishness, apes English values, and thereby symbolically represents the greed and ambition that lurk even in the English bosom, even in the country husband and wife. In short, the Jew expresses the spirit of the nation, the new, commercial England.

The ideological climax of the play calls for retreat, an escape from London and a return to the older, simpler world of precommercial England. The husband announces this solution when he instructs his wife, "You must strip yourself of your Puppet-Shew Dress, as I will of mine; they will make you ridiculous in the Country, where there is still something of Old *England* remaining" (*MLT,* 42–43). So, just as the Jew is typically dressed up as the foppish beau in so many of these comedies, the country husband and wife must dress down: they have cross-dressed out of their class just as the Jew attempts to cross-dress out of his ethnic otherness. After all, the transformations of husband and wife have made them strangers to each other and to their family members, as if in London they appear in deliberate disguise. While the father asks, "Is this be-powder'd, be-curl'd, be-hoop'd Madwoman my Daughter?" she claims to recognize neither her father nor her husband: "Father, I am sure you don't know me; nor you, Mr. *Thomas*, neither;—nor I won't know you" (*MLT*, 37). After the husband "*Gives him [the Jew] a Box on the Ear*" and "*Kicks him off the Stage*" (*MLT*, 39) in a kind of ritual expulsion, Fielding returns the couple to the sanctuary of the country, having learned their lesson in the dangers of fashionable London life—namely, not to trespass the bounds not only of the country but also of their class. The husband must prove first that he has learned to remain within his station, so he declares, "I own I was a Footman, and had rather be a Footman still, than a tame Cuckold to a Lord" (*MLT*, 38). In this way the play is a critique of transformations of class identity (like those ethnic transformations I analyzed in my previous chapter)—the sudden transformations of footman to country squire, of country wife to fashionable town lady, of Jew to beau gentleman. And the Jew here is the pivotal figure: not only is his transformation the most radical and the most bogus—Miss Lucy asks in disbelief, "Is this a Beau, and a fine Gentleman?" (*MLT*, 21)—the Jew is seen as the central power of such bogus transformations because he holds the magic power of money to make them happen. The procuress tells Lucy about the Jew, "He'll make you a fine Lady," and the Jew attempts to seduce her by claiming, "If you will suffer me to kiss you, I will make you the finest of Ladies" (*MLT*, 22). The newly emergent middle class typically climbs the social ladder on the money of Jews; and in the gendered picture of this climb, England as woman is in danger of prostituting herself to Jewish money.

While the father in *Miss Lucy in Town* remains the reliable guardian of his daughter and oversees her retreat to the country, later in the century the father or guardian figure is seen as entirely implicated in Jewish money. This deepens the doubling between the mercenary English and rich Jewish characters, and makes clear the negotiation that invites the Jew to enter English culture through a kind of bribery. In Mrs. Margaret Holford's *Neither's the Man* (performed at the Theatre-Royal, Chester, c. 1798), for example, the heroine's guardian has approved "the richest Jew in the city" (Mordecai again) and "a pretty fribble" (Lord Filligree) as potential husbands.[33] The unstinting ambitions of the middle class tirelessly seek either increase in money (the Jew) or rank (the lord) or both. Since the Jew and the lord once again are merely different versions of each other, "they are seldom seen asunder" (*NM*, 10). Coarse money and ugly looks (the Jew) are paired with effete title and effeminate manners (the lord). The heroine requires that the "frightful old Jew" (*NM*, 27), with a "swarthy complexion and dusky beard" (*NM*, 25), remake himself for her—that is, that he submit himself to the kind of transformation I explored in chapter 2. When she insists that he shave his beard and dine on pork in a kind of mock conversion, we see that his greed is deeper than his religious principles in what becomes a conventional critique of Jews in Georgian England: "Vell, my comfort ish, dat a man may be a Jew at heart, though he hash a shmooth chin, and feeds upon shwine's flesh" (*NM*, 55). His swarthy complexion, his dusky beard, his dietary laws, and his lisping dialect mark the Jew as other on the Georgian stage. At the same time, the apparent doubleness of Jewish identity opens the possibility that any Englishman (who has a smooth chin and eats pork) may be "a Jew at heart."

The ideological denouement of *Neither's the Man* becomes one of the telling fables of this culture. The heroine rejects both money (the Jew) and status (the lord), hence neither's the man. She makes the meritorious choice of the poor lover, and thereby is doubly rewarded when she discovers that her lover turns out to be rich and well-born. Play after play, through a kind of ideological sleight of hand, manages to look as if it disqualifies money and status but nonetheless confers them both as rewards on the deserving heroine. This means, however, that the question the heroine asks when she learns of her lover's wealth and status haunts both the end of *Neither's the Man* and the culture of commercial England in general: "What becomes of my poor generosity?" (*NM*, 77). Is English generosity always only virtual, only gratuitous? Are wealth and status always the final rewards in commercial England?

Like *Neither's the Man*, many of these plays expose the guardian figure as a mercenary who is susceptible to Jewish bribery. In another marriage plot that is really a plot of prostitution, the heroine's aunt in *The Fair Refugee or The Rival Jews* wants to marry her to "Mr. Solomons the Rich Jew," who will provide the aunt with a yearly income "provided the Nuptials are consummated" (*FR*, 26). And in John O'Keeffe's popular comedy *The Young Quaker* (1783), it is the absence of the father, who abandoned his daughter many years ago, that makes her susceptible to Jewish seduction. In this variation on *The Harlot's Progress* the old Jew Shadrach works his seduction of the young girl who arrives friendless in London by substituting himself for her missing father: "As you have nobody to depend on now but me, you'll never find your father in dis great town." His sexual pleasures are to be the payment for the money he lays out to support her in London: "I vill draw a bill upon your beauty, which your virtue must accept; you pay me vid your honour, and den Cupid, my little clerk, vill give you a receipt, and I vill stamp it vid a kiss." He plays the father's role—"I'll take you under my protection"—at the same time that he plays the role of the seducer: "I must force you."[34] Such plays suggest that the English guardian figure has sold out to Jewish money, making the daughter available to be bought and sold.

Richard Brinsley Sheridan's immensely popular *The Duenna* (1775), "constantly given all over Britain until the 1840s,"[35] produced the clearest example of the father and the Jew as co-conspirators against the daughter. Instead of the guardian-father protecting the daughter from the Jew (as in *Miss Lucy in Town*), or being a partner in the heroine's scheme to expose and escape the Jew and other fortune hunters (as in *Love à la Mode*), in *The Duenna* the father tries to sell his daughter to the Jew, and actually functions as the Jew's double, admitting that he married the heroine's mother for her ducats. Although set in Spain, the play really exposes English commercial practices, as the following ironic barb aimed at England makes clear: Antonio, the heroine's choice, while poor, is of "as antient and as reputable a family as any in the kingdom," but her father takes his cue from England, for "in England they were formerly as nice as to birth and family as we are—but they have long discover'd what a wonderful purifier gold is—and now no one there regards pedigree in any thing but a horse."[36] So the avaricious father who wishes to sell his daughter to a rich Jew is modeled on English practices, and the historical record in England does in fact show that "with many of the marriages contracted between upper-class Jews and Gentiles, the wealth the Jewish partner brought to the marriage was undoubtedly the key element in securing the union."[37] And just as the father is interested only in the Jew's money, the Jew is interested only in the father's money: the heroine, for all her beauty and grace, is simply an object of economic negotiation. In these comedies and farces, the Jew is consistently seen as a fortune hunter: the Jew's attempt to make money by matrimony, or "matrimonishy,"[38] is articulated through a pun that comically reflects the Jew's dialect, "monish" being the common transcription of the word "money" in the dialect of the stage Jew.

The duenna and the Jew became the comic center of the play. Celebrated favorites of the London stage, the popular iconic duo was pictured in *The Duenna & Little Isaac* (figure 7), a print made in 1784 by William Paulet Carey after a painting by Thomas Rowlandson. Sheridan demonstrates the

Jew's shortcomings as a lover through an extended courtship scene in which he makes love to the duenna, mistaking the servant (dressed as Luisa) for the rich heroine. At first he is startled by her ugliness, but he quickly reconfirms his goal: "'Tis well my affections are fixed on her fortune and not her person" (*D*, 250). The scene functions as a kind of emasculation of the Jewish male suitor, though from the outset Sheridan feminizes him. Before they meet, Isaac is seen "admiring himself" (*D*, 243) in a looking glass: he is the feminized beau Jew who is vain about his looks. He is afraid of female beauty and afraid of lovemaking; he confesses that he "cou'd'nt be more afraid if I was going before the Inquisition" (*D*, 249). So, the trial of his masculinity is even more intimidating than the trial of his Jewishness, as the two trials are collapsed into one. By the same token the duenna is masculinized, with "a pretty sort of velvet down" (*D*, 251) on her lips, realizing his worst fear: "I only desire she mayn't have a beard" (*D*, 247). In kissing her, then, he narcissistically makes love to himself in a homoerotic embrace that further undermines him as a suitor to the heroine. In the parodic lovemaking scene between Jew and duenna, the male and female roles in courtship are in fact reversed: the Jew is courted by the brazen duenna, who seats him before her, takes his hand, and showers him with compliments.

As the double of the Jew, the duenna underscores and copies the Jew's motives and strategies in this commercially driven world. When she hopes that he will shave his beard, he retorts in an aside—"The razor wou'd'nt be amiss for either of us" (*D*, 251)—which symbolically marks her as male, Jewish, and the other half of "us." The duenna is the double of the Jew insofar as she pursues him for his money, even being willing to overlook his ugliness, just as the Jew pursues the duenna (whom he thinks is Luisa) for her fortune despite her looks. Both the duenna and the Jew try to advance themselves through the marriage market. The duenna disguises herself as her mistress as part of her plot to catch the rich Jew. Both the duenna and the Jew, then, are performers; both try to pass. But in the courtship scene between the Jew and the duenna, the Jew is shown as duped, with the tables turned on him: he becomes the object of the duenna's avarice and successful passing. In short, the Jew is outsmarted by "a Jew at heart."

The duenna is modeled on the Jew (down to the beard) because the Jew is always the central symbolic figure of social ambition in these comedies. Isaac is especially susceptible, for example, to the compliment the duenna pays him—"So little like a jew, and so much like a gentleman" (*D*, 250); he has, after all, "forsworn his country" of Portugal and turned "christian these

Figure 7: *The Duenna & Little Isaac*. Courtesy of the Library of the Jewish Theological Seminary.

six weeks" (*D*, 237), in order to rise in his new host culture—a case in which "the child of circumcision" has converted in order to woo "the child of commerce." In this he is like the Jew in *Neither's the Man*, who happily agrees to shave his beard and eat pork as a way of wooing the heroine and entering English culture, or like the converted Jew in *The Israelites; or, The Pampered Nabob* (1785), who declares about the fortune of a rich heiress: "Thirty thousand—I'll have her—get naturalized, slip in for a borough, live upon loaves and fishes."[39] Conversion becomes for these Jews a means to infiltrate England and live upon the fat of the land through a rich English woman. The Jew is never shown in these plays as a religious figure; in fact these Jews easily set aside religion as a means of serving their financial and social ambitions. As the beau Jew in *The Fair Refugee* asserts, "A Gentleman never troubles himself about Religion" (*FR*, 32). Jewish identity is understood in these plays primarily in opposition to an accepted and venerated civic code of morality, which Jews and Christians alike transgress. In other words, the Jew becomes the vehicle for a critique of social mobility that reaches well beyond him, and in this way he simply represents an entirely Judaized England, an England where both converted Jews and Judaized Christians are "Jews at heart."

While the Jew's efforts are focused on successfully invading his host culture, the comic formula of these plays consistently requires the defeat and even the dismissal of the Jew as lover. As in *The Merchant of Venice*, the heroine and her servant outsmart the Jew by cross-dressing, but in *The Duenna* the women change class roles rather than gender roles because the play is about social climbing. Likewise, the women outsmart the Jew here not in the court of law but in the marriage market, because in eighteenth-century commercial England the Jew's money moves him from outcast usurer (Shylock) to interloping suitor (Isaac)—in fact, the suitor chosen by the father for his daughter. If, on the one hand, the playwrights of eighteenth-century England move the Jew into the marriage plot as a suitor in part as a response to the actual intermarriages that were taking place in the culture at large, on the stage the Jew is allowed only a mock courtship, and if he wins at all, he wins only the old duenna disguised as the heroine. So, when the audience last sees Isaac, he is in flight from his double, the bearded duenna; in their exit, they make way for two Christian marriages to take place. In short, these courtship plots function as a kind of national fantasy: the Jews are made hideously ugly, even while they are self-admiring and overadorned, with the suggestion of effeminacy (Beau Mordecai in *Love à la Mode* is a "lunatic *castrato*"),[40] and hence are excluded from the marriage plot, as if to demonstrate at least one economic arena in which the Jew fails. Having learned his lesson, the Jewish speculator in English womanhood can exclaim with Mordecai in *Neither's the Man*: "A fine shpeculation, upon my vord . . . dish ish de lasht time I shall consharn myself about shtock, of vitch a voman ish de proprietor" (*NM*, 76; ellipsis in text). Not only does the Jew's ultimate emasculation occur at the hands of women, his financial defeat is recurrently restaged by showing him baffled in his traffic in women.

Even when the Jew is finally rehabilitated on the Georgian stage, he never has the role of the legitimate and successful suitor of a Christian woman. His rehabilitation takes place within another trope, the figure of the guardian or father. In this role the Jew displaces the morally corrupt Christian father, the English merchant who thinks only of money. So, the rehabilitated stage Jew is an old man, entirely desexualized, with only a fatherly interest in a young Christian woman. He offers no sexual threat whatsoever, and rather than attempting to steal the heroine and in some sense Judaize her, he becomes her protector and facilitates her marriage in a Christian family. The Jew in such plays has no family members himself; he is a figure of isolation, without relations and shunned by the Christian community; he is pure instrumentality itself, put to use to serve the (financial) needs of the Christian community. The prototype of this figure is Sheva in Cumberland's celebrated *The Jew*, but he appears as well in farces by the successful dramatist Thomas Dibdin, who copied the character from Cumberland. But before looking at these plays I wish to analyze an earlier play by Cumberland that provides the prototypes of merchant, father, and Jew that the playwright deliberately and self-critically revised two decades later in *The Jew*.

In *The Fashionable Lover* Cumberland constructs the kind of plot that makes clear the intersection of the ethnic and the commercial that I am identifying as a central new development in Georgian comedy: the multiethnic spectacle of Jew (Napthali), Scot (Colin Macleod), Welshman (Dr. Druid), and Frenchman (La Jeunesse) is made to include the English merchant, who takes his place in this cast of character types. The merchant Bridgemore is a middle-class social climber who attempts to make his daughter "a woman of quality" (*FL*, 6)[41] by marrying her to a lord. The Jew Napthali enters the plot as a mask for the English merchant. Bridgemore makes people think that it is Napthali the Jew to whom Lord Abberville is indebted, but it is the English merchant, "under cover of this Jew," who is the real "usurer" (*FL*, 16). Hiding his own greed and ambition behind the mask of the Jew, the English merchant represents the Judaized world of commercial England, an England turned over to Jewish (or commercial) values. The city merchant takes on the kind of vampiric qualities traditionally associated with Jews, sadistically telling Napthali about Lord Abberville's gaming: "The dice are little weapons, but they make deep wounds: what between those that win and us that lend, he bleeds at both arms" (*FL*, 42) in a mock crucifixion. Foreign Jew and English merchant are doubles—"us that lend" and feed off the lord. In this way, the English merchant is seen as even more despicable than the foreign Jew; while claiming that "there's people enough at home can poison their native country" (*FL*, 7), the English merchant does not realize that he himself is such a poisoner. Even worse than the foreign Jew (with strange name and dialect), the English merchant is a kind of traitor, ruining his own native land. In such a view England is vulnerable not simply to foreign but also to native corruption—from the Jew within, the Judaized Englishman, the Englishman as Jew. And such a view was not limited to the stage but became a widespread mode of English self-critique, with the Jew serving as the double of the Englishman. In horrified condemnation of the governor of Madras's conduct in India and his amassing of an immense fortune, Horace Walpole claimed, "Rumbolds & Co. have robbed the Indies of their climate as well as of their gold and diamonds, and brought it home in ingots. . . . I believe it will not be long before we are outcast like the Jews, and become pedlars like them up and down the earth, with no country of our own."[42]

The lord in Cumberland's play is not a simple victim but rather a special version of London corruption—the fashionable lover of the play's title, a rake and a gamester who has foolishly gotten himself in debt to the Jew and the merchant. It is through the character of Colin Macleod, whom the lord calls his "Highland savage" (*FL*,2), that the lord is morally rehabilitated, even as the theatrical rehabilitation of the Scottish character on the English stage represents the most palpable motive of the play. In short, the English author rescues the Scottish character just as the Scottish servant rescues the English master. The Scottish servant is contrasted to the Jewish broker: while the Jewish broker encourages the corruption of the city merchant by justifying his usury, the Scottish servant intervenes on the corruption of the lord by critiquing his profligacy. So the Jew functions as a corrupting mirror for the merchant, grounding his identity in greed, while the Scot functions as a chastising mirror for the lord, teaching him the lesson of useful economy. As Lord Abberville says of Colin, "He is the glass in which I see myself, and the reflection tortures me; my vices have deform'd me; gaming has made a monster of me" (*FL*, 29). The conventional parsimony of the stereotypical Scot, a standard target of anti-Scottish discourse, here is turned into a useful virtue from which the profligate lord can learn. In fact, in a deliberate echo of the national debate on the subject, Cumberland uses the Highland Scot to support the critique of commercial England: "In England, he that wants money, wants every thing; in Scotland now, few have it, but every one can do without it" (*FL*, 17). So, in *The Fashionable Lover* the Scot is rural innocence and useful economy, while the Jew is city corruption and self-seeking avarice, which means finally that the Scot drives the Jew away: Colin confesses, "I promised him a beating, and I kept my word" (*FL*, 52). Here and in *Miss Lucy in Town* the rich Jew, the corrupter of English values, is aggressively ejected from the community by a provincial character of innocence and humble birth.[43] And just as Fielding's country husband and wife are returned to the country at the end, Cumberland's lord is returned to his Highland retreat, under the ministering protection of the Highland servant and far from such predators as the city merchant and the Jew. The servant saves the master; the Highland savage saves the fashionable London lord.

While the lord is rehabilitated through the intervention of his Scottish servant, the rehabilitation of the English merchant is more complicated. Cumberland knew that the audience would not allow an unconditional critique of the merchant class, and in fact during the first-night performance there were signs of disapproval from the audience—disapproval of the praise of the Scotsman and the criticism of trade: "This Piece some thought to have been written from some political view, as the Scotch are, in a manner, deified at the expence of the English, and several indecent reflections were occasionally thrown out against the Citizens of London, one of which, in the first Act, concerning the dignity of Tradesmen . . . created an almost general hiss, and had well nigh stopped the procedure of the Performance."[44] While Cumberland refused a simple rehabilitation of Bridgemore, he compromised by producing toward the play's end another English merchant, who is Bridgemore's antithesis. The recreant merchant (Bridgemore) is divided from the good merchant (Aubrey) in an especially telling way: the first is the false guardian, the latter the good father. In fact, Bridgemore is seen doubly in the role of the father, as if to emphasize his function in this role: the English merchant is the father who is willing to cheat in order to make his daughter (Lucinda) a woman of quality and the guardian who steals from his ward (Augusta Aubrey) and finally abandons her. It is in his latter role that he becomes chastised by his double, the good merchant-father who returns to rescue his child whom he left with Bridgemore to protect. It is Aubrey's function to intervene in the other merchant's activities, and to define the proper values of the English merchant at the climax of the play: "Learn of your fraternity a more honourable practice; and let integrity for ever remain the inseparable characteristic of an English merchant" (*FL*, 60).

While the commercial plot ends with a moral about the honorable English merchant, constructed in the shadow of the recreant merchant, the ethnic plot ends with a moral about the tolerant English citizen, constructed in the shadow of the ethnic prejudice the Welshman shows toward the Scot. The last lines of the play exhort the prejudiced Welshman, who is pitiless in his attacks on the Scotsman, not "to join the cry with those, whose charity, like the limitation of a brief, stops short at Berwick, and never circulates beyond the Tweed. By Heaven, I'd rather weed out one such unmanly prejudice from the hearts of my countrymen, than add another Indies to their empire" (*FL*, 63). The sentiment for toleration is so deep, so strong, that the only way to measure it is to allow it, at least temporarily, to supersede the desire for imperialist conquest and acquisition. In this way the national goal of commerce seems to hang in the balance with the national goal of toleration. The final moral of the play about ethnic prejudice takes two strategic detours here that leave it significantly incomplete. First, the final moral is safely aimed against the Welshman, when it was in fact the English who were in the midst of a serious bout of virulent Scottophobia; and second, the final moral lets stand the anti-Semitism that was the conventional vehicle used to attack the commercial interests of the English.

When Cumberland decided to rehabilitate the Jew on stage, after rehabilitating the Irishman and the West Indian in *The West Indian* and the Scotsman in *The Fashionable Lover* in the early 1770s, he began with what looks like a self-critical revision of his earlier work. Cumberland revises his account of the English merchant whose greed is supported by Jewish principles and Jewish counsel by showing the usurious English merchant critiqued and ultimately educated by the high-principled Jew. In 1794 in his celebrated comedy *The Jew*, Cumberland makes Sheva the moral center of the play, and Sir Stephen Bertram, the English merchant, is the ambitious middle-class father who values money above all else, including his daughter. This is a radical revision of not only *The Fashionable Lover* but also *The Merchant of Venice*, where the test of values consistently used the Jew as the extreme example of material values and the merchant as the spokesman for love and generosity. It is Sheva the Jew, not the Christian, who is the educator in the finer values of pity, forgiveness, generosity, and mercy. As in *The Fashionable Lover*, the critique against the English merchant shies away from being a generic critique, but here it is made by the Jew himself, who tells Sir Bertram, "You have no great deal of pity yourself, but I do know many noble British merchants that abound in pity, therefore I do not abuse your tribe," and Sir Bertram is forced to confess: "I am confounded and ashamed; I see my fault, and most sincerely ask your pardon."[45]

The literal father, the English merchant, the man who cares only about money, and the symbolic father, the Jew, the man who cares only about making the young lovers happy, are the antithetical poles around which the action of the play is built. Here the Jew's role has been radically changed again, countervailing the prevailing Georgian paradigm: he is not the foppish suitor, the fortune-hunting Jew whose courtship intrudes on a Christian marriage, but the kindly father-figure who makes a Christian marriage possible, again set off against the English merchant as father. By supplying Eliza with the ten thousand pounds that Sir Bertram requires of a potential daughter-in-law, the Jew clears the path to the young lovers' marriage and to the father's eventual forgiveness of his son. But at first Sir Bertram reads Eliza's newly found riches as some nefarious plot by the Jew that the merchant attempts to unmask: "Which of your money-making tribe ever had sense of pity? Show me the terms, on which you have lent this money, if you dare! Exhibit the dark deed, by which you have meshed your victim in the snares of usury; but be assured, I'll drag you to the light, and publish your base dealings in the world" (*J*, 39–40). The solution to Jewish deceit is to illuminate and to publish the dark deed, to produce the spectacle of Jewish crime, to make the Jew visible—in other words, the goal of Georgian England's anti-Jewish theatrics. This rhetoric of exposure is important because it ironically parallels the genuine unmasking of the Jew that the play itself has undertaken as its central goal: the revelation of the Jew's inner humanity and generosity. In short, the conventional, anti-Semitic unmasking of the Jew is superseded by the tolerant act of removing the layers of prejudice that mask the Jew and make him a stock figure of hard-hearted usury.

In counterpoint to the scene in which Sir Bertram attempts to unmask Sheva, the scene between Charles Ratcliffe and Sheva earlier in the play functions as a scene of genuine recognition. Sheva's claim is directed equally at Charles and the audience when he invites all to see him remove the mask: "You shall see what I have shown to no man, Sheva's real heart" (*J*, 18). By unburdening himself of his loneliness and the centuries of persecution that he and his coreligionists have suffered, and by generously offering financial assistance to Charles, the Jew unmasks himself. In such a scene the play attempts to move beyond the Christian's exposure of the Jew to Jewish self-exposure, from representation to presentation. This is an attempt to put Jewish identity, and its revelation, in the hands of the Jew himself. So, below the surface of this scene we sense the traditional recognition scene of drama, where fathers find long-lost sons, brothers find long-lost sisters, but here the characters in Cumberland's play find an unexpected family member in the Jew. After all, the denouement of the play is a series of such recognitions, when Charles declaims to all the characters: "My benefactor; yours, Eliza; Frederic's; yours, dear mother! all mankind's: The widow's friend, the orphan's father, the poor man's protector, the universal philanthropist" (*J*, 64). Such a recognition scene is meant to suggest the ways in which the strategies of the theater are being reinvented for a reevaluation of Jewish identity. At the same time, the Jew's identity seems dissolved in a universal abstraction, and the Jew without his own family—"No, no sister, no broder, no son, no daughter" (*J*, 17)— seems to exist only to facilitate Christian marriage and Christian procreation. No procreator himself, he dissolves in some version of Christian brotherhood; he will live on not in any of his own progeny but in the successful regeneration of this Christian family, and his earlier prediction—"My family is all gone, it is extinct, my very name will vanish out of memory when I am dead" (*J*, 25)—still seems to ring true. Christened the universal philanthropist, the Jew Sheva seems to disappear.

Moreover, this unmasking of the Jew is seen as so radical, so disorienting, that Sheva feels almost as if he has no identity, at least socially, publicly, apart from that which has been assigned to him over the centuries—namely, to play the miser, the cheat, the usurer, the man with no affections or human ties. After all, the name "Jew" in England functions even in the Jewish community with the same meanings as in the Christian; Sheva's coreligionist servant Jabal complains, for example, "He is no Hebrew, no more a Jew than Julius Caesar; for . . . he gives away his money by handfuls to the consumers of hog's flesh" (*J*, 28). Even at the end of the play, when all wish to praise him for his good deeds, Sheva disallows the praise because the terms sound so alien, because he cannot recognize himself in these terms. He even reverts to a kind of masking: "You make me hide my face" (*J*, 64). Charles tells him, "You have long masked your charities. . . . You must now face the world, and transfer the blush from your own cheeks to theirs, whom prejudice had taught to scorn you. For your single sake, we must reform our hearts, and inspire them with candour towards your whole nation" (*J*, 64). But the Jew replies: "I am not used to hear the voice of praise, and it oppresses me: I should not know myself, if you were to describe me: I must refute the praises of that gentleman" (*J*, 64). In the ultimate recognition scene, then, the Jew fails to recognize himself in the praise of others. The Jew is unknown not simply to others but even to himself, in the larger theater of public life, without the conventional taunts and stereotypes that construct and represent him—that is, without the anti-Semitic discourses that, over the centuries, have become part of the name and identity "Jew." Sheva redefines the Jewish mask: it is not the mask that the Jew wears to pass as a Christian in order to infiltrate Protestant England, but the mask that the Christian community has required the Jew to wear for centuries—the mask that even the Jew himself cannot simply take off (as he hides his face).

Sheva's generosity is figured at least in part as a kind of repayment for the good deeds of the Ratcliffe family. So, while Sheva rescues Charles Ratcliffe from poverty, Sheva himself has been rescued, twice, by the Ratcliffe family. Sheva is well disposed toward Charles from the beginning because Charles has saved him from being "mobbed and maltreated" (*J*, 14); he owes "the debt of gratitude" (*J*, 25) to Charles, who acted "to save a poor jew from a pitiless mob" (*J*, 14). Moreover, in the course of the play Sheva discovers that Charles is the son of the man who saved him many years ago from the Inquisition in Spain. So again Sheva is quick "to pay the debt of gratitude that I do owe to you, and to your fader" (*J*, 58). Hence Sheva can describe his "debt" in the following terms to Charles' mother: "Your debtor in no less a sum than all I possess, the earnings of a life preserved, first by your husband, and now again by your son" (*J*, 64). Even Mrs. Goodison is brought into the web of rescues when she recalls that "Mr. Sheva . . . rescued me from the like distress when my poor husband died" (*J*, 48). This complex network of rescues and debts of gratitude radically revises debt as the foundation of the intersection between Jews and Christians. Financial debt, the debasing bond of Jewish-Christian relations, is transformed into moral debt. In this way the play tries to move the basis of the intersection between Jews and Christians from the legally binding financial contract toward the freely given gift.

The sheer popularity and profitableness of *The Jew* led others to copy it. Thomas Dibdin, an immensely successful playwright, tells the story of how William Dowton, an actor whose first appearance in London was as Sheva in *The Jew*, "lamented he could not get the character of a comic Jew to perform in town: he wanted one quite as benevolent, but more farcical, than Mr. Cumberland's Sheva."[46] In response to Dowton's request, Dibdin set about writing *The Jew and the Doctor*, a farce that premiered at Covent Garden in 1798 and that begins with the same problem as *The Jew*: a father who "value[s] women . . . by weight"[47] argues with his son, whom he wants to marry a rich woman, but the son is already smitten with a poor one. But here the young heroine is literally—not just figuratively—the ward of an old Jew. Abednego adopts Emily as a foundling, raises her as a Christian, and bestows on her a fortune that makes her eligible for marriage. Emily acknowledges that Abednego has "always been a *father* to me" (*JD*, 8, emphasis in text). Such plots function as fantasies of national wish-fulfillment: rich, fatherly old Jews (Sheva and Abednego) enter Christian family plots in order to repair breaches between fathers and sons as well as between different families, to facilitate Christian marriages, and finally, to leave a fortune to young Christian couples. Is this the bribe that English audiences required to take the Jew to their hearts?

In such revisionist comedies, the Jew consistently is the moral teacher of the Christians, suffering their prejudices and educating them in the benefits of tolerance and the dangers of materialism. Here Abednego lectures the old father, Bromley: "If Christians *profess* forgiveness of injuries, Jews can sometimes practice it" (*JD*, 12, emphasis in text)—a line stolen from *The Israelites; or, The Pampered Nabob*, in which a similarly benevolent Jew is the kind guardian of a Christian woman ("I will show you there are some Jews who practise what many Christians only profess").[48] And as in *The Jew*, Jews and Christians are knit together through a series of moral bonds and obligations that transcend the mere financial relations that fuel the plot. Emily asks her guardian Abednego, "How, Sir, shall I ever repay your goodness. Alas! the debt of gratitude commenced with my birth" (*JD*, 10). But the Jew refuses literal repayment, both from his ward and from her real father, who reappears at the end to claim his daughter and to pay Abednego. The Jew responds: "I'll tell you how to *pay* me. If ever you see a helpless creature vat needs your assistance, give it for ma sake—And if de object should even not be a Christian, remember that humanity knows no difference of opinion; and that you can never make your own religion look so well, as when you shew mercy to de religion of others" (*JD*, 31, emphasis in text). Similarly, in Dibdin's *The School for Prejudice*, which premiered at Covent Garden in 1801, after Ephraim has guarded and then restored the missing money owed to the Widow Howard and she tries to compensate him, he retorts: "So, after I've been so honest vayever I can, you vant to pay me for it, and make a rogue of me; but I sha'n't let you do noting of de kind."[49] In other words, the Jew refuses the reward that inevitably goes to the Christians at the end of all these plays, money. So, in these plays the Jew guards and restores a Christian inheritance, rescues an abandoned child and raises her as Christian and finds her a worthy (not fortune-hunting) husband, facilitates the marriages of young lovers (against misguided and obdurate paternal interdiction), and typically ends by lecturing the community on the virtues of tolerance and mercy. In short, the Jew has become the guardian of English money, English innocence, English marriage, and in the end, English conscience.

The immense impact of these revisionist plays was publicly acknowledged, sometimes grudgingly or even satirically. The theater itself, through intertextual citation, remarked on Cumberland's success when an aspiring playwright in a comic prelude, George Colman the Younger's *New Hay at the Old Market* (which premiered at the Haymarket in 1795), claims he has figured out the formula for popular dramatic writing: "The fashion of Plays, you know, now, is to do away old prejudices; and to rescue certain characters from the illiberal odium with which custom has mark'd them. Thus we have a generous Israelite."[50] Cumberland's *Jew* immediately became the source of ongoing debate, so a reviewer of Colman's afterpiece shot back in the *Monthly Mirror* (July 1796): "Why should Colman ridicule, as he does in his *New Hay*, the *tender* MISANTHROPE and *benevolent* JEW of Cumberland?" (p. 185). And in the same periodical in December of 1802, a theater critic grudgingly admitted about the Jews, "The stage has lately become the vehicle of their panegryic," pointing in particular to Cumberland: "When was offered a compliment more pointed, flattering, and liberal, to any sect or nation, than Cumberland has paid to the Jewish race in his *Sheva*?" (p. 405). But most reviewers applauded Cumberland's intentions "to rescue an injured and persecuted race"[51] and to counteract the way in which the stage Jew "has been exhibited for the entertainment of the public."[52]

The Jew inspired wide debate and controversy, well beyond the purview of the theater. William Cobbett published an essay in 1806, for example, that became part of his *Political Register*'s ongoing attack on what he saw as the new "Jewish Predominance," the result of "the growth of the commercial spirit among us." In the midst of an attack on Jewish predominance—"But now they are the companions of our feasts, the pride of our assemblies, the arbiters of our amusements"—the essayist pointed a blaming finger at Cumberland: "Mr. Cumberland should consider, that he has indiscreetly over-done the part; and, that a Jew who gives away his money for the mere pleasure of doing good, without shew or profit, is such a monstrous caricature as no real Jew can see without contempt. It is only with us simpler Christians that the play has had any influence, and I will not dispute with Mr. Cumberland, that it may have assisted us to shake off those suspicions and prejudices which so long held our Jewish inmates in the condition of rats, always persecuted but never extirpated, nor prevented from purloining our victuals."[53] So, *The Jew* bamboozles well-intentioned Christians but not "real" Jews about the nature of Jewish identity. And in 1830, almost four decades after the premiere of *The Jew*, Cobbett was still publishing articles that complained about Cumberland, his Jew, and the London stage's attack on intolerance: "Have we not still . . . *enlightened blacks*, and *generous Jews*! Though *pensioned* CUMBERLAND is dead, are there not a plenty of the same cast left behind him?"[54]

Cumberland's comedy produced such wide and heated interest because it was recognized as part of the larger Enlightenment goal of critiquing Shakespeare's Shylock and thereby European (including English) anti-Semitism. In 1781, for example, in presenting his translation of Gotthold Lessing's *Nathan the Wise* to the English public, R. E. Raspe explained that the play "was intended as an antidote against that rancour of religious bigotry, with which the Jews are still treated in many parts of Germany." But why bring the play to England? Because, "though the unnatural and abominable character of Shylock continues to fan the expiring flame of inquisitorial bigotry, and universal toleration is far from being fully established, it is hoped, however, that Nathan will be suffered to counteract the poison which barbarous ages have left in the minds of fanatics, and Shakespeare and political factions may, some time or other, stir up again and put into fermentation."[55] And some years later, in 1805, another translator came forward, to offer his English version of *Nathan* to the public as a supplement to what Cumberland might not fully have achieved: "The altered sentiments and conduct of the German public towards the Jews began in Nathan the Wise. The consequent alterations of Prussian Legislation result from Nathan the Wise. Cumberland's Comedy of the Jew, which has favoured in England an analogous temper, . . . does not appeal to so high a class of feelings."[56]

Cumberland had set a new and radical standard by which the staging of Jewish identity in England was to be judged, and in so doing he had initiated a much larger debate, for to question the place of Shylock and Sheva in English culture was to raise questions that went to the heart of English national identity. So, with Shylock and Sheva as starting points, nothing short of a national public debate was conducted in the periodical literature of the time, where theater reviewers, anonymous citizen-correspondents, and editors hidden behind pseudonyms debated the Jewish question, not forgetting that such a debate had its origins more than half a century earlier in the controversy over the "Jew Bill." A typical example of such journalism appeared in the *Monthly Visitor* in 1797, based on a group of friends debating the question,

"Which is most consistent with the character of an Israelite, Shakespeare's Shylock or Cumberland's Sheva?" The author argues that Shylock, "instead of being a caricature, is not only the best portrait of an Israelite in the English drama, but one of the truest copies of nature to be met with throughout our author's works," in exposing Jewish "duplicity, cruelty, and revenge, together with the auxiliary vice of avarice." But, while Shakespeare's is the truer representation, the portrait of Sheva, though "both inconsistent and unnatural," "entitles him [Cumberland] to a larger share of praise, for striving to free an oppressed people from the taunts and insults of the ignorant and malevolent. For my own part, I am proud, I feel my bosom glow with the most pleasing sensations, when I reflect, that I am in a country where the mist of prejudice is daily passing away; and where Jews are treated with fellow-feeling and humanity. Thanks to the benevolent genius of Cumberland! . . . For though he has failed in endeavouring to present us with a copy of nature, he has done more; he has kindled into a flame the latent sparks of philanthropy, [and] roused the dormant feelings of humanity."[57]

These remarks encapsulate the schizophrenia of the culture and the stage's persistent duality with regard to Jewish identity: while the cruel and vengeful Shylock was seen as an accurate picture of Jewish identity, the culture at the same time praised itself for its tolerance in allowing and applauding *The Jew*. England was wise enough to know that Jews were Shylocks, but also tolerant enough to make believe they were Shevas. In this light Cumberland's portrait of the benevolent Jew is really not about Jews at all, but about the benevolent Englishman. As a reviewer of the third edition of *The Jew* explained, "The extraordinary success with which it has been attended, may be esteemed a proof, that liberal sentiment holds no mean rank in the catalogue of our national virtues."[58] In short, the debate over Shylock versus Sheva could embrace both characters. Anti-Semitism and philo-Semitism lived, indeed flourished, side by side in (tolerant) England.

The kind of debate that the *Monthly Visitor* published was in fact conducted frequently in the press at the turn of the nineteenth century, and I am arguing that the debate over the "Jew Bill" turned into a debate over Shylock and the plays that directly challenged for the first time Shakespeare's portrait of Jewish identity. For example, such a debate emerged in the *Monthly Mirror*, developing over the course of a couple years from articles and letters on Shylock and Sheva to extended dialogues between correspondents on the nature and the history of the Jews. In June 1804, "On the Character of Shylock," an anonymous letter addressed to the editor, took the form of a response to another writer who had made "an apology for Shylock." The current correspondent applauded the fact that "within a few years several dramatic productions have been performed where the character of a Jew is placed in the most amiable point of view; few of the modern comedies have received more applause than Cumberland's excellent play" (p. 406). Two letters to the editor (both signed "N.S.") that appeared in June and December 1805 significantly broadened the question: "Remarks on the Character of the Jews" (deliberately pushing beyond the scope of "On the Character of Shylock") and "The Jews in this Country." The first is a philo-Semitic account of the "almost uninterrupted series of oppressions" suffered by the Jews, arguing that "it is under such circumstances as these that the present character of the Jews has been formed" (pp. 381–84). The second applauds the laws of England, but sharply understands the social stigma that still attaches to the English Jews: "Codes of jurisprudence cannot regulate the spontaneous emotions, the innate sympathies of the heart; we have still to divest ourselves of narrow prejudices." This letter writer sets side by side, as reminders of English prejudice, "the Venetian usurer, so finely pourtrayed by our favourite bard," and the "Jew Bill," recalling that "in the middle of the last century, the circumstances attendant upon the act of the British legislature for naturalizing the Jews, evince sufficiently the dispositions by which our own countrymen were animated. The feelings manifested at that time must reflect an equal disgrace upon the mass of the people who entertained them" (pp. 374–76). Early in the following year, in February 1806, a letter to the editor entitled "The Jews" (and signed "Samuel B—") answers these letters by beginning with a conventional nod toward Enlightenment tolerance that soon turns to an invective of prejudice that suggests instituting ghettoes (after the manner of Germany) in England, for the writer is horrified at "that assimilation of affection—that sympathy of feeling" (pp. 86–89) that some Christians have invited. And in April of 1806 this letter is answered in a letter entitled "Further Observations Respecting the Jews" by the earlier correspondent, N.S., who attacks the paranoiac fear of the Judaization of England that is the bugbear of English anti-Semitism: "Must we naturally become converts to judaism by treating its professors with the same general benevolence that one human being should ever feel for another?" (pp. 230–34). The kinds of arguments articulated here in the *Monthly Mirror* and in the public press generally not only recall the debates over the "Jew Bill" by actually citing them but also anticipate the parliamentary debates on Jewish civil disabilities that were soon to be initiated.

But, while Sheva, Abednego, and Ephraim achieved the goal of inciting a national debate, their shortcomings were all too obvious. Each was a dual creature, at once pathetic and comical, as if the stage, even with its high-sounding attacks on prejudice, could not entirely relinquish certain elements of the comical stage Jew. Farce regularly punctured the tender moments of these plays. In *The Jew and the Doctor*, for example, the Jew obsessively quotes the price of every item with which he comes into contact, and his moral speeches are typically interrupted by his acknowledgment, "I always minds de main chance" (*JD*, 10). Audiences applauded the main didactic purpose, which seemed a vague effusion of tolerance that rose above the play, while still laughing at the oddities and peculiarities of the miserly Jew, especially since his great wealth did not stay in his hands but was transferred to the Christian community. It was a well-calculated negotiation made by actors, playwrights, and managers. *The School for Prejudice*, with a good deal of self-satisfaction, announced its goal "to banish prejudice from us all!" (*SP*, 84) and to "terminate the Reign of Prejudice," and audiences laughed at the Jew's comical dialect and his miserly eccentricity at the same time that they were drawn into such self-gratifying celebration: "A British Audience scorns . . . [Prejudice's] gloomy sway" (the epilogue). In other words, a British audience laughs prejudice away.

Moreover, one of the central problems of these plays was that they functioned so simply and directly in reaction to Shakespeare's play: the Jew becomes a philanthropist instead of a usurer. This is ethnic recuperation engineered through a simple binary opposition, no more than an exaggerated reversal of Shylock. The effect often produced in audiences was a self-satisfied sense of having co-opted and converted Jewish identity. What I mean here is that audiences typically saw Sheva as a Christian, despite his protestations to the contrary. One typical reviewer claimed, "The author has made the Jew act like a *Christian*, in opposition to Shakespeare's Shylock."[59] The play did try, if unsuccessfully, to guard against this particular interpretation. Charles Ratcliffe compliments Sheva along these lines (in the language of *The Merchant of Venice*): "Thou hast affections, feelings, charities—. . . . I'll call you christian, then, and this proud merchant [Bridgemore] jew." This is the conventional way of critiquing commercialized England through a slur that keeps in place the derogatory meanings of the name "Jew" while shifting that name to the Christian merchant. But Sheva refuses the apparent praise—"I shall not thank you for that compliment" (*J*, 17)—because he is unwilling to lose his own identity, in what is in fact a subtle and covert form of conversion. Nonetheless, audiences persisted in reading Sheva as a Christian: "In doctrine he is a Jew; in good works, he will thank you to call him Christian."[60]

The strained effort of these plays, their double-mindedness about Jewish identity, their exaggeration of Jewish benevolence, and especially their patent ideological agenda, opened the door for the theater to seek other ways to critique the conventional stage Jew. In my next chapter I examine another stage strategy for fighting the anti-Semitism of *The Merchant of Venice* in particular and the English stage Jew in general—namely, a metatheatrical comedic structure that exposed and deconstructed the theater's own stage craft, its own construction of the Jew as a popular staple of the London stage. If audiences suspected that what Cumberland had produced was a Christian in Jew's clothing, the stage was ready to perform a further unmasking— namely, to show in more profound ways that the stage Jew was no more than a Christian in Jew's clothing, quite literally. In other words, the stage began to expose the ways in which Christian actors, playwrights, and audiences co-operatively produced a stage Jew that was simply the invention of Christian culture, Christian prejudice—written, acted, and applauded by Christians. The theater took the radical and self-critical step of revealing that the stage Jew was no more than a sight gag and a sound gag. In the trope of the cross-dressing Gentile, the theater revealed that the stage Jew was simply the sum of his costume and props—his beard, his hat, his dialect—and thereby exposed the culture's theatrical construction of Jewish identity.

CHAPTER FOUR

"Circumcised Gentiles," On Stage and Off

IT IS NOT surprising that the general public became fascinated with—even to the point of mimicry—a people who had been officially banished from England from 1290 until 1656, and who were suddenly seen in the opening decades of the eighteenth century as a defining feature of the new commercial identity of England. In this chapter I examine the ways in which the figure of the Jew in Georgian England became a highly visible and self-conscious theatrical construct, the product of professional actors on the stage and the public at large off the stage, from the time when the fiasco of the "Jew Bill" put the Jews on the national agenda in the 1750s through the opening decades of the nineteenth century. The many plays containing Jewish characters in London theaters in the second half of the eighteenth century allowed, and perhaps even encouraged, the public at large to participate in the performance of Jewish identity: the stage Jew often existed as a farcical exaggeration that was easily mimicked at masquerades and in street theater. I begin by recording the multiple ways in which the general public embraced the act of passing for a Jew, frequently in more or less overt political demonstrations. Passing for a Jew was not mere comic sport; it became the means of expressing a deepening anxiety over the increasingly fluid border between Jew and Gentile, and the location of Englishness in relation to Jewishness. And of course such a border began to look all the more fluid precisely insofar as Gentile Englishmen successfully passed for Jews, whether on the stage, at a masquerade, or in street theater. I then turn to the way in which, through the trope of the cross-dressing Gentile, the stage examined its own representations of Jewish identity as well as the theatricalization of Jewish identity in the culture at large.

While in my preceding chapter I showed how the new visibility of Jews became a central topic in *The Connoisseur*, I now wish to emphasize how this new visibility led to a growing preoccupation with mimicking Jews. *The Connoisseur*'s opening number focuses its tour of London on the site of representation itself, following in the footsteps of a famous actor, Charles Macklin (though not identified by name): "When a comedian, celebrated for his excellence in the part of Shylock, first undertook that character, he made daily visits to the centre of business, the 'Change and the adjacent coffee-houses; that by a frequent intercourse and conversation with 'the unforeskinn'd race,' he might habituate himself to their air and deportment" (January 31, 1754). An actor leads the search not simply for Jews but for a mode of representation; how to represent and to mimic this strange people who now populated the city became an important object of inquiry. Jewish representation entered a new phase in Georgian England because for the first time in several centuries the Jew evidently was no longer merely a figure of fantasy but was in fact available for empirical observation. Visible and accessible, Jews were suddenly before everyone's eyes, at the coffeehouses, at the Royal Exchange, in the theater pit and boxes—there, in other words, to be copied and mimicked.

Playing the Jew became a popular public phenomenon in an era that was already obsessed with performance, with the theatricality of everyday life. This was a time when the border between theater and everyday life was at its most liminal—the time, for instance, of amateur theatricals and masquerades, when theatrical amusement meant not merely attending the theater but bringing the theater into one's own lived experience, the time when everyone was an actor as well as a spectator. Amateur theatricals became the craze, and even became the object of satire on the stage itself from the 1770s through the 1790s.[1] As one contemporary observer noted, "The phrenzy for spouting and acting . . . has not only shown itself in the parlours of private houses, but even descended into the kitchen and stables, the very footmen and grooms becoming Romeos and Alexanders."[2] Plays themselves satirized this frenzy: Arthur Murphy's *The Apprentice*, for example, records "a meeting of prentices, and clerks, and giddy young men, all intoxicated with plays!," sets a comical scene in a spouting club, and makes fun of a young man who obsessively acts as if he is in play, even in the most unlikely circumstance.[3] And this kind of amateur playacting spilled over into the popular masquerades of the time, where ethnic disguise in general and the Jewish disguise in particular became especially popular, a fact that Terry Castle's *Masquerade and Civilization* (1986) overlooks, reproducing for example an engraving from 1771 entitled "The Masquerade Dance" in which one man is dressed as a Jew (Castle identifies the group dancing merely as "all-male").[4] There are frequent journalistic accounts of masquerades that record the appearances of "a Jew Pedlar, talking German and broken English,"[5] and "two Shoeblacks, formerly Jew Brokers,"[6] as well as frequent examples of what I have called the multiethnic spectacle—that is, masquerades at which one could see "a Spaniard," "a Highlander," "an admirable droll Mungo," and "a Jew and Jewess,"[7] or "a Mungo," "two or three Quakers," "several female Jew Pedlars," and "an old-fashioned French Fop,"[8] or "an Israelite money-lender," "a Highlander," and "a Welsh pauper."[9]

The novel and the periodical essay also represented the popularity of Jewish performance. In Samuel Richardson's *Pamela* (1740), for instance, the heroine recalls a masquerade at which someone appeared as a Jewish rabbi, and a fictitious epistle in *The Spectator* reports on a masquerade at which "a *Jew* eat me up half a Ham of Bacon."[10] Novels such as Tobias Smollett's *Expedition of Humphry Clinker* (1771) and William Godwin's *Caleb Williams* (1794) portray characters who hide their identities by assuming a Jewish disguise, while in Edgeworth's *Harrington*, "good Christian beggars . . . dressed up and daubed" as Jews—"the tone, accent, and action, suited to the parts to be played."[11] In Jane Austen's *Mansfield Park* (1814), a novel that anatomizes theatricality, Henry Crawford declares: "I could be fool enough at this moment to undertake any character that ever was written, from Shylock or Richard III down to the singing hero of a farce. . . . I feel as if I could be any thing or every thing."[12] Henry's claim to "be any thing or every thing" starts with what might seem the greatest performative stretch of all, playing the Jew. Nonetheless, it was a role that had become immensely popular. In fact, what I have already characterized as a conscious embrace of the new commercial identity of England at the beginning of the eighteenth century might also be seen as an unconscious symptom that came to characterize the culture at large throughout the century—namely, Addison's declaration, "I have been taken for a Merchant upon the *Exchange* for above these ten Years, and sometimes pass for a *Jew* in the Assembly of Stock-Jobbers at *Jonathan's*."[13]

The phenomenon of passing for a Jew flourished in the most liminal theatrical spaces. During the Old Price riots at Covent Garden Theatre in 1809,[14] when rioters protested the new ticket prices, there is the record of a Gentile cross-dressed as a Jew. This Jewish performance takes place off the stage but still in the theater, and suggests how complex and how powerful transgressing the border between stage actor and public spectator became in Georgian England. The management had hired some Jewish pugilists, most notably Daniel Mendoza and "Dutch Sam," to contain the rioters, and soon the Jews themselves became one of the primary objects of opprobrium during the months that the riots dragged on, in handbills, placards, mottos, and epigrams: "Turn out the Jews"; "And lo! it came to pass, that John Bull was sorely vexed, and smote the Israelites"; "Oppose Shylock and the whole tribe of Israel"; "Shall Britons be subdued by the wandering tribe of Jerusalem"; "The Covent Garden Synagogue, Mendoza the Grand Rabbi"; "Genius of Britain support our cause / Free us from Kemble and Jewish laws"; and so on.[15] During the particular episode that I have in mind, the pit "joined in expressing a sort of mock indignation against a man, who appeared in the garb of a venerable Jewish rabbi," the "assumed" dress consisting of "a large black beard, and slouched hat." In this way the popular convention of the stage Jew became the property not of the actors on the stage but of the audience in the pit. Anyone could assume the role of the Jew, and audience members, in their dispute over rising theater prices, in effect could stage their own performance of Jewish identity. The mock Jewish rabbi "suffered himself to be pushed about the pit, by his companions, without betraying the slightest symptoms of displeasure. While he was the object of attack, many exclaimed, 'a Jew! a Jew! turn him out.' The sham Israelite kept up the deception until he was quite exhausted."[16] By 1809 London audiences had become acculturated to the performance of Jewish identity, so that this audience's performance of the pelted rabbi reproduced what it had seen on the stage, week after week; it was copying off stage the scapegoating of the Jew that occurred on stage in a variety of plays, both old and new.

The audience's shouts to turn out the Jew were aimed not at a real Jew but at a mock Jew, and in this way functioned to realize the power of the audience in the form of a ritualized expulsion. The performance of the rabbi buffeted by shoves and jeers in every direction, the object of derision and ostracism, reenacted what was perhaps the most dramatic event of Anglo-Jewish history—namely, the expulsion of the Jews from England in 1290. In fact, the guardianship of Englishness was connected in Georgian England with what were seen as patriotic performances of the expulsion of the Jews. On another evening during the Old Price riots, real Jews were in fact ejected from the theater in what became in its own way a celebration of Anglocentrism. "Repeated exclamations now came from the audience of 'Turn out the Jews;' and a ruffianly [*sic*] Hebrew, who was in the pit on the preceding night . . . now again grossly insulted the whole audience." A scuffle ensued, the Jew was turned out into the lobby and then knocked down, and he finally retreated with some other Jews. "A cry soon resounded from the pit, signifying that the

Jews were turned out, and three loud huzzas were given immediately by the audience, followed by 'God save the King,' in universal chorus."[17] We have here a mini-opera that stages, off stage in the pit, the kinds of mottos that the rioters constructed to represent the Jews as a threat to Englishness, not to mention the kinds of operatic farces that audiences were used to seeing on stage.

Such incidents suggest how the public could empower itself to formulate English identity through the theatrical performance of the expulsion of the Jew. They recall an episode recorded in the *London Evening-Post* a half century earlier, at the time of the clamor over the "Jew Bill": "On Saturday Night last amidst the Rejoicings for the celebrating his Majesty's Birth-Day in the Borough of Southwark, the populace dress'd up the effigy of a Jew, and burnt him in a large Bonfire" (November 13–15, 1753). The Jewish effigy was a popular theatrical device used to represent the Jew as a kind of puppet figure in important ideological battles. There was, for example, the drunken Tory mob that paraded with a Jewish effigy in 1753.[18] Such representations made their way into plate 1 of William Hogarth's *Four Prints of an Election* (1755–58), where the Tories parade with a Jewish effigy marked "No Jews."[19] Like the Jewish rabbi of the Old Price riots, the Jewish effigy functions as part of a ritualized public performance of expulsion, and suggests, through a kind of theatrical dressing up of a figure as a Jew, the ways in which the public used the lessons it learned nightly at the theater about staging Jewish identity.

While the performance of Jewish identity sometimes had a specific political agenda—as in the cases of the "Jew Bill" or the Old Price riots—I wish to argue that the public's appropriation of the performance of the stage Jew was a response to what was seen more generally, with increasing anxiety, as the newly porous borders between (foreign) Jew and (English) Gentile in the culture at large. This fluidity between identities was everywhere in evidence. For example, it was during the Georgian period that the name "Jew" began to slip and slide, opening up the overlapping middle ground between Jew and Gentile, Jew and Englishman. As early as May 27, 1727, in *The Craftsman*, we read: "Among the Christians with whom I reside there are a peculiar Sort called Stock-Jobbers. The Christians themselves nickname them Jews, as a mark of Reproach. . . . Those, who are the natural Jews, may be known by their Complexions and a sort of lingua Franca." So, there are "natural" Jews, and there are Jews by habit, behavior, or performance. During the clamor over the Naturalization Bill, those who campaigned against the bill substituted the word "Jew" for "Whig," the Pelhams were called the Jewish brothers, and their supporters the Jewish candidates. In fact, the Jewish effigy paraded in Oxfordshire actually represented a Whig candidate—a vivid and politically charged example of the cross-dressing Gentile (cross-dressed against his will).[20] Similarly, during the Old Price riots Kemble was nicknamed "Mr. Jew Kemble," and caricatures of him depicted him with a very large nose.[21] And when a stockbroker in the audience criticized the Old Price rioters, they immediately called out, "Put him in the *Stocks*, he is a *Jew*."[22]

It was probably Charles Lamb who best summed up this culture's confusion and discomfort: "I do not relish the approximation of Jew and Christian, which has become so fashionable. . . . Jews christianizing—Christians judaizing—puzzle me. I like fish or flesh."[23] This new "approximation" was quite evident in the culture at large, including the newly familiar social relations between Jews and Gentiles, not to mention the increased fervor to convert Jews to Christianity, as well as such sensational events as the conversion of a nobleman like Lord George Gordon to Judaism in the late 1780s, or the claim that the English were descended from the ancient Jews, made famous by Richard Brothers in the 1790s. There was in this culture, then, the paranoiac dissociation of English identity from Jewish identity, using exaggerated stage markers to locate Jewish difference and epitomized by the ritualized performance of the expulsion of the Jews from England, at the same time that English Gentiles began more and more to socialize with Jews, to marry Jews, and to name themselves Jews, usually pejoratively but not always (as in the cases of Gordon and Brothers), while Jews sometimes converted, sometimes took Gentile names, and generally assimilated in large numbers.[24] In short, the theatrical performance of Jewish identity was often used to rigidify the border between Gentile and Jew precisely as it began to become more and more porous.

At the same time, the performance of Jewish identity—in which Jew and Englishman seemed coterminous, even mixed—-could become a strikingly material realization of the culture's paranoiac fears about the new "approximation" between Jew and Gentile. After all, the performance of Jewish identity required the Gentile to be hidden and absorbed in the body of the Jew. So the confusion between Jew and Gentile (or Christian) was noted as a genuine puzzle that was particularly manifest at masquerades: "We had a *Jew Pedlar* who play'd his part to a miracle, appeared both in dress and behaviour a very Jew, and yet in real life, I am told, he has every good quality, and is an excellent *Christian*,"[25] or again, "A Jew Old Cloaths-man['s] . . . language was so perfectly characteristick, that we were inclined to suppose him a *true* counterfeit; but on his putting his vizor up, our doubts were solved by our discovering that the *principle was Christian*."[26] In such cases the performance of Jewish identity posed the central problem of how to locate the sameness and difference between Jew and Christian in this culture, and Jews themselves, at masquerades, could play with such puzzles of identity, as in the case of Sampson Gideon, the famous financier, appearing at a masquerade "in a Friar's dress."[27] In the remainder of this chapter I focus on the ways in which Georgian theatrical culture used and explored the embodiment of Jewish difference in general and the exchange of Jewish and Gentile bodies in particular. In this culture we have numerous examples of the public's growing spectatorial appetite for the embodied figure of the Jew, and I now turn to an especially grotesque version of the new visibility and accessibility of Jewish identity in order to explore the ways in which the Jewish body became a focus of this culture's attention. I quote from the *Public Advertiser*'s report (December 14, 1771) that followed the Chelsea murder case, when four Jews were executed on the charge of murder:

> The Curiosity and Impatience of the People to see the dead Bodies
> of the Jews exposed at Surgeons Hall on Tuesday late was so great,
> that it was with the utmost Difficulty that any Gentlemen of the
> Faculty could gain Admittance; the Mob was never so numerous
> and unruly upon a like Occasion. . . . The professor of Anatomy and
> Mr. Bromfelld were obliged to climb in at a Window, to the no small
> Diversion of the Crowd, which at last became so great, that it was
> impossible to open the Gates to any one. . . .
>
> As Mr. Bayford was returning from the Hall after the Lecture,
> he was stopped by the Wife of the Jew Doctor, earnestly begging the
> Body of her Husband for Interment; which Request however could
> not be complied with, as the Skeleton of this Criminal is to be hung
> up in Surgeons Hall.

What the opening number of *The Connoisseur* described as the goal of "penetrating into the most secret springs of action in these people" has become, twenty or so years later at Surgeons Hall, a mob inspection of the secret sites of the Jewish body; the hunt through the streets of London described in *The Connoisseur* has become a scavenger hunt. And while *The Connoisseur* concluded that "one might almost doubt, where money is out of the case, whether a Jew has 'eyes, hands, organs, dimensions, senses, affections, passions,'"[28] at Surgeons Hall these parts are nakedly displayed—"exposed"—in death. The skeleton of the Jew hung up in Surgeons Hall mimics the Jewish effigy paraded through the streets or burned in celebration. In such cases the mob functions as spectatorial audience, whether on the real or the mock Jewish body. I wish to press the special theatricality of such a scene in which the Jewish body is displayed in a public arena: the events at Surgeons Hall suggest how the public at large, outside the domain of the conventional theater, could be constituted as spectators in what amounted to a kind of theater of the dead.

But the fascination with the Jewish body did not stop here, as the *Public Advertiser* makes clear: "Two eminent Tooth-Drawers of this Town had a Scramble for the Teeth of the four Jews: One of the Gentlemen, however, had nearly extracted three whole Sets before the second Operator arrived, who was therefore obliged to content himself with the Teeth of the fourth poor Wretch, (the Doctor) which he soon dislocated, and put into his Pocket, and they will probably ere long adorn the Mouths of some of the *Bon Ton*; a Jew's Eye is proverbially precious,—why not a Jew's Tooth?" While for us an eerie anticipation of the Holocaust, for an eighteenth-century audience this account echoes the often repeated story in which King John draws the teeth of a Jew to extort money from him; in this sense, the account is part of a cultural tradition that demonstrates English attitudes toward the Jews, except that the newspaper account is meant to satirize the apparently more polite and fashionable world of Georgian England, where the teeth of executed Jews eventually adorn the beaux and belles of London. So, in a culture in which the actor and the masquerader attire themselves in the long whiskers and slouch hat of the Jew, the English demimonde wears the Jews' teeth in an especially grotesque mirror of the performance of Jewish identity, a telling example of the fascination with the intersection of Jewish and Gentile bodies. The newspaper account moves from the inspection of the dead Jewish body, to its invasion—the extraction and dislocation of the teeth—to end finally with its incorporation into the Gentile body. This movement from inspection to invasion to incorporation suggests an allegory of the steps by which Jewish identity was, at this historical moment, popularly staged by this culture. It inadvertently warns about the ways in which the newly popular theatrical staging of Jewish identity functioned transgressively and suggests that the spectatorial obsession with the new Jewish visibility was in fact rapacious. Did the performance of Jewish identity require the absorption and incorporation of the Jewish body in the Gentile body, and was the stage Jew being constructed on the corpse of Jewish identity, a uniformly static and grotesque figure that parasitically fed off a real and diverse population?

The picture we have here of the Gentile invasion of the Jewish body functions as a corollary to—even as a defense against—the fear of the Jewish invasion of the Gentile body, most notably expressed time and again during the uproar over the Jewish Naturalization Bill. In fact, I wish to claim that an important new figure, the circumcised Gentile, emerged during the propaganda campaign against the "Jew Bill" and led directly to the popular phenomenon of the cross-dressing Gentile. The anxiety over the naturalization of foreign-born Jews in 1753–54 took its most potent form in the fear of a Judaized England, expressed in many forms in newspapers, pamphlets, and satirical engravings that imagined St. Paul's converted into a synagogue, Jews sitting in Parliament, and most notably, the mass circumcision of Englishmen. The figure of the circumcised Gentile was especially popular in the satirical prints of the time. In *A Scene of Scenes for the Year 1853* (a prediction of an entirely Judaized England one century after the 1753 "Jew Bill") a figure is being circumcised, while several bishops and judges who had supported the "Jew Bill" witness the circumcision as they await their turn. In *A Stir in the City*, a satire on the General Election of 1754, a group of butchers is introduced to perform the rite for any voters who wish to become Jews, with the cry: "Are ye ready for circumcision?" In *The Jews shaving the Par*l*m**t*, set in a barber shop with a Jewish barber, a seated Gentile cries out, "They will Circumcise us next." The satirical print *The Circumcised Gentiles, or a Journey to Jerusalem* shows a Jew, with the typical markers of beard and slouch hat and dialect, along with two Gentile figures who have been converted and circumcised. It is no surprise, then, that a typical quip at this time nicknamed the "Jew Bill" "your Circumcition Bill [*sic*]."[29]

The opponents of the "Jew Bill" claimed that "the unconverted Jews can never be incorporated with us,"[30] and I am arguing that the proposal in the "Jew Bill" to incorporate the Jewish body into the English body politic led to two opposing but corollary images: the assimilated Jew (the Jew who has become an Englishman) and the Judaized Englishman (the Englishman who has become a Jew)—in the latter case, the English body incorporated into the Jewish body, represented in the demonstrably corporeal figures, first, of the circumcised Gentile, and then, of the cross-dressed Gentile. What all these figures have in common is the merging and meeting, or even worse, the indistinguishability, of (foreign) Jew and (English) Gentile. Hence the renewal of medieval claims that visible markers be reinstituted to identify

Jews, and the efforts of the theater to mark Jewish difference. According to a political weekly of 1753, *The Protester*, Jews are marked by nature: "Their very Breed . . . is in general of the lowest, basest, and most contemptible Kind, distinguishable to the Eye by peculiar Marks, odious for that Distinction, and what, if once communicated to a Family, becomes indelible."[31] But if these marks go unnoticed or are hidden, the Jew can be deliberately marked; an advertisement in the *London Evening-Post* explains how *An Historical Treatise concerning Jews and Judaism in England* demonstrates "that a Jew has no Right to appear in England without a yellow Badge fix'd on the upper Garment" (September 13, 1753). In many ways, the theatrical props of beard and hat and dialect were the ways in which, through performance, the Jew was marked in Georgian England; they became the theatrical equivalents of the yellow badge. With "Jews christianizing, Christians judaizing," the stage was performing the important social function of untangling this confusion by marking the Jew clearly and unambiguously.

In this way not just the immediate social and political events of the time but the larger history of the Jews informed the performance of Jewish identity in Georgian England. The accoutered stage Jew reminds us that the history of the Jews is in so many ways the history of the signifying body par excellence—in fact, arguably the most well-known and most dire history of the use of the inscribed body, from the bodily mark of circumcision to the well-known stereotypical bodily signs (from noses to odors) used to locate and expel the Jewish body in Christian societies throughout Europe from the Middle Ages through the twentieth century. This history includes the special identifying marks of both garment and body (from the specially colored hat or badge to the concentration camp number) that various European cultures imposed on Jews as an unmistakable sign of Jewish identity. It is no accident, then, that when the Jew emerged as a central stage character in Georgian England, the question of such bodily markers was recalled and reinvented. The theater, the spectacle of the moving, speaking body, reinvested the Jews with its own set of markers—the long beard, the slouch hat, the garbled dialect.

In fact, such stage markers became the means of re-Judaizing the Jew, reinventing even the real Jew as Jewish, as super-Jewish. The re-Judaization of the Jew was necessary because "in matters of dress, manners, speech, living habits, and cultural aspirations, they were ceasing to be identifiably Jewish."[32] So street theater, the masquerade, and the stage could assume the function of re-Judaizing the Jew, making the conventional markers show and stick.

Satirical prints worked in the same way; in *The Grand Conference or the Jew Predominant* (1753), for example, Sampson Gideon (whose fame made him an extremely popular figure in Jewish caricature at the time) is represented as speaking with an accent more commonly associated with foreign-born Eastern European Jews, despite the fact that he was a London-born Sephardi.[33] This figure of the Jew super-Judaized, forced to play the role of the theatrical Jew, reached its most remarkable articulation in Charles Dickens's *Our Mutual Friend* (1865), when the Jew Riah performs publicly the role of hardhearted Jewish usurer, a Shylock, as the cover for the real usurer, the Gentile Fledgby—a scenario that Dickens took from a Georgian play, Cumberland's *The Fashionable Lover*. So, precisely insofar as Jews were assimilating (and the government was pressing to naturalize more of them) there developed the need to mark them further, to reinvent the assimilating population as alien through representation. And I have been recording the ways in which the theater in particular and the public in general, in the figure of the Jew on stage, at the masquerade, and in street theater, embraced and employed these markers.

While it was the work of the theater to invent and to disseminate such markers, the theater also began to expose their artificiality, to subvert the culture's wholesale theatricalization of Jewish identity. The surplus of Jewish representation and the supertheatricalization of Jewish identity led in fact to a crisis in representation. The numerous new plays with Jewish characters, the public's broad embrace of Jewish performance in street theater and masquerades, and the exaggerated, satirical, and highly conventionalized nature of these theatrical representations eventually led to the specific theatrical trope I now wish to examine: the trope of the cross-dressing Gentile. I mark here that historical moment when a surplus of Jewish performance produced another new theatrical phenomenon—namely, the pivotal scene when, on stage, a Gentile character dons the costume and mimics the dialect of the Jew, thereby exposing the performative nature of Jewish identity in Georgian culture generally. So, in the theater at this time, audiences experienced a double—a doubling—phenomenon: plays that unself-consciously and mimetically presented Jewish characters, and plays within which a Gentile character, in a critical scene, would suddenly appear dressed up and speaking like the stage Jews the audience had seen presented mimetically perhaps only the night before. Even this experience was in fact eventually staged in a single theatrical entertainment when in some plays there occurred the extraordinary meeting between the cross-dressed Gentile and the "real" Jew whose part he was playing, in what was supposed to be an uproariously funny, and what became an ontologically searching, encounter between "fake" and "real" Jews. Such scenes in which the audience was exposed to the performance of Jewish identity—especially scenes where the "fake" Jew was believed over the "real" Jew by the other characters in the play—challenged the conventional mode of representing Jewish identity on the stage.

The apparently seamless performance of Jewish identity on the stage in the numerous new plays containing Jewish characters began to be punctured, then, when the action of a play was interrupted to disclose, almost as a kind of confession made on the part of the theater, the way in which the performance of Jewish identity was staged. In other words, what was normally hidden backstage, as part of the actor's craft, was suddenly announced publicly on stage in an extraordinary piece of metatheater: we witness the Gentile plan to equip himself with beard, with slouch hat, with dialect, and we see him appear moments later transformed into a Jew, and sometimes we see that persona stripped from him right on the stage, returning him to his Gentile identity. In this way what I am calling the surplus of representation overflowed into metarepresentation, metatheater, when the audience was suddenly given a view of not simply the stage Jew but also the staging of "the Jew," the act of (mis)representation itself.

If the conventional Georgian stage Jew was meant to represent the differences between Jew and Gentile, the trope of the cross-dressing Gentile also, at least initially, depended on and in some ways affirmed these differences; no such cross-dressing was possible if the differences between Jew and Gentile were not apparent. The actual act of performing the Jew, the elaborate scheme of passing, meant that the Jew and the Gentile were recognizably different. So, at one level, the trope of the cross-dressing Gentile served the function of marking the Jew, of making him a comical exaggeration, even of controlling him like a puppet. Functioning as a largely unthreatening version of the figure of the circumcised Gentile, the trope of the cross-dressing Gentile was a theatrical experiment, forgoing the knife and the indelible mark of circumcision for the hat and the beard and the dialect, within the artificial and controllable arena of the theater: it was an experiment at playing becoming the Jew, even being lost and absorbed in the Jew. Moreover, the trope was a controlled experiment that could be reversed: all of the theatrical markers of Jewish identity could be laid aside, as they were when the cross-dressing Gentile reemerged, as he always did, without his Jewish disguise. While from one vantage point the trope represented the absorption of the Englishman in the Jew (and his successful reemergence), the trope also functioned as an experiment that realized the communal or national desire to infiltrate the Jewish body, incorporate it, in order to imitate and control it, to make it do one's own bidding. Finally, however, the trope of the cross-dressing Gentile did not simply stage this desire but explored and eventually exposed it, in what became the most signal hallmark of the trope—namely, its self-referentiality. From the beginning, all the plays that employed the trope of the cross-dressing gentile self-consciously explored theatricality in general and the construction of Jewish identity in particular.

The typical organizing feature of these plays is a comic marriage plot in which the *senex iratus*, a father or guardian, refuses access to his daughter or ward, and either the hero or his servant cross-dresses as a Jew in order to gain access to her. In George Colman the Younger's farce *Love Laughs at Locksmiths* (1803),[34] for example, we have a plot in which the guardian keeps the heroine locked up, and the hero gains access to her through disguising himself as a Jew. In this play the heroine is at once the captive ward of the guardian and the captive model of the artist, for the guardian is a painter who, "although he lets nobody behold the original, many . . . have seen the resemblance" (10). The play asks, Is it possible for the spectator to reach the original, behind the mask of the copy? The artist holds the original captive, bending it to his own uses; and the world he makes is of "sham men and women" (21), "busts and pictures . . . representing figures as large as life" (26)—in other words, the world of optical illusion, the world that these plays consistently show the cross-dressing Gentile occupying. The comic gag here depends on showing that the man who insists on monopolizing the original for himself, and showing only the resemblance to others, is in fact fooled (at least initially) by the figure of the cross-dressing Gentile, when the hero cross-dresses as a Jew to fool the old guardian. Once the guardian discovers the disguise, the guardian mimics a Jew by copying the hero who mimics a Jew: this multiplication of false Jews becomes part of the trope in some of the plays, in a potentially infinite play of representation and reproduction that occurs in the cultural construction of Jewish identity. So, in an allegory of the representation of Jewish identity, the painter who in his work copies the original (his ward) now copies the copy (a Jew).

In Andrew Franklin's farce *The Wandering Jew; or, Love's Masquerade* (1797),[35] there is a similar self-consciousness about various forms of representation, and the play's humor and meaning work through a number of optical illusions and sight gags that draw attention to the power of art. In the main plot we have a painter, whose dummy model several times incites confusion between the real and the copy, when, for example, the hero puts on the clothes of the mannequin and then is mistaken for a "walking model" (18). And in another scene, two characters place their heads in the holes that have been cut out of life-size portraits, making to the astonishment of everyone "living portraits" (54). This obsession with the real inhabiting, hidden in, obscured by, or animating the artificial becomes a consistent context for exploring theatrical impersonation in general and the figure of the cross-dressing Gentile in particular. The hero impersonates not only the Wandering Jew but also an Italian count, Count Gran Contrasto del Camera Obscura, with the name here a play on the entire theme of illusion, representation, and artistic reproduction. In his impersonation of the Italian count, he must admit that he can speak no Italian, but neither can the woman he attempts to fool, so that he can speak "in Hebrew, Greek, Latin, Welch, or Irish" (24) and successfully fool her nonetheless. The ignorance of the spectator, then, is a central requirement in the successful performance of the other, and the parochial "English spectator" (25) is time and again singled out as the butt of the humor in these plays. In another scene, a character remarks about having been to the theater to see the actor Jack Bannister in a play (27), and of course the audience knows that it is Bannister who is playing the Jew and the Italian in this play. The actor (Bannister), who plays the hero playing a Jew and an Italian, is told: "You'd make an incomparable actor! Do, go on stage" (23).

These plays thrive on this kind of inside joke between the actor and the audience, where all the fictions of theatricality are shared between the actor and the knowing audience member (as opposed to the gullible spectator pictured on stage). In other words, the metatheatrical dimension of these plays keeps displacing the work of seeing and knowing onto the stage itself, where the play's characters enact the role of the audience by being consistently gulled. In this way the cross-dressing actor and the sophisticated audience member collude, refusing the spell of theatrical illusion. It is in this way that these plays work to minimize character and story—what might be called the center of mimesis—in order to maximize the infinite play of dialects, makeup, and costumes, the equipment of performance itself. It is no accident, then, that the hero is often a former actor; in fact these plays characterize the actor as hero—only the dissembling actor can outsmart the old guardian.

We can see this emphasis on the hero as actor, as role-player, in Theodore Hook's farce *The Invisible Girl* (1806).[36] In this play, only one character (played again by Jack Bannister), aptly named Allclack, does all the speaking.

In the course of the play he impersonates a Jew, a lord, and his own mother. In its reduction of speaking roles to just one and in its entire focus on the many roles a single actor can play, this farce makes it especially clear that the slight plot of these plays exists merely to serve the series of performances given by the actor. We have here the hero as actor in the comic marriage plot and the actor as hero in the theater of impersonation. The series of cross-dressing performances swallows the plot just as the hero-actor swallows the other characters (he is "allclack"). The plot exists to stage a series of cross-dressings, and so becomes neither more nor less than the site of a special kind of theatrical spectacle, a place where a kind of double watching and double listening occurs. A double act of recognition structures such performance-plays. On the stage misrecognition occurs when the gulled spectator mistakes Jack Bannister for Allclack for a Jew. But in the audience, a form of recognition occurs when the enlightened spectator recognizes that Allclack is impersonating the Jew, and even that Bannister is impersonating Allclack. In this spectacle of cross-dressing, performativity is put on display. One actor can play all the roles because theater is about performance, not mimesis. Instead of hiding its secrets, its constitutive conventions, theater exposes them in these plays and makes sure that the audience recognizes them.

While in *The Invisible Girl* a real Jew exists, but only as a mere ghostly presence who at one point in the play silently beholds his speaking double in the actor's performance, in William Moncrieff's *Rochester; or, King Charles the Second's Merry Days* (1818)[37] the telling absence of a real Jew is marked by the multiplication of fake Jews. In *Rochester* both Rochester and Buckingham put on "a Jew's dress and beard" to enter the old guardian's house and to court the heroine. When both are so dressed (unbeknownst to each other), Rochester hears Buckingham's cry, "Ould clothes" (38). Rochester worries that his disguise will be discovered by the real Jew, the Jew who cries "Ould clothes." This is the phrase he himself cried a moment ago—after all, the script of Jewish identity is both unalterable and universally known. So even the cross-dressing Gentile, while aware of his own theatrical construction of Jewish identity, is gulled into believing the fiction of the cross-dressing Gentile. The power of such theatrical constructions, or our willingness to believe in them, seems universal. When Buckingham, cross-dressed as an old-clothes man, sees the cross-dressed Rochester, he similarly exclaims: "Here's a real Jew here; I hope he won't detect me" (38). But Buckingham has nothing to fear: Rochester is not "a real Jew," and the stage, in Andrews's *Dissipation*, had already shown in 1781 that even a "real" Jew cannot detect a cross-dressing

Gentile, when a Frenchman absconds with a Jew's daughter by putting on the costume of a rabbi and speaking the dialect, thereby fooling the Jewish father. The power of the stereotype knows no bounds: it fools Gentile and Jew alike, and it even fools those who work the fictitious construction themselves.

It is only when both cross-dressing Gentiles in *Rochester* raise the price they are willing to pay for some old clothes (in an effort to gain admittance to the house that holds the heroine) that each begins to realize the other cannot be a Jew—that is, each begins to fail to live up to the stereotype of the greedy Jew: "I suspect this fellow never can be a genuine Jew" (39). When one of the cross-dressed Jews accuses the other of being an imposter, the gullibility of the Gentile about what constitutes Jewish identity is made clear when the old guardian responds: "How can he have such a beard, and not be a Jew?" (40). In order to prove that the other is an imposter, Rochester says (in a comical rendition of Othello's famous speech): "I'll shave him directly. I took the uncircumcised dog by the throat and smote him thus—dere—(*pulls off* Buckingham's *beard*)" (40). The beard is shown as a false marker compared to the true marker, circumcision. The scene ends farcically with each fake Jew pulling off the other's beard. In other words, each cross-dressing Gentile undresses the other—that is, undoes the construction of Jewish identity for all to behold. It is an important moment in the self-reflexivity of the trope of the cross-dressing Gentile: we are shown the way in which the trope undoes itself, exposes itself. At the same time, there is no "genuine Jew" in the play; he has been displaced by the multiplication of false Jews. The "genuine Jew" becomes, if not a fiction, at least an absence. Jewish identity exists only in an apparently endless line of simulacra. The real Jew—whatever that is—is banished from the stage in favor of multiple doubles. The spectator is left to choose between two copies, and once their impersonations are discovered, no "real" Jew takes their place. In the absence of the stereotype, nothing appears.

What happens when a so-called genuine Jew enters a play to interrogate the cross-dressing Gentile? While this is imagined in *Rochester*, when both cross-dressing Gentiles fear being discovered by a real Jew, such a scene does in fact occur in John Allingham's *Transformation; or, Love and Law* (1810).[38] Here the attorney Makesafe uses his servants as sentinels to guard his house against the young hero's entrance. He imprisons his ward while he guards both her and her fortune against her will. The cross-dressing hero is an actor aptly named Cameleon, pinpointing this increasing association in the trope of the cross-dressing Gentile: in Thomas Dibdin's *Family Quarrels* (1802) the servant Proteus is a former actor; in the same author's *Humphrey Clinker* (1818), the hero Wilson is also a former actor; even Mr. Hardy in Hannah Cowley's comedy *The Belle's Stratagem* (1780) goes not to a Jew but to an actor in order to learn how to impersonate a Jew. In all these cases, access to Jewish identity occurs through the stage; the protean actor, chameleon-like, is the man who knows the tricks of performance that can create the figure of the Jew.

Transformation makes explicit the case for the power of the actor and the gullibility of the spectator when Cameleon recalls his days as a strolling player, working with the Strutt family. Mr. Strutt, who is eulogized as "a fine actor," is comically characterized as being "four feet high" and having "squinted, waddled and snuffled" in real life, "yet in Macheath he was thought to excell." Mrs. Strutt is another example of the enigma of the mesmerizing power of acting: "twice as high" as her husband, she "hobbled" in real life but excelled in dancing roles and in playing Columbine (10–11). Are such characterizations a eulogy to the mysterious, self-transformative powers of the actor, or a comic satire on the public and its desire to be fooled or at least its love of impersonation and masquerade?

The hero in *Transformation* plays three roles—a woman, a Jew, and a Yorkshireman—where the trope of cross-dressing emphasizes the comical otherness of the roles played. Makesafe gives his two servants a description of the three people whom they are allowed to let enter the house—"so exact a description, that it will be impossible for you to mistake them" (5). When Cameleon decides to impersonate these three figures in order to gain access to the imprisoned heroine, he models his impersonations on these written descriptions. Never having seen the actual people, the actor copies not from life but from a written description—in other words, from a representation—so that his performance is at a double remove. The play here suggests the way in which the performance of Jewish identity on the stage, or even the representation of Jewish identity in general—in novels, engravings, pamphlets—may in fact be a copy of a copy. While the written descriptions that the servants record incites in them a desire for authenticity, for the original—"Their portraits are so very interesting, that I long to be acquainted with the originals" (7)—the servants meet the copies of the originals, namely, the actor Cameleon impersonating the originals. The written descriptions recreate and expose the myth of the distinguishing feature or real marker that stamps identity and so makes it recognizable. Malachi, the Jewish moneylender, is described as having "a red beard, and a red head, a broad brimmed hat . . . , and a long dark coat, almost down to his heels" (7). Intended to assist the servants in recognizing the Jew with whom Makesafe has business, these features actually assist the actor Cameleon in his job of mimicry—they become the recognizable marks by which he can gull the servants. Performance is exposed here as occurring through the citation of a text, the dominant culture's text of Jewish identity. The spectator recognizes Jewish identity through the representations that have been dictated: "Write what I dictate" (5), Makesafe tells his servants, as he describes the Jew.

The farce examines the power of representation, both in written descriptions and in performed behaviors, through a series of (mis)recognition scenes. By staging encounters between the cross-dressing hero and the people he is impersonating, the farce shows how the servants are unable to tell the copy from the original; in each case the servants mistakenly choose the cross-dressed Cameleon, the actor, as the real person. In the case of the Jew this farce marks an important development in the trope, because here the cross-dressing Gentile encounters the Jew he is impersonating, thereby deepening the issue of theatricality: even when compared with the "real" Jew, the cross-dressing Gentile is believed, taken for real. Such a scene calls into question the entire notion of the "genuine Jew" as it figures in all modes of representation, because of course the "genuine Jew" (19) in the play is himself only a performed mask, played by an actor. When one of the servants sees the two Jews, he exclaims: "All the people walk about today in company with their own ghosts" (19). Representation is exposed as a deadly form of reproduction, in which the original and the ghostly double are inextricably entwined, enmeshed with each other. The original, the authentic, no longer exists. When the two Jews see each other, both exclaim; when named, they bow simultaneously. The name "Jew" names only a fiction.

In this light, Jewish identity seems displaced from itself: the servant addresses Malachi, "Are you yourself—or is that you?" The servant then takes out his written description of the Jew, and examines the two Jews minutely. "Are you he—or is he you? For one of you certainly must be the other, that's clear" (19). Jewish identity is entirely destabilized; it seems to exist outside itself. In a comical song in which Malachi attempts to authenticate his identity, he sings, "I am de true Malachi, vat ish call'd the original Jew, / Vat shells every thing as sheep as can be" (20), just as Cameleon the actor copies him. The "original Jew" seems to exist only in his double, in the stereotype of the cunning peddler, the man who gulls us in the first place by telling us that he "shells every thing as sheep as can be." The original Jew, then, is already a copy, as is the man who plays the original Jew here, just another actor. The so-called original Jew of course is the Jewish peddler that has been conventionalized in play after play, in graphic print after print. Even the so-called genuine Jew is amazed at the copy of himself that he sees, allowing him to make an anti-Semitic comment to his convincing double: "You must be de tevil!—or you would not be so like me" (21). The Jew sees himself outside himself and, as it were, momentarily authenticates the negative stereotype of Jewish identity; the stereotype is so profound, so thoroughly diffused in the culture, that even the Jew (mis)recognizes himself by it.

This scene exposes not only how performable the other is, according to a communally scripted description of otherness, but also how spectators are socially constructed in their belief in certain conventional visual and aural identity markers—what we call stereotypes. So, in such a scene, the spectator himself is shown as a social construction manipulated by ideologies of difference and otherness. The servant tries to solve the dilemma through his belief in spectatorship, in the great English tradition of empiricism: "You, sir, come here, and let me look at you—and you, sir, if you please" (19). This scene repeats the kind of inspection of Jewish identity that occurred frequently on the stage, when a Jew's exaggerated dress was marked and mocked by another character on stage, but now the spectator is puzzled because two Jews are under inspection, with the serious suspicion that one is real and the other fake. Previously, Jewish identity was always recognizable precisely insofar as it was distinguishable from English (or some such "normative") identity (and vice versa); but here, Jewish identity must be distinguished from its copy, so to speak.

Finally, the (English) spectator's own identity is challenged, insofar as the recognition of the other is the ground of one's own identity, when the servant exclaims: "Next time I come into the room, I shall expect to see my double here ready to fight it out with me—whether I am myself or somebody else" (25). A new question now emerges: Who is the man who (mis)recognizes the Jew? Does the subject/spectator himself become someone else, alienated from himself, doubled, when he sees double, when he can no longer adequately recognize the Jew as other? Moreover, one must wonder about the status of the audience proper in such a scene: while the audience typically shares the joke of the cross-dressing Gentile, in the scene that I am now examining the audience could be genuinely fooled in its attempt to distinguish between the cross-dressed hero and Malachi, depending on the performance choices the actors make in playing the scene. In such a case even the apparent sophistication of the theater audience is overthrown, when the gulled spectator on the stage mimics and mocks the gulled spectator in the audience. The recognition of Jewish identity has become a puzzle that even the spectator in the audience cannot solve. In this way the destabilization of Jewish identity functions to destabilize the normative English spectatorial position.

Structured through a variety of metatheatrical strategies aimed at the audience (such as the shared jokes between actors and audience members or the figure of the gulled spectator on stage), these plays began to function intertextually as the basis of a specific cultural community, so much so that they became part of a theatrical project collectively shared by playwrights, actors, and audience. This is illustrated particularly well in *The Belle's Stratagem* when Mr. Hardy, in order to cross-dress as a Jew at a masquerade, copies not from nature but from the stage, by going "to my favourite little Quick [to] borrow his Jew Isaac's dress. . . . He shall teach me—Ay, that's it—I'll be cunning little Isaac."[39] Here, in *The Belle's Stratagem*, Cowley depends on her audience's recognition of a direct citation of Sheridan's *The Duenna*, in which the well-known actor John Quick was celebrated for his performance of the Jew Isaac Mendoza. Cowley points to the artificiality of the Jew in Sheridan's play by having Mr. Hardy borrow from the actor the Jewish costume and learn from him how to perform the Jewish character type. And when the famous character of "cunning little Isaac" appears at a public masquerade (in the person of Mr. Hardy), the pure theatricality of the stage Jew becomes apparent: the construction of Jewish identity is mobile, able to be imported to a number of settings and performed by a number of (even unprofessional) actors. This kind of intertextual citation acknowledges the audience's knowledge of Sheridan's celebrated play, and even of the particular players on the London stage, for in certain productions of *The Belle's Stratagem* it was Quick himself who played Mr. Hardy citing Quick, another one of those metatheatrical jokes shared between actor and audience that underscored the artificiality of constructions of Jewish identity. In such ways the audience became a constituent player in the theater's demystification of the stage Jew. In a similar intertextual strategy, forty years after the first production of Sheridan's *School for Scandal* in 1777, John Tobin rewrites Sheridan's play as *The Faro Table; or, The Guardians* (1816) and forces on Sheridan's Sir Oliver, now named Mr. Barton, what Sir Oliver avoids, namely, cross-dressing as a Jew. But such a revision was inevitable, because certainly by the time of Tobin's play no one in the audience could have taken Sir Oliver's protests seriously: "How the Plague shall I be able to pass for a Jew?"[40] The question had been answered too often, on stage and off. So, the trope of the cross-dressing Gentile became the necessary supplement that haunted the stage Jew and the theatricalization of Jewish identity generally. In the cases of both Cowley and Tobin, for example, the trope functioned as a citation of an earlier play and a corrective demystifier. In this way, audiences were involved in reviewing the staples of the theatrical repertory, as they were being (re)written through the addition of the trope of the cross-dressing Gentile.

In such ways these plays began to imagine and even to constitute an English theatrical community engaged in working out the question of Jewish identity from play to play and from performance to performance. As a fluid theatrical sign, Jewish identity began to move with ease between and among a variety of plays, and the act of cross-dressing articulated and signaled such movement. The trope of the cross-dressing Gentile demonstrated that anyone could borrow the script of Jewish identity, anyone could occupy the position of the Jew; Jewish identity was an infinitely performable script, to be cited and renewed and circulated time and again. The plays, the performers, and even the audiences of the London stage seemed to be participating collaboratively in the (re)formulation and demystification of the Jew as a collective construction. When we recall that four of the most popular plays in the last quarter of the eighteenth century were *The Duenna*, *The School for Scandal*, *The Belle's Stratagem*, and *The Merchant of Venice*,[41] we realize that the theater and its public in some profound sense were given over to this question of Jewish identity. And when we recognize, for example, that *Transformation* played as the afterpiece to *The Duenna* at the Lyceum on December 4, 1810, or that as late as 1824 the cross-dressing Gentiles from *The Belle's Stratagem* and *Love Laughs at Locksmiths* were sharing the repertory at the Haymarket with a conventional stage Jew like Shadrach from O'Keeffe's 1783 *Young Quaker*, we realize the ways in which the subversive trope of the cross-dressing Gentile intersected with the more conventional theatrical repertory, and continued to interrogate for many years the question of the English theater's construction of Jewish identity. With its corollary features of the masquerade, the optical illusion, the gulled spectator, the figure of the double, and the (mis)recognition scene, the trope of the cross-dressing Gentile became the broadest and most probing inquiry into the nature of the representation of Jewish identity that had ever been produced in England. In play after play, the trope investigated and subverted the representation of Jewish identity as a coherent and fixed theatrical construct—even as a kind of social institution—shared by the culture at large.[42]

CHAPTER FIVE

Novel Performances and "the Slaves of Art"

All we know of the style of . . . [Irish] melodies, reached us through
the false medium of comic airs, sung by some popular actor, who,
in coincidence with his author, caricatures those national traits he
attempts to delineate.

—Sydney Owenson, *The Wild Irish Girl*, 1806

After travelling east, west, north, and south, my cousin
Craiglethorpe will know just as much of the lower Irish as the
cockney who has never been out of London, and who has never, in
all his born days, seen an Irishman but on the English stage; where
the representations are usually as like the originals, as the Chinese
pictures of lions, drawn from description, are to the real animal.

—Maria Edgeworth, *Ennui*, 1809

It has been my object to describe these persons, not by a caricatured
and exaggerated use of the national dialect, but by their habits,
manners, and feelings; so as, in some distant degree, to emulate the
admirable Irish portraits drawn by Miss Edgeworth, so different
from the "dear joys" who so long, with the most perfect family
resemblance to each other, occupied the drama and the novel.

—Walter Scott, *Waverley*, 1814

IN THE OPENING decades of the nineteenth century a group of important
novelists based in Ireland and Scotland shared the common goal of attempting to counteract the London stage's caricaturing of minority ethnic identity.

In previous chapters I have shown how the Georgian stage defined and perpetuated ethnic caricatures, and eventually began, not always successfully or comprehensively, to question and even to deconstruct such stereotypes. I now turn, in this chapter and the next, to the ways in which novelists such as Maria Edgeworth, Sydney Owenson, and Walter Scott attempted to recuperate minority ethnic identity by unhinging it from the theatrical stereotypes that had popularly defined it for so many decades. I argue that my restoration of the stage history of the ethnic other in the preceding chapters illuminates the strategies and goals of the early nineteenth-century British novel, when novelists typically embedded in their novels direct citations to this stage history, and constructed their novels as a direct response to such popular stage figures, as the epigraphs above suggest. So, I read this novelistic tradition as entirely implicated in a theatrical history that these novelists signal quite explicitly but that scholars have typically neglected. This requires understanding the ways in which the novel examined and defined its goals in the broadest sense in relation to this stage history. Finally, I widen the parameters of what was once marginalized as the regional novel and sharpen our understanding of the various projects undertaken by the national tale and the historical novel, by restoring the figure of the Jew to the novelistic discourses of this period, and more generally by articulating the ways in which the theater functioned as a profoundly influential paradigmatic form that the novel attempted to counteract through absorption and revision.[1] This has the unexpected result of showing the ways in which the novel continued to define ethnicity theatrically, even while attempting to deconstruct the stage's stereotypes.

I begin by briefly suggesting some of the ways in which the novel and the stage intersected during this period, a topic that has been unduly neglected. First, it is important to recognize the ways in which early nineteenth-century novelists both understood the theatrical history they inherited and participated in the theater of their day. Walter Scott, for example, purchased a share in the patent of the Edinburgh Theatre, became one of its trustees, and oversaw the production of a play by Joanna Baillie, writing its dramatic prologue, attending its rehearsals, and later that year entertaining such theatrical luminaries as John Philip Kemble (the famous actor and theater manager) and his celebrated sister, the actress Sarah Siddons, when she performed in Edinburgh.[2] Scott wrote a lengthy review of a biography of Kemble, and even more important, in his long essay "The Drama" attempted at once a theoretical and historical inquiry into the nature of the theater from the Greeks to current developments on the Georgian stage. In such works he made sweeping claims for the profound importance of the theater: "The drama is in ours, and in most civilized countries, an engine possessing the most powerful effect on the manners of society"; "our ordinary language and ordinary ideas are modified by what we have seen and heard on the stage."[3] But it is Scott's essay on Richard Cumberland that in many ways functions as a guide to the kinds of ethnic figures and ideological questions that would inform the early nineteenth-century novel, for Cumberland was the playwright who most clearly anticipated this novelistic tradition insofar as he undertook most consistently the critique of the stage's ethnic caricatures. Even the arc of Cumberland's career is a kind of microcosm of what happened in the novel— namely, first the figures of the Irishman and the Scot were recuperated, and only later the figure of the Jew. Scott praises the Irishman in *The West Indian* because Cumberland "enjoyed repeated opportunities of forming a true estimate of the Irish gentleman," while the portrait of the Scotsman in *The Fashionable Lover*, because it was "not . . . drawn from nature," has little "to distinguish it from the Gibbies and Sawnies which had hitherto possession of the stage, as the popular representatives of the Scottish nation." Scott also praises Cumberland's "generous intention,"[4] but not entirely successful attempt, to recuperate Jewish identity in *The Jew*, something Scott himself attempted in *Ivanhoe* (1819).

We see here in Scott (and even in Cumberland) the growing consensus of the period about the challenges of ethnic recuperation—namely, that even the best intentions can fail and that first-hand knowledge is required. Cumberland himself admitted he had "no other guide for the dialect of my Macleod than what the Scotch characters of the stage supplied me with."[5] And novelists also succumbed to such theatrical caricatures, as Scott's complaints about Robert Bage's novels make clear: "his Irishmen [are] not beyond those usually brought on the stage; his Scotchmen [are] still more awkward caricatures, and the language which he puts in their mouths not similar to any that has been spoken since the days of Babel."[6] So, the problem of how to escape the circle of ethnic theatrical misrepresentation was explicitly articulated by both playwright and novelist. During this period there emerged what often was taken to be a new prerequisite of ethnic representation, namely, that it should be based not on theatrical convention but on empirical knowledge and perhaps even on native intelligence—that is, on the knowledge that ethnic writers themselves bring to portraits of their fellow countrymen.

While some novelists experienced Georgian theatrical culture largely as a set of theoretical and historical problems that fueled their own novelistic projects, others had a far more intimate connection to the ethnic caricatures that appeared on the stage. Sydney Owenson, for example, writes of her father's "brilliant success in Sheridan's Sir Lucius O'Trigger, and Cumberland's Major O'Flaherty, in both of which he had been the *remplacant* of Mr. Hirst and Mr. Mudie, who knew as much of Ireland as they did of New Zealand. Their English audiences, however, be it said, were satisfied, for they had not yet got beyond the conventional delineation of Teague and Father Foigarde, types of Irish savagery and Catholic Jesuitism. Cumberland and Sheridan both thanked my father for redeeming their creations from caricature."[7] Owenson's remarks here on the distinction between English caricatures of the stage Irishman and her father's determined efforts to rise above such caricatures point to what had increasingly become a critical way of understanding the stage—namely, through the important differences that distinguished between Irish and English audiences and actors. In this light both father and daughter had the same goal in different media—the redemption of the stage Irishman. Owenson reports Cumberland's response to her father's performance of Major O'Flaherty: "Mr. Owenson, I am the first author who has brought an Irish gentleman on the stage, and you are the first who ever played it *like* a gentleman."[8] In this history of firsts, Sydney Owenson claimed herself to have produced "the first purely Irish story ever written."[9] Immediately after the success of *The Wild Irish Girl* she went so far as to write a comic opera for the Dublin stage in which she created the role of an Irishman for her father, who then went on to reprise his role of the Irish major in *The West Indian*. So, during the period when she was writing her Irish novels, she was inventing Irish figures for the stage, reinvigorating her father's career of stage Irishmen, and even participating in a war of words with John Wilson Croker on the state of the Irish stage.[10]

As the case of Owenson makes clear, these ethnic stage figures and the plays in which they appeared did not simply precede these novels as a historical legacy. Many of these plays, while first produced as early as the 1750s, enjoyed a lively stage life through the opening decades of the nineteenth century and beyond, and so in some sense competed with the novel's representation of ethnic identity. And just as novels were consistently rewriting the works of the stage, novels in turn were consistently being rewritten for the stage. For example, within the first year of its publication, Scott's *Ivanhoe* was produced on the London stage under such titles as *Ivanhoe; or, the Jew's Daughter*, *Ivanhoe; or, The Jew of York*, *Ivanhoe; or, the Jewess*, and finally, dropping the name of the dull Saxon hero entirely, *Rebecca; or, the Jew's Daughter*[11]—titles intended to remake *Ivanhoe* about the Jewish characters in general and about Rebecca in particular as a way of capitalizing on the appetite of theater audiences for ethnic spectacle.

Playwrights adapting novels for the stage even invented Jewish characters for the delight of stage audiences: while Tobias Smollett had his young hero Wilson appear disguised as a Jew in *The Expedition of Humphry Clinker*, when Thomas Dibdin adapted the novel for the stage he invented the character of Mordecai, a Jewish peddler accoutered with dark gabardine, long beard, and lisping dialect, all borrowed and mimicked by Wilson (in another example of the trope of the cross-dressing Gentile).[12] So, just as novelists regularly attacked the stage and revised its plots, playwrights were quick to co-opt, revise, and redirect for their own purposes the most popular novels of the day.

In short, plays and novels at this time collaborated and competed with each other on the topic of ethnic identity. By this I mean that while my emphasis in this chapter and the next is on the ways in which a certain novelistic tradition found its purpose in critiquing the theater's stock ethnic caricatures, the history of early nineteenth-century representations of ethnic difference is more complicated, because these stage caricatures frequently worked their way into the novel without critique, without demystification, without reconstruction, just as the theater itself continued to stage plays that reproduced such caricatures as well as plays that self-consciously undermined and exposed them.

Perhaps the most telling case here is Maria Edgeworth. She was writing plays, and having them performed at Edgeworthstown, both before and during her career as a successful novelist, and she even published two collections of plays. She spoke of succumbing to, and then escaping, "the Mania of Playwriting,"[13] and deemed herself "a disappointed playwright."[14] The entire family performed in these plays, her father built elaborate stage machinery and little theaters in the house, and she and her family often participated in charades: there is a particularly memorable picture of an evening of charades, with impersonations of a London black beggar, Scott's Gypsy Meg Merrilies, and a Spanish gentleman, in the spirit of what I have called the multiethnic spectacle, with Edgeworth herself taking the part of "an Irish nurse in a red cloak, come all the way from Killogonsawce, 'for my two childer that left me last year for foreign parts,'"[15] a dramatization of a character very much like the old nurse in her novel *Ennui*. She sent two of her early plays to Richard Brinsley Sheridan, who rejected both. In fact, one of her major Irish tales, *The Absentee* (1812), began as a play with that title; it was submitted to Sheridan for production, but he claimed that he did not have enough actors to play the Irish roles and that the Irish subject matter would be unpopular with London audiences.[16] So one of the major Irish novels produced in the early nineteenth century began its life as a play, and only after rejection in this form did it become a novel. Moreover, the novel's skewering of an Irish lady who affects London ways, and especially London speech, is taken directly from a stage comedy by Edgeworth's fellow Irish writer, Charles Macklin—namely, *A True-born Irishman*.

It therefore may come as no surprise that in her fiction Edgeworth sometimes transcended the stock ethnic figures of the stage and sometimes uncritically imported them wholesale. In the first case, contemporary reviewers recognized her ability precisely insofar as she rejected and transcended in her fiction the common stereotypes of the stage: "The Irish characters are inimitable;—not the coarse caricatures of modern playwrights—but drawn with a spirit, a delicacy, and a precision, to which we do not know if there be any parallel among national delineations."[17] But she also sometimes fell back on such coarse stage caricatures. Some of her early fiction reproduced the strategy of another comedy by Macklin, *Love à la Mode*, which continued to be performed through the opening decades of the nineteenth century and was thus contemporaneous with Edgeworth's fiction. In *The Absentee*, for example, the Jew is named Mordecai, the same name that Macklin used for his stage Jew, and both play and novel are centered in the project of overturning the stage's stereotype of the Irish while reproducing a highly theatricalized caricature of a Jew. Moreover, Edgeworth's Mordecai is patently a descendent of an even older stage Jew, namely, Shakespeare's Shylock: "Nothing will do but my money or your bond."[18] In a variety of fictional works such as "The Good Aunt" (contained in *Moral Tales* [1801]), *Belinda* (1801), and *The Absentee*, Edgeworth created multiethnic plots in which she attacked various ethnic prejudices (against blacks, Welsh, Irish, Scots, mulattoes) at the same time that she reverted in each case to the highly conventional stereotype of the stage Jew. So, while in many of Edgeworth's tales a wide population of outsiders is meant to be the object of our sympathy, the figure of the Jew consistently becomes a kind of communal scapegoat. Borrowing the formula of so many of the stage's multiethnic spectacles, Edgeworth imagines the ever-widening circle of the project called Great Britain capable of maintaining itself, of including Scot and Irishman, Welshman and black, only if some group remains beyond the pale, playing the part of other. The function of the Jew in such texts is to confirm the legitimate place of a wide variety of others in Great Britain while still maintaining a closed circle of Britishness that cannot be entered by everyone. At the same time, Edgeworth's career offers perhaps the most powerful example of the way in which the novelist at the beginning of the nineteenth century not simply succumbed to, but also eventually eschewed and even critiqued, such theatrical caricatures, including the stage Jew, writing what is generally considered a landmark philo-Semitic novel, *Harrington*.

The emphasis of this chapter and the next is on analyzing how such novelists worked to move beyond the powerfully influential ethnic caricatures of the London stage. The first step in such a process depended on recognizing the immense power of what Edgeworth called "the arts of misrepresentation"[19]—namely, the power of theatrical and other forms of representation to (mis)construct ethnic difference and (mis)direct our sympathies. For novelists like Edgeworth, Owenson, and Scott, it was precisely in the nature of the relationship between metropole and periphery that misrepresentation had always already intervened, producing a prejudiced misrepresentation of the ethnic other. This is the thrust of Edgeworth's remark in *Ennui* that the only Irishman many Londoners have seen is England's stage Irishman. So, the plots of these novels engineer the direct encounter between the (English) self and the (ethnic) other, but even here the focus remains on the ways in which the relationship continues to be mediated by representation. Even as the English hero discovers that the ethnic other has been veiled by a thick network of misrepresentations, his actual encounter with the other reveals a new set of complex cultural texts and practices that typically make the other unknown and even untranslatable to him. The populations on both sides of the divide are consistently at the service of representation rather than vice versa, and these novelistic plots explore and expose the ways in which access to minority ethnic cultures is never direct. So, while such plots have typically been understood as the hero's movement from the metropole to the periphery, I am suggesting that they describe the journey from one set of representations to another. In this light these novels become at least as much about the processes and mechanisms of representation as they are about Irish or Scottish or Jewish identity. In this way these novels self-consciously contemplate their own function as forms of representation, acknowledging at some level that they can offer only another (corrective) form of representation, as opposed to delivering up the ethnic other unmediated.

As texts about representing the ethnic other, these novels do not respond to the theater simply by critiquing the stage's stock ethnic figures. Quite the contrary, the predominance of scenes of performance in these novels—singing, acting, reciting—signals that they do not simply dismiss theatricality. The novels explore a wide range of theatrical acts and contexts within which to understand not only the encounter between the English hero and the ethnic other but also ethnic identity in itself. In the first case, theatricality provides a model for a kind of sympathetic identification that can move the English hero toward understanding and identifying with the ethnic other. In this way these novels set the test of cross-ethnic identification for the English hero and ultimately for the English reader. In the second case, theatrical performance is increasingly seen as a legitimate event that is in fact constitutive of ethnic communities. In opposition to the theatrical spectacle of ethnic difference staged for an English audience in a London theater, these novels begin to describe how theatrical performance can function within an ethnic community as a central means of constituting itself, its own communal solidarity.

In reacting against the London stage's caricatures of ethnic minorities, these novels develop a host of strategies that complicate the representation of ethnicity, especially demonstrating the kinds of differences in speech, geography, class, and religion that existed within such groups, in order to deconstruct the homogenous, single-note Paddys and Sawnies that were produced on the London stage. But perhaps the most conspicuous and consistent innovation of these novels is the way in which they regender ethnic difference, inventing the beautiful female ethnic other to displace the caricatured (and sometimes demonized) male ethnic other of the theater. By installing the ethnic woman as the love interest of the English hero, these novels move the prejudiced English hero out of his private (and prejudicial) world of reading into an actual encounter with an ethnic woman who mediates her culture through representation, through various cultural artifacts and performances. In short, the ethnic woman in these novels functions to intervene on the English hero's prejudices in order to instruct him in the uses and abuses of representation.

Edgeworth's *Belinda*, published in 1801, opens the century with a subtle investigation of the role of the different arts in civil society, and immediately interrogates its own form by claiming not to be a novel. Acutely aware of the social powers of representation in general, novelists in the early nineteenth century developed a sharp self-consciousness about their own formal and ideological goals. Hence, the kinds of redefinitions and renamings that preoccupied these novelists, whether it was Edgeworth calling *Belinda* "a Moral Tale—the author not wishing to acknowledge a Novel,"[20] or Owenson denominating her novels "national tales,"[21] or Scott's long list of novelistic options that he eschewed in *Waverley* (a "Sentimental Tale," "a Tale of other Days," "a Romance from the German," "A Tale of the Times," and so on).[22] Edgeworth in particular was reacting to the conventional charges against both the theater and the novel, articulated most succinctly by Rousseau when he claimed, "Great cities must have theaters; and corrupt peoples, Novels."[23] The two forms were frequently linked in formulaic anathemas. *London Magazine*, for example, stigmatized circulating libraries by aligning them with theaters, warning that Parliament would soon declare their owners, "like the players, 'rogues and vagabonds,' the debauchers of morals, and the pest of society."[24] In the course of her novelistic career, Edgeworth was continually preoccupied with such questions as whether theatergoing and novel reading were parallel activities, and whether the powers of such activities could be turned to the public good.

With its continuous citation of novels, poems, plays, and paintings, *Belinda* is a novel almost painfully self-conscious about the medium of fiction, the connections among different forms of representation, and the moral consequences of all aesthetic experiences. One of the most salient features of *Belinda* is the way in which it consistently blurs the line between private reading and public theatricals, especially as a way of interrogating such aesthetic experiences and their moral consequences. In chapter 13, at "a reading party" (*B*, 164) a gentleman famous for his public readings reads aloud from a French play, and in addition Clarence reads aloud from Sheridan's *School for Scandal* (from which Edgeworth will import a Jew for a climactic chapter in *Belinda*). I wish to argue that this reading party functions as a model for a series of more or less public acts of reading that occur throughout the novel, and that reading becomes consistently theatricalized in *Belinda*, threatening the division between private reading and public theatricals, dramatized most famously in Jane Austen's *Mansfield Park* (1814) where Fanny Price escapes to read in private as a protection from the public—and corrupting—theatricals that are being performed elsewhere in the house.

While *Belinda* certainly critiques the theatricality of fashionable life in Georgian England—the world of masks and masquerades—it is another, often neglected definition of theatricality that surfaces and revises these scenes of reading: namely, the function of theater as a shared, communal activity, repeatedly praised in Georgian England for its ability to bring together a wide diversity of people. This was praise that Rousseau himself was armed against, in his disclaimer in *Letter to M. d'Alembert on the Theatre* (1758), "People think they come together in the theatre, and it is there that they are isolated."[25] I am arguing that in *Belinda* scenes of reading are theatricalized precisely insofar as they disrupt the private scene of isolated reading by making it communal. Even private letters, addressed to only one recipient, are shared, particularly through the agency of Lady Delacour. Early in the novel she takes from Belinda's hands a letter addressed to the heroine, and later in the novel she proposes that she and Belinda read together the lengthy letter Clarence has addressed only to herself. Lady Delacour regularly puts the private into public circulation, for the knowledge of more than one reader or spectator.

The private act of reading becomes theatricalized in *Belinda*, then, when texts are shared, mediated, dialogized—when they become community property and aspire to do the communal work that is the domain of public theater, not private reading. Scenes in which the act of reading is shared demonstrate the social consequences of reading—namely, that reading influences and even shapes our common knowledge and our social relations. Moreover, by making the act of reading public, such scenes become moral goads and even tests, and thereby disclose, and perhaps even constitute, the moral and social values of the characters publicly. When, for example, Lady Delacour in public opens a volume to a moral apothegm that is strikingly pertinent to her own life story and asks Belinda to join her in reading it, she accuses Belinda of deliberately leading her to this passage, as if one reader has morally instructed and enlightened a second reader in a communally based model of reading. And later, when Belinda's suitor, the West Indian plantation owner, reads aloud to her and Lady Delacour from a famous abolitionist poem "The Dying Negro," it is as if Mr. Vincent's credentials as a tolerant Englishman are being performed by him and evaluated by others. Some editions of the poem carried a preface that indeed suggested a test of values that the West Indian reader would fail because he would be unable to sympathize either with the poem or with the newspaper clipping that was its basis (recording a runaway slave's suicide after being recaptured and prevented from marrying the white woman he loved): "The Author trusts, that in an age and country, in which we boast of philanthropy, and generous sentiments, few persons, (except *West-Indians*) can read the above paragraph, without emotions similar to those, which inspired the following lines."[26] Born and bred in the West Indies, "his knowledge of English literature . . . not as extensive as Clarence Hervey's" (*B*, 347), Mr. Vincent gives a public reading that tests his nationality and national values when he reads in the person of the native Englishman and abolitionist Thomas Day, and in the voice of the persecuted slave. In the same scene, Lady Delacour challenges Clarence, who is suspected of seducing a young woman, to read aloud another poem by Day that tests his moral worth, warning him: "If you have any 'sins unwhipt of justice,' there are lines, which I defy you to read without faltering" (*B*, 350). Reading aloud—as opposed to reading in private—can expose you. For this reason a test of the rival suitors for Belinda's hand becomes a trial by reading in public.

The novel's most extended illustration of the dangers of reading in private occurs in the subplot of Virginia. Even before demonstrating the deep impression that reading has made on Virginia, we learn of how it has provided Clarence with the central (misguided) project of his adult life: "He read the works of Rousseau: this eloquent writer's sense made its full impression upon Clarence's understanding, and his declamations produced more than their just effect upon an imagination naturally ardent" (*B*, 362). After a sojourn in France where Clarence is shocked by the dissipation of the Parisian women, Rousseau's picture of the innocent Sophie in *Emile, or Education* (1762) so charms him that "he formed the romantic project of educating a wife for himself" (*B*, 362). Clarence eventually finds a young girl who has been raised in utter seclusion, and he moves her to Windsor and changes her name from Rachel to Virginia: "He was struck with the idea that she resembled the description of Virginia in M. de St. Pierre's celebrated Romance; and by this name he always called her" (*B*, 370). At this point Virginia becomes twice-over the product of Clarence's reading—her (textual) identity is formulated on models he encounters in his reading of Rousseau and St. Pierre. His Virginia is a copy of a copy; hence, she is now called Virginia St. Pierre, with a romance writer as her father. Her paternal name signals that she is almost literally a fiction; St. Pierre is her author. Losing interest in his project, Clarence largely abandons Virginia to her own devices, and the girl named after a fiction learns to live solely upon fictions: "all her notions were drawn from books; . . . her appetite for books . . . was insatiable. Reading, indeed, was now almost her only pleasure" (*B*, 379–80). Virginia is not simply allowed the act of private reading; she in effect has no other choice.

The pattern of the private act of reading interrupted, inspected, and communalized becomes all the more apparent in the story of Virginia precisely because her entire education has been based on private reading. Hence the novel especially underscores the moment when Mrs. Ormond finds Virginia reading alone and attempts to share the act. Already well practiced in her career as a reader of romances, Virginia finds a copy of *Paul and Virginia* (1787); she knows that her name has been taken from this romance, so she is mesmerized by reading the book, as if she were reading her own story, until she is interrupted by Mrs. Ormond, who awakens Virginia from her almost trancelike state of reading and asks to see the book. This is the pivotal event that the novel stages time and again, when the private act of reading is interrupted, when a (private) text is shared, opened to communal participation, made public. Repeating the scenes in which Lady Delacour takes a letter out of Belinda's hands, or a book out of Mr. Vincent's hands, Mrs. Ormond attempts to take Virginia's book. But Virginia "held the volume fast," refusing to give it up and provoking Mrs. Ormond to ask, "Will not you let me read over your shoulder, along with you?" (*B*, 380).

Mrs. Ormond's question is a direct invitation to undertake a kind of double or communal reading. Virginia eventually yields the book even though she declares she does not want Mrs. Ormond to see the passage she has been reading. After being allowed to read the passage in which St. Pierre's Virginia seeks protection from her mother, Mrs. Ormond declares, "And am not I a mother to you?" at which "Virginia threw her arms round Mrs. Ormond, and laid her head upon her friend's bosom, as if she wished to realize the illusion, and to be the Virginia of whom she had been reading" (*B*, 381). In this way Virginia is about to absorb Mrs. Ormond into the plot of the romance, to deactualize her real life and make her part of the private fantasy world she herself inhabits. Clarence's desire—that she be St. Pierre's Virginia—has become her desire; she knows no other. And Mrs. Ormond's attempt to share the act of reading, to open it up and make it communal, fails precisely because Virginia, unlike the other readers in the novel, has been so totally absorbed by the world of books. When Mrs. Ormond claims to understand her, Virginia rejects her: "No, indeed, you do not: you cannot. . . . How could you possibly know *all* my thoughts and feelings? I never told them to you; for, indeed, I have only confused ideas, floating in my imagination, from the books I have been reading" (*B*, 381). In other words, Virginia has no knowable, no social, self; she exists as a pastiche of her reading, a tissue of fictions, even to herself.

Virginia's identification with her namesake from St. Pierre's text becomes more and more complete: she tells Mrs. Ormond, "I thought I was not myself, but the Virginia that we were reading of the other night. . . . There were high mountains and rocks, and cocoa-trees and plantains." She pictures herself reproduced from "the prints of that book" (*B*, 387). But Clarence has already reproduced her in this way, in a vicarious act of (re)authoring on his part: as if to realize more fully his reproduction of Rachel as Virginia, he has the girl painted as St. Pierre's Virginia. She is revealed for the first time to the reader of *Belinda* and to the characters in the novel as an exotic image, not as a real person, at an exhibition of paintings. Alienated from herself, even alienated from her national identity, Rachel is reproduced as the unreachable Virginia, removed from real life in the idealized and illusory portrait of her—a "foreign beauty . . . if one may judge by her air, her dress, and the scenery about her—cocoa-trees, plantains" (*B*, 190). She is figured through her exoticization: she is a foreigner, an unknowable other, perhaps a colonial subject (as her name suggests). Even Clarence himself, late in the novel, recognizes the subjugated state of Virginia, when he implores her, "Do not consider me as your master—your tyrant" (*B*, 399). Here the term "master," which circulates freely throughout the novel (frequently as "massa," the word used by the black West Indian servant Juba), manages to complicate Clarence's role as tutor with both class and race inflections. Virginia is mastered both by her master-tutor and by the series of master-texts that she serves. This makes of Clarence a kind of West Indian of the imagination, and suggests that, just as Belinda is in danger of being mastered by her literal West Indian suitor (as we will see), even her purely English suitor, Clarence Hervey, has engaged in a relationship modeled on West Indian subjugation. Subdued and mastered in such ways, at the end of the novel Virginia becomes the center of a symbolic negotiation that affirms the institution of slavery, when she is given in marriage to the man who saves her father's life during a slave rebellion on his plantation: Virginia becomes "payment of your father's debt of gratitude" (*B*, 476). A slave to the imaginings of Clarence, she now has the monetary value of a bought and sold slave. So, while Clarence's project of educating a wife for himself apart from the world of fashion depended on this distinction—"What a difference . . . between this child of nature and the frivolous sophisticated slaves of art!" (*B*, 371)—he ends by making this child of nature into his own special slave of art, pictured in her West Indian costume, giving up her identity to that of St. Pierre's Virginia, subjugated to the project of Rousseau's *Emile*. This figure of the child or woman enslaved by representation, by art, becomes one of the central figures in the novelistic tradition I am analyzing.

For all of *Belinda*'s Enlightenment pretensions to reason, the subplot of Virginia's reading shows us the work of art as a kind of talisman, as potent in England as it is in the West Indies or Africa. The efficacious power of the talisman and the fetish is ostensibly the subject of critique in the novel: when the black West Indian servant Juba, for example, is frightened by the figure of an old woman all in flames, we are told of the superstitious nature of blacks, and we see the way in which what the text calls "the ignorant negro" (*B*, 222) learns the illusory nature of his vision—it is merely a phosphorescent illusion concocted to frighten him. But his credulity is repeated in those scenes which show us that Lady Delacour and Virginia also fear and love phantoms. Lady Delacour sees a spectral vision three times, and Virginia's "imagination, exalted by solitude and romance, embodied and became enamoured of a phantom" (*B*, 469). An embodied image herself, Virginia falls in love with a picture, and her future husband is presented to her at the end of the novel in a portrait in which he is painted as St. Pierre's Paul, enabling her full absorption into the world of romantic fictions. In such cases we see how the black Juba and the white Virginia are equally the "slaves of art," equally susceptible to the powers of "the black art" (*B*, 40). In fact such apparently primitive, non-Western phenomena—what one might call the magical arts—exist in a variety of forms in Enlightenment England, as the novel demonstrates. There is, for example, the episode in which the effigy of Mr. Moreton functions to underscore the belief in the power one has over another through the medium of representation, reminding us that the effigy functioned as a popular form of street theater in Georgian England.

While the novel may attempt to demystify such apparently magical forms of representation, it nonetheless admits their psychological power and their social efficacy. *Belinda*, then, exposes and anatomizes the human susceptibility to a variety of forms of representation, and argues that this susceptibility is universal: the border between civilized and savage—to use the terms of the Enlightenment—is here quite permeable. There is a continuum between the African practice of obeah and the Western practice of the novel and other arts. After all, if the novel claims "the astonishing power, which the belief in this species of sorcery has over the minds of the Jamaica negroes; they pine and actually die away, from the moment they fancy themselves under the malignant influence of these witches" (*B*, 221), contemporary attacks on the novel and the theater represented them as a kind of sorcery: *Belinda* reports about Virginia's mother that she was "a sentimental girl, who had been spoiled by early novel-reading" (*B*, 408) and who "died of a broken heart" (*B*, 366). In fact, I would argue that the modernity of Edgeworth's view does not dismiss such susceptibilities as merely foolish but shows (in anticipation of Freud) the psychopathology of the mechanism of identification and the ways in which the work of art facilitates such psychopathological states. In this way, *Belinda* anticipates such novels of the 1890s as Oscar Wilde's *The Picture of Dorian Gray* (1891) and George du Maurier's *Trilby* (1894), in which poison books, living portraits, mesmerized singers, and hypnotic photographs are at the center of fables about the profoundly dangerous powers of the artist and the arts.

While *Belinda* on the one hand keeps a sharp eye on the kinds of manipulations and misrepresentations that art (or the magical arts) can work, it nonetheless in the end relies on its English readers' prejudices by concocting a divisive race plot that valorizes Englishness and uses the most conventional theatrical strategies to caricature and finally exclude ethnic minorities. In this way *Belinda* formulates the central challenges of Edgeworth's entire career and of this novelistic tradition's implication in the dominant theatrical and Anglocentric conventions of Georgian England. While the novel at first seems headed in the direction of recuperating certain ethnic minorities, it winds up valorizing Englishness, rejecting the West Indian (who in Cumberland's *West Indian* in fact succeeds in marrying the Englishwoman), demonizing a Jew, and reproducing a comical version of black identity. For a purely English marriage to conclude the novel, Clarence must be cured of his foreign (both French and West Indian) ways—his reliance on Rousseau's radical theories and St. Pierre's primitive romance—and be re-anglicized, rejecting his exotic, creolized Virginia for the English Belinda. Similarly, Belinda must reject Mr. Vincent, the West Indian who has been sent to England to be anglicized but in the end is sent by the novelist out of England into exile.

The novel accomplishes the indictment of Mr. Vincent through a highly theatrical scene that has recourse to a familiar cultural scapegoat in a chapter entitled "A Jew." Imported directly from those multiethnic spectacles centered in marriage plots in which a non-English man (unsuccessfully) courts an English woman, this chapter disqualifies the West Indian Mr. Vincent's suit for the hand of the Englishwoman by disclosing that he is stained by a double racial mark when the skeletons in his closet—"Juba, the black, and Solomon, the Jew" (*B*, 446)—are exposed. The two are made to share an especially prominent stage marker, their comical dialect: "Each went on talking in their own angry gibberish as loud as they could, till at last the negro fairly dragged the Jew into the presence of his master and Mr. Perceval" (*B*, 447). (The French valet in the novel, another foreigner finally ejected from the plot, also speaks the "gibberish" characteristic of stage Frenchmen [*B*, 260].) While the crime of slavery is never made explicit here—in fact, it seems elided and displaced onto the crime of "having recourse to Jews—a desperate expedient" (*B*, 445)—nonetheless the Jew suddenly appears in the plot in order to underwrite the man who has made his wealth through the institution of slavery. In having "recourse to Jews" like Mr. Vincent, the calculating novelist apparently indicts Vincent not on account of his slaveholding but on account of his indebtedness to the usurious Jewish moneylender, though even Vincent's gambling reminds us of his association with slavery, for as a young man he daily played "at games of chance, with his negroes" (*B*, 422). And both Juba and Solomon, hidden in Mr. Vincent's bedchamber and repeatedly given their racial nametags as if they were ethnic caricatures on the stage, are literally bound together in a wrestling match, inseparable in the mutually associative stain they put on Vincent's character.

While I have been arguing that theatricality sometimes provides in *Belinda* a dialogized public sphere for broader, even communal, understanding, in this chapter Edgeworth falls back on those theatrical conventions that solidify difference and lock ethnic minorities in the kind of mutual misunderstanding that locates them, like their "gibberish," outside the purview of the central English plot. And while this theatrical scene does contribute to further understanding by making Vincent's secret debts public, this advantage accrues only to the members of the English plot. As Lady Delacour explains to Belinda, Jew and black here have only one function, their pure instrumentality in facilitating the marriage of English hero and heroine, "for without that wrestling match of theirs, the truth might never have been dragged to light, and Mr. Vincent would have been this day your lord and master" (*B*, 451). This scene, then, saves the English heroine from being enslaved by Vincent, the West Indian, reminding us that, while the Jew is "signing the bonds" (*B*, 445), earlier in the novel Belinda was careful to remain "free": "She would not bind herself by any promise, or engagement, to Mr. Vincent" (*B*, 345). During the period of his temporarily postponed marriage to Belinda, then, Mr. Vincent is exposed as wed to a Jew, "signing the bonds, and . . . completing the formalities of the transaction" (*B*, 445) that binds him not to Belinda but to "A Jew"—after all, "his passion for play" (*B*, 421) has been shown to compete with, and finally supersede, his passion for the heroine, and he winds up choosing "a gamester's life" over a "lover's" (*B*, 424).

At first hidden behind a theatrical "curtain" (*B*, 446), the Jew recalls a long line of stage Jews when he is finally dragged on stage in *Belinda*, not only the Jewish moneylender in Shakespeare's *Merchant of Venice* and Sheridan's *School for Scandal* but perhaps most tellingly also Napthali in Cumberland's *Fashionable Lover*. In addition to a plot in which a father makes a fortune in the West Indies and returns to England to reclaim the daughter he has abandoned, both Cumberland and Edgeworth show us a faithful servant belonging to a minority who attempts to rescue his master from a Jewish moneylender: Cumberland's Scot and Edgeworth's black are recuperated at the same time that they function to support an anti-Semitic stereotype. In both cases the Jew is represented less as the object of prejudice than as its purveyor: Napthali calls Colin "that devil Scotchman," while "Solomon had an antipathy to the sight of a black" (*B*, 447). And in both cases the Jew is subjected to physical abuse: the Scot declares, "I promised him a beating, and I kept my word,"[27] while the black "seized the Jew by the throat" (*B*, 446). The comicality of Edgeworth's scene derives from the spectacle of "the wrestling match" between Jew and black, especially because of the Jew's "terrour" (*B*, 447) at the sight of a black, as in the farce *In and Out of Tune*, where the Jew is similarly frightened by a black ("It ish de devil himself").[28] Edgeworth attempts to balance this comedy with pathos over the black's response to the exposure of his master as a gambler and bankrupt: "No torments, in the power of human cruelty to inflict, could, in all probability have extorted from this negro one of the tears, which affection wrung from him so plentifully" (*B*, 449). In other words, the horrors of slavery are superseded (and even suppressed) in Edgeworth's picture of the pathos of the grateful Negro, facilitating the way in which the chapter focuses on "a Jew" and the novelist's own strategy of having "recourse to Jews." But even Juba is reduced to comic stagecraft in this scene; the heroic black of "The Dying Negro" is reduced to the duped servant who, believing his rich master cannot be in debt to the Jew, inadvertently exposes (rather than rescues) his master. Juba, bearing the same name as his master's dog, exits the novel entirely infantilized: "He sobbed like an infant" at the thought that "massa is gone!" (*B*, 449). In such ways the novel submits to what Lady Delacour in the last paragraph calls "the rule of the stage" (*B*, 478).

I now wish to show why and how the xenophobic elements of *Belinda*, many of which were borrowed from the stage, get turned around in Edgeworth's *Harrington*, which eschews the valorization of the English woman over the exotic woman and deconstructs the theatricalization of the Jew. If *Belinda* shows Edgeworth yielding in the end to many of the most Anglocentric theatrical conventions of the day, *Harrington* is Edgeworth's most incisive study of the powers of theatricality both to caricature and to recuperate minority ethnic identity. *Harrington* repeats in important ways the subplot of Virginia in *Belinda*. In the cases of both Virginia and Harrington we see the mastery of the child-adolescent by the master-tutor and by master-texts; both Virginia and Harrington fall prey to a kind of psychic possession. But *Harrington* is of special interest because it explores such issues in an attempt to perform an etiology of anti-Semitism and the critical role the stage plays in this form of prejudice.

The novel's initiating moment shows us a nursery maid who instills anti-Semitism into the young child in her care, feeding him multiple stories of rapacious Jews, so that he confesses, "I became her slave."[29] Perhaps even more powerfully than in the story of Virginia, Edgeworth makes clear that she is exploring extreme pathological or even preternatural mental states in her young character: we hear of Harrington's "Jewish insanity" (*H*, 43), and Harrington himself says, "I should have flourished a favourite pupil of Mesmer, the animal magnetizer" (*H*, 7), so profoundly is he under the spell of his nursery maid, the stories she tells him, and the stories he reads on his own in a variety of popular texts. Enslaved by representations of anti-Semitism, the child is bound in a psychological "prison-house" (*H*, 4) with no will of his own, but to do her bidding, as if he is hypnotized, mesmerized, awaiting to be awakened.

Edgeworth turns to the stage to examine a critical moment in the history of anti-Semitism in England and to show the means by which her hero can be awakened. Set in a London theater during the celebrated performance of

Charles Macklin in *The Merchant of Venice*, chapter 7 allows Edgeworth to explore the powerful hold the stage Jew has on Georgian audiences and the means by which an English audience might be liberated from both the play and the anti-Semitism it supports. In some sense, the chapter is a return to the original scene of the crime of anti-Semitism in England, the production of Shylock. Before the play begins, the hero observes a woman with a foreign air, at first thought to be an "East Indian . . . by her dark complexion" (*H*, 58) but then recognized as a Jew. Since her face is at first blocked from his view, he changes his position "so that I had a better view of my object, and could observe her without being seen by any one" (*H*, 59). This emphasis on the invisibility of the male spectator, and on his double spectatorship—that is, on the subtle play between watching the stage and watching the audience—becomes the hallmark of the chapter. Once Shylock appears on stage, "I forgot everything but him. . . . The Jew fixed and kept possession of my attention" (*H*, 59). In this section of the chapter, then, the stage Jew supersedes the view of the Jew who sits before him, in a kind of allegory about the cultural power of images of the other. Already profoundly interpellated through the medium of representation—through the stories his nursemaid tells and the books he reads—Harrington is once again taken possession of, so that he longs to be absorbed entirely into the play, into its anti-Semitic illusion, repeating and extending the way in which Virginia functioned as the slave of art in *Belinda*, desiring the fullest absorption in the illusory world of representation: "In my enthusiasm I stood up, I pressed forward, I leaned far over towards the stage, that I might not lose a word, a look, a gesture" (*H*, 59). Harrington's appetite for the spectacle of Jewish identity—not unlike that of London audiences generally—is so strong that he attempts to erase the border between himself and the stage, forgetting the illusion of the play. Even though he has met the actor backstage, and knows that he is only playing a part, "I forgot it was Macklin, I thought only of Shylock" (*H*, 59).

When the curtain falls, the chapter moves into its middle section: Harrington hears both "thunders of applause" and "a soft low sigh near me; I looked, and saw the Jewess!" (*H*, 59). Both the sound and the sight of the Jewish woman before him break the illusion, and at this moment the dissonance between the majority population and the minority of one shatters the spell of the play: he witnesses the different ways in which the play is received, depending on one's ethnic and religious identity. The soft low sigh of the Jewess disrupts for him and for Edgeworth's readers the fiction of the so-called universal humanism of Shakespeare. It is at this moment, when her identity as other is most apparent—when her reaction to the play is set against everyone else's—that Harrington is given his first complete view of her: "I had, for the first time, a full view of her face and of her countenance, of great sensibility, painfully, proudly repressed. She looked up while my eyes were fixed upon her—a sudden and deep colour spread over her face and mounted to her temples" (*H*, 59). While he sees on the stage the mask of the Jew, a Gentile masquerading as Shakespeare's Shylock, in the audience, beside him, he sees the mask fall from Jewish identity, as he sees Berenice's pain and her embarrassment at being seen.

Harrington's experience of the play radically changes at this point: "My imagination formed such a strong conception of the pain the Jewess was feeling, and my inverted sympathy, if I may so call it, so overpowered my direct and natural feelings, that at every fresh development of the Jew's villainy I shrunk as though I had myself been a Jew. Each exclamation against this dog of a Jew . . . I felt poignantly" (*H*, 60). The hero's identification with the woman's pain causes him to feel Shylock's pain, the Jew's pain, so that a kind of conversion occurs: "I shrunk as though I had myself been a Jew." The series of identifications with the woman, with the Jew, and with Shylock form a continuum which at this moment defines the act of sympathy as an act of inversion ("my inverted sympathy") that disturbs the hero: the natural—the male, English spectator, possessor of the imperial gaze—becomes in the course of the scene identified with the female and the ethnic other. By his own confession the hero shrinks, his direct and natural feelings are overpowered, and he feels poignantly. We have here the double bind of cross-ethnic and cross-gender identification. Edgeworth wants the full conquest of her hero's anti-Semitism at the same time that she understands the ways in which such a conquest requires his radical transformation— that is, the entire submission of his conventional power as an Englishman.

The third and final section of the chapter is signaled once again when the hero changes his position in the theater, reminding us of the ways in which this episode is about the powers of (male) spectatorship: "During the third act, during the Jessica scenes, I longed so much to have a look at the Jewess, that I took an opportunity of changing my position. . . . I was so placed that I could see her, without being seen; and during the succeeding acts, my attention was chiefly directed to the study of all the changes in her expressive countenance. I now saw and heard the play solely with reference to her feelings" (*H*, 61). At first such a passage suggests a continued identification with the female, an immersion in her feelings, and thereby a new way of reacting to Shakespeare's play, of experiencing first-hand what it is to be a Jew. But there is also a growing sense of mastery in the hero's experience, as his submission to the other begins to be replaced by the reassertion of his own identity as male spectator. I refer here to the sense in which Berenice begins to become an erotic spectacle that rivals and finally supersedes the spectacle of Jewishness on the stage: "I anticipated every stroke which could touch her, and became every moment more and more interested and delighted with her, from the perception that my anticipations were just, and that I perfectly knew how to read her soul, and interpret her countenance" (*H*, 61). The sympathetic understanding of Jewish suffering begins to blend into the masterful interpretation of the female/erotic experience. His imaginative anticipation of "every stroke which could touch her," like his earlier realization of the suffusion of blood through her face, eroticizes her through her suffering and victimization. In fact, Berenice's pain at the performance apparently provokes a kind of sexual arousal in the hero, and leads him back into the world of illusion, of private erotic fantasy: "I saw the struggle to repress her emotion was often the utmost she could endure; and at last I saw, or fancied I saw, that she grew so pale, that, as she closed her eyes at the same instant, I was certain she was going to faint" (*H*, 61–62). He helps her out of the theater, when he notices in her "a great dread of exposing herself to public observation" (*H*, 62). In understanding her dread we realize how profoundly the hero has acted as a kind of peeping Tom throughout this episode, watching her without being seen.

While this scene is perilously balanced between sympathetic identification and erotic mastery, a problem to which I will return, it nonetheless theorizes the powerful potential of sympathy with the other as a performative, or theatrical, act. It should be clear that a similar structure links this episode in the theater to the episode of Virginia's private reading in *Belinda*: what is studied in both episodes is the act of reception. In both cases the apparently private and closed reader-text circuit is opened to a second reader or spectator. We have, then, in both cases a triangular structure of representation and identification: both scenes begin with a character entirely absorbed in an aesthetic experience, Virginia in a book and Harrington in a play. Both scenes explore a character's attempt to share another's aesthetic experience: Mrs. Ormond tries to read *Paul and Virginia* over the shoulder, and through the eyes, of Virginia, and fails; Harrington tries to see *The Merchant of Venice* through Berenice's eyes, and succeeds—he feels the pain of the Jew. The difference between the two scenes suggests the importance of seeing a work of art not simply directly but through the eyes of another. I mean here that Berenice has the power to awaken Harrington from his infatuation with the play, and to demystify the play for him, to make plain its dangers and its prejudices, while Mrs. Ormond is powerless to do the same for Virginia, who seems forever lost in her aesthetic experience. For this reason Virginia simply remains enclosed in the world of her illusory fictions, while Harrington moves from his identification with the play to his identification with Berenice. This triangular structure intervenes on the basic process by which representation typically functions, namely, by mediating between us and the world—that is, the representation of Shylock mediates Harrington's view of Jews. It is precisely because Edgeworth understands the immense power of representation to shape our view of the world—say, in Harrington's explanation of how profoundly the authority of books shaped his anti-Semitism—that she theorizes what one might call the second, pedagogic stage in representation— namely, when another reader or spectator mediates our view of the mediating representation.

The episode in the theater in *Harrington* is so important because it intervenes in contemporary debates about the social functions of works of art. The hero's sympathetic identification with Shylock and with Berenice is precisely the kind of identification that was at the heart, on the one hand, of the powerful critiques of both the theater and the novel at the time, and on the other hand, of concepts of the act of sympathy in which spectators put themselves in the place of sufferers to feel their pain. In the first case, I recall such touchstone critiques as Rousseau's influential *Letter to M. d'Alembert* and Austen's *Mansfield Park*, as well as *Belinda*, which warns against the powerful dangers—fetishistic, talismanic, mesmeric—of the work of art and its capacity to compel us to enter its world of often dangerous illusions. Social critiques of the theater and the novel focused on them as media of identification, attacking "this identifying propensity"[30] that led the self outside itself, outside its proper realm, thereby threatening to overturn the entire social order. In the second case, I recall Adam Smith's theory of sympathetic identification in *Theory of Moral Sentiments* (1759), which Edgeworth quotes in *Practical Education* (1798) and the heroine reads in *Belinda* (*B*, 228). For Smith, the act of sympathy is an act of identification that many commentators have described as theatrical, for it is a kind of role-playing. According to Smith, as spectators we become the sufferer by an act of imagination in which "we place ourselves in his situation, . . . we enter as it were into his body, and become in some measure the same person with him . . . by changing places in fancy with the sufferer."[31]

Edgeworth brilliantly situates herself between these two extremes, acknowledging the power of both. In her explorations of the science of the child's development, which she and her father did so much to found and to foster, she became acutely aware of the profound impressions that representations make on the child and the adolescent. We have in her work an unusually modern understanding of how the social self is constructed through representation. Again and again, in her novels and in her pedagogical writings, she analyses what happens when people in general but especially children and women (those especially vulnerable to the dangers of identification and imitation) fall under the spell of the heroes and heroines of novels and the stage. Edgeworth's initial translation of Smith's notion of imaginative identification occurs at the level of pedagogy. Her entire pedagogic project is shaped in order to have a positive influence on the child through the means of identification: she describes how "to inculcate the plain precepts of real life, not by eloquent harangues, but by such pictures of real life, as may make a child wish to put himself in the place of the character intended to excite his emulation."[32] And the narrator in her novel *Ormond* (1817) claims, "Young readers readily assimilate and identify themselves with any character, the leading points of which resemble their own, and in whose general feelings they sympathize."[33] But Edgeworth revises Smith precisely at the point that she realizes sympathy and imitation may be dangerous. She fears the full power of sympathy and hence sets its limits: she speaks of children "catching faults by sympathy," and, citing Smith, she warns that "a person governed by sympathy alone must be influenced by the bad as well as by the good passions of others."[34] And we do have in the episode in the theater in *Harrington* Edgeworth's attempt to draw a limit to her hero's sympathy: "No power of imagination could make me pity Shylock, but I felt the force of some of his appeals to justice; and some passages struck me in quite a new light on the Jewish side of the question" (*H*, 60).

At the same time, by setting the powerful scene of sympathetic identification in the theater, Edgeworth emphasizes the performative nature of the act of sympathy and documents not simply the danger but also the value of this kind of theatrical yielding of self, this self-annihilation, considered the hallmark of the actor by various Georgian theorists of acting.[35] Edgeworth in fact pushes such a performative theory to its limit by imagining the self to be filled not merely by another but by the threatening ethnic other. So, while there is ever present in the episode a warning about "catching faults by sympathy," at the same time the episode allows the hero to come as close as possible to experiencing anti-Semitism first-hand, to seeing through Jewish eyes, as it were. Harrington understands the power of anti-Semitic representation by seeing its effects on Berenice, and he experiences her pain by putting himself in her place: it is the death of the English Protestant male ego, if only for a moment.

The radicalness of such a moment might best be realized when we compare it to the attack on the theatricals in *Mansfield Park* (which Edgeworth records reading on December 26, 1814),[36] and Fanny Price's attempt to legitimize the privacy of the self through the privacy of reading, as opposed to the public and shifting selves that operate in theatrical performance. I am reading Edgeworth against such a formulation by claiming, first, that she complicates and even critiques the act of private reading (in *Belinda*), and second, that while she understands the dangers of theatricality, she also understands its profound value (in *Harrington*). The triangular structure of identification and representation that I have located in her novels moves toward imagining the idea of sharing another's point of view; this is the function of the second reader or spectator. Such scenes embrace the public and the theatrical, as opposed to the absolute values of the private and the so-called real. In such comparisons I hope to make clear the way in which the novel, at this historical moment, engages a debate about the social functions of different aesthetic forms, and negotiates in particular the differences between the private act of reading and the public act of theater. Reading Edgeworth against Austen (to set the limits of the debate), we see the abandonment of the self to another, to the other, as opposed to the retrenchment of the self, its paranoiac self-protection, withdrawal, and seclusion in *Mansfield Park*.

The endorsement of such self-abandonment through the theatrical crossing of the boundaries of gender and ethnicity lies at the heart of the authorial process for Edgeworth. First, I recall her description of the genesis of her first novel, *Castle Rackrent*, when she describes her relationship to one of her Irish servants: "His dialect struck me, . . . and I became so acquainted with it, that I could think and speak in it without effort . . . he seemed to stand beside me and dictate; and I wrote as fast as my pen could go, the characters all imaginary."[37] Edgeworth's first novel, then, is the result of the kind of psychic and theatrical possession that I have been describing, where the act of authorship replicates the activity of sympathetic identification. Such an act is grounded in actorly self-annihilation, allowing the author in effect to be authorized by another, even by the other. In a kind of trancelike automatic writing, the Anglo-Irish landowner loses herself to the Irish manservant. In this way Edgeworth produces a landmark novel written in non-standard English that, as she announces in the preface, "the *ignorant* English reader"[38] may not entirely understand.

A similarly theatrical crossing of boundaries stands behind *Harrington*, which was written in direct response to a Jewish reader who wrote to Edgeworth to complain of the anti-Semitic portraits that were prominent in her earlier fiction.[39] The act of Jewish reception, then, is the founding moment of *Harrington*. In this light the episode in the theater simply copies the act of triangulated authorial production: Edgeworth produces *Harrington* only after she looks over the shoulder of Rachel Mordecai and sees through Jewish eyes the earlier anti-Semitic texts that she herself has produced. Mordecai's experience of Edgeworth's earlier fiction has the same effect on the author that Berenice's experience of *The Merchant of Venice* has on Harrington: in both cases, a Jewish woman functions as a kind of textual mediator, an enlightened master-reader.

In my next chapter I explore the way in which the focus in *Harrington* on the ethnic woman as the channel through which the English hero begins to understand a minority ethnic culture is in fact a central strategy shared by a group of novels in which, first, ethnic difference is renegotiated through the figure of a beautiful, exotic woman, and second, the encounter with the exotic woman is mediated by representation. In *Harrington*, for example, the hero encounters Berenice on the grounds of representation, at a performance of *The Merchant of Venice*, repeating the way in which Maria Edgeworth herself encounters Rachel Mordecai on the grounds of the author's own previous texts. Moreover, the emphasis in *Harrington* on the woman engaged in the production and evaluation of ethnic identity—the woman writer, reader, and character—actually signals a much larger movement in the negotiation between the stage and the novel at the time. In *Harrington* the movement of the hero's gaze from the conventional male figure on the stage to the romantic female figure in the audience, I will argue, suggests a profound ideological move that the novel as a genre makes in the early nineteenth century.

CHAPTER SIX

"For Our English Eyes"

Regendering Ethnic Performance in the Novel

A MAJOR PARADIGM shift in the representation of ethnic identity occurred early in the nineteenth century: the depiction of ethnic identity moved from the caricaturing of the male other in the eighteenth- and early nineteenth-century theater, to the romantic representation of the female other in the nineteenth-century novel. As we have seen in the course of this book, the eighteenth-century's stage portraits were virtually always male. During a period of extraordinary social mobility, when the metropole (in the eyes of many of the English) was overrun with Scots, Jews, and the Irish, the male ethnic stage figure was a way of responding to a kind of ethnic panic, frequently expressed by representing English womanhood plagued by ethnic fortune hunters and seducers. The nineteenth-century novel inverted this paradigm in a series of important cross-ethnic romantic pairings, often written by women authors.[1] The ethnic woman—Glorvina, Flora, Rebecca, Mirah—entered the cultural imagination of Britain, and the love plots of the novel began to focus on cross-ethnic romance, in both *Belinda* and *Harrington* (as I have shown), and perhaps most famously in Walter Scott's *Ivanhoe*, where the romantic attraction between Ivanhoe and Rebecca is finally disallowed, but not before Scott has produced the first sufficiently celebrated Jewish female character to challenge Shakespeare's Jessica. There are many other examples: Horatio and Glorvina in Owenson's *The Wild Irish Girl* (in many ways the prototype of this tradition), Waverley and Flora MacIvor in Scott's *Waverley*, Tancred and Eva in Benjamin Disraeli's *Tancred* (1847), and Daniel and Mirah later in the century in George Eliot's *Daniel Deronda* (1876). Even Germaine de Staël's widely influential *Corinne, or Italy* (1807) brings together Lord Nelvil and

163

Corinne according to this pattern. In such examples, the English male hero is attracted to a "foreign" woman in a plot that is typically configured as a kind of (male) ethnographic study of (female) ethnic difference that introduces the hero to another, alien culture.[2] Waverley's exploration of the Scottish Highlands, for example, fuses with his fascination with Flora, and Deronda's interest in Mirah, he admits, forces him to confront for the first time the question of anti-Semitism, and hence he wanders through ghettoes, visits synagogues, buys Jewish books, and studies Hebrew grammar, as a means of reeducating himself (and courting Mirah).

This new emphasis on the ethnic other as woman in the early nineteenth-century novel encounters its own set of theatrical dangers. For example, in exploring the performative act of sympathetic identification, the novelists in this tradition ask whether or not it is possible to disentangle the threads of identification—sympathizing with the other, becoming the other, and mastering the other. Is putting oneself in the place of the other through sympathy a form of displacing the other through mastery? Similarly, many of these novelists focus on the obsessive desire of the English male hero to reproduce the female other through representation, in a sense to re-author her. In other words, the sympathetic identification with the female other in such cases often merges with the attempt at mastering her through copying her. The foreign woman in such plots is in danger of becoming nothing but spectacle, the object of the hegemonic gaze, an object of study and subjugation for the English hero, and therefore in danger of becoming simply another form of the theatricalized ethnic other.

These novelists use a theatrical model most clearly by casting the English hero in the role of spectator. With a father who was used to playing stage Irishmen both for English and for Irish audiences, Owenson uses patently theatrical situations in *The Wild Irish Girl* to explain how the power dynamics and cultural differences between the Irish and the English are negotiated, particularly focusing on the Irish (woman) as the object of the English (male) gaze. As in *Harrington*, the young English hero is prejudiced in youth by his reading: in Owenson's novel the hero reports that "the barbarity of the Irish . . . fastened so strongly on my boyish imagination"[3] through the reading of books about Ireland. And both novels are first-person narratives, locating the English male spectator as the central position from which everything is observed. Edgeworth and Owenson were writing for a foreign audience[4]—that is, for English readers—and used the English hero's perspective to copy English attitudes (that is, English prejudices) and to demonstrate the process by which those prejudices could be uprooted.

Early in Owenson's novel the English hero is cast in the role of spectator not at the theater but at a Catholic mass. This scene anticipates several similar novelistic scenes of spectatorship in which the English Protestant hero enters a house of different religious worship—a Catholic church in *Corinne* and a synagogue in *Harrington* and later in *Daniel Deronda*. All four scenes suggest the ways in which the hero's encounter with religious difference is experienced as a kind of theatrical spectacle. In Edgeworth's novel, the theatricality of the scene is most fully realized when a figure dressed up to look like the Jewish figure that terrified Harrington when he was a child makes its appearance; the synagogue, reduced to stage craft and stage effect for the English Protestant spectator, simply becomes an extension of the scene in which he sees the frightening Shylock on the London stage, only here in the synagogue he does not have Berenice to demystify the theatrical figure.

In Owenson's novel, Horatio has his first glimpse of the Irish heroine during her observance of the Catholic mass with her father. With the ruined cloisters of a chapel in a ruined castle, the Prince dressed in "the ancient costume of the Irish nobles" (*WIG*, 47) as if he were in a play, the oddity of the nurse as if modeled by "the genius of masquerade" (*WIG*, 49), otherness is consistently defined as theatrical spectacle. The scene is dominated, like the episode in the theater in *Harrington*, by the male spectator's attempts to observe the exotic heroine. The hero describes himself, like the gathered peasants, as a mere member of the audience, "straining my eyes" (*WIG*, 46) to see the figures of the Prince and his daughter as they enter the chapel. But the face of the heroine consistently eludes him: "Not once was the face turned round," and even "when I shifted my position, the envious veil intercepted the ardent glance" (*WIG*, 48–49). The shifting of the male hero's position in both *Harrington* and *The Wild Irish Girl* records the shifting of the dominant, Anglocentric position in relation to the ethnic minority; the face of the foreign woman is at first hidden from view, and then only by degrees revealed and observed, in an allegory about knowing the other. The religious service, heightened by the ethereal nature of the heroine and the grandeur of her princely father, works its power on the hero-spectator: "What a religion is this! . . . how seducingly it speaks to the senses. . . . What a captivating, what a *picturesque* faith! Who would not become its proselyte, were it not for the stern opposition of reason—the cold suggestions of philosophy!" (*WIG*, 50). In both novels, then, the theatrical spectacle works on the English Protestant spectator by bringing him to the edge of conversion, a trope for the radical completeness of sympathetic identification: Harrington feels like a Jew in the theater (as we saw), and Horatio imagines becoming a proselyte of Catholicism, even fantasizing being the Prince of Inismore ("I . . . almost wished I had been born the Lord of these beautiful ruins" [*WIG*, 52]).

The pedagogic project in both *Harrington* and *The Wild Irish Girl*—the removal of the ethnic and religious prejudices of the English hero—is always at least partially vitiated by the objectification and the eroticization of the ethnic other. In the course of Owenson's novel the hero's English Protestant ego is reasserted through his controlling male gaze; though an outsider at the mass, he soon penetrates to the inside of this community and begins on a course of absorbing and incorporating Ireland into his own vision. So, while these novels succeed in eschewing the caricature of the male ethnic stereotype, they at the same time explore the ways in which the female ethnic other becomes spectacle, a theatricalized object on view for an English male audience. From his first partial viewing of the Irish heroine, the English hero in *The Wild Irish Girl* is consistently defined through his position as spectator. So, the scene in which Horatio watches Glorvina unobserved in the theater of the ruined cloister is followed by a scene in which he is clearly cast as a peeping Tom: on seeing that her casement is open in the evening, he climbs a wall in order to get "a perfect view of the interior of that apartment" (*WIG*, 52). His punishment for this act of scopophilia occurs when he falls and seriously injures himself, becoming entirely dependent on Glorvina and her father. Injured, he enters her domestic space under an alias, in disguise, anticipating a similar act of ethnic spying when Deronda under false pretenses intrudes on the Cohen family's pawnshop, even to the point of interrupting the Jewish Sabbath. While calling another character an "arch spy" (*WIG*, 133), Horatio himself becomes the chief spy in the novel, time and again observing the heroine while unobserved, even deliberately hiding himself from view.

In these novels the English hero consistently walks the fine line between ethnographer and spy, and typically enters the minority culture disguised. Horatio disguises himself as an "itinerant artist" who has come to Ireland "to take views, and seize some of the finest features of its landscapes" (*WIG*, 55–56): the artist who "takes" and "seizes" repeats, at the level of spectatorship and representation, the conquest of Ireland that his ancestors accomplished when they literally seized and took this castle from the Prince's forebears. His entrance into the virgin world of Glorvina is a kind of rape ("I had penetrated thus far into this remote corner" [*WIG*, 56]), and his role as unobserved spectator in the novel consistently functions almost as a kind of sexual violation: "Those precious moments . . . gave her to my view" (*WIG*, 65). His disguise as an artist in this way predicts his symbolic mastery, through the powers of representation, of both the Irish landscape (mythologized into the "picturesque" for the tourist) and the Irish heroine. In fact, Ireland and its erotic embodiment, Glorvina, typically fuse in the novel. To know Ireland through knowing Glorvina sweetens the pedagogic and ethnographic projects, and thereby marks in such plots the pure functionality of the ethnic heroine, diminished into an object of study: "I am merely interested for this girl on a philosophical principle. I long to study the purely national, natural character of an Irishwoman" (*WIG*, 65); "and even this little Irish girl, with all her witcheries, is to me a subject of philosophical analysis" (*WIG*, 132).

The artist-hero, hired to instruct Glorvina in drawing, actually copies her on the sly. He exclaims in triumph, "I took her likeness" (*WIG*, 97), "the countenance of Glorvina . . . I have most happily caught" (*WIG*, 101). While she remains "unconscious of my observation" (*WIG*, 97), he draws her when she thinks he is drawing the castle, so again the ethnic woman is unwittingly observed, and here not just observed but also "caught" and copied. Similarly, the Englishman manages to transform through his hidden gaze those scenes in which she seems to be performing for herself or for her father into scenes in which she performs for him. On the one hand, the artist's reproduction of the young woman instead of the ruined castle suggests a focus on the vitality of the current nation as opposed to its tragic past. On the other hand, the scene suggests that Glorvina is like Clarence's Virginia in *Belinda*, the colonized other, held captive and reproduced in a portrait meant to serve the fancy of the English male hero. In *Daniel Deronda*, the same idea surfaces when Hans paints and thereby reproduces Mirah as the biblical Berenice, and he and Deronda argue over the ethics of making such portraits, especially without Mirah's knowledge. In all three cases, the exotic woman seems all surface and image, reproduced in the erotic service of the visual imagination of the Englishman.

In Owenson's novel, when Horatio reveals to the heroine the drawing he has made of her, we again have a scene of triangular representation: "Looking over my shoulder, she beheld not the ruins of her castle, but a striking likeness of her blooming self" (*WIG*, 100). Just as Mrs. Ormond tries to read the book over the shoulder of Virginia, Glorvina tries to read the picture over the shoulder of Horatio. But while in the former case Mrs. Ormond tries to awaken Virginia from dwelling in the fantasy romance on which Clarence has modeled her, Horatio is happy to see Glorvina mesmerized by the portrait he has made of her. Hero and heroine gaze not at the real woman but at her reproduction, at what *Belinda* calls "the slaves of art"—the woman reproduced by the English hero as exotic other to serve his erotic interests. The ethnic other seems divided from herself literally by having the English male artist stand between her and the portrait he has made of her; in this way he doubly mediates the view of her that she sees. Supposed to be the antidote to the books that prejudiced him against the Irish, to be the empirical thing-in-itself, Glorvina ironically becomes another form of representation, authored by him. Whereas in the triangular scene of representation in *Harrington* the English hero's observation of the play through the eyes of Berenice exposes the difference between the original and the copy of ethnic identity, here in Owenson's novel the hero's and even the heroine's eyes are riveted on the representation, on the copy, of ethnic identity. In this way the scene of triangulated representation becomes a scene not of demystification but of interpellation: the English hero uses the mediating form of representation to incorporate the Irish heroine into his fantasy of her.

In this scene we learn that Glorvina copied his face on the day he arrived, so these copies—his copy of her, her copy of him—are meant to function, at least in part, as a kind of mutual education in difference as the English hero and the Irish heroine attempt to understand each other. Along these lines, she and her priest educate him in Irish manners, customs, and language. Like Deronda sitting up at night studying a Hebrew grammar after meeting Mordecai, Owenson's English hero reports that he is "deep in the study of the language, history, and antiquities of this ancient nation" (*WIG*, 88). And Glorvina teaches him the Irish language by making him a sort of copyist: "Glorvina . . . makes me repeat some short poem or song after her, that I may catch the pronunciation (which is almost unattainable), then translates them into English, which I word for word write down" (*WIG*, 89). Like Staël, Owenson (called "the Irish de Staël")[5] makes her heroine the spokeswoman for the culture of her nation, introducing the English hero to the antiquities of Ireland in the same way that Corinne introduces Lord Nelvil to the antiquities of Rome. It is through the beautiful foreign woman that the Englishman might learn of a culture besides his own and give up his prejudices. To love the ethnic female other is to love the vast array of aesthetic and cultural objects that her culture has produced: it is a project based on the confusion between an individual woman and an entire culture.

On one level, Glorvina sees translation as a porous border that allows a limited form of access between different cultures; she happily reads Macpherson's English translations of Ossian, for example, and produces translations of Irish poems for Horatio's lessons. On another level, she warns the English hero: "Let me, however, assure you, that no adequate version of an Irish poem can be given; for the peculiar construction of the Irish language, the felicity of its epithets, and force of its expressions, bid defiance to translation" (*WIG*, 92). The untranslatability of Irish is the novel's most direct attempt to focus the special and unassimilable features of Ireland on its language, and thereby to counteract the comical dialect of the stage Irishman, invented by the English for English audiences. The scenes of Glorvina at her harp singing Irish songs, for example, are meant to function as the theatrical antidote to the caricatured stage Irishman speaking in dialect, producing bulls in his brogue. The untranslatability of Irish, whether in Horatio's language lessons or in Glorvina's songs, locates the Irish language not simply beyond the ken of Englishmen but beyond the possibility of caricature: it is the unreachable, untranslatable, incomprehensible sublime, at the farthest remove—geographically and linguistically—from the dialect of the London stage Irishman. In fact, Glorvina's Gaelic songs copy the strategy her father used in interrupting the comical dialect of the stage Irishman by breaking into Gaelic song and speaking in his own native language when on stage—a performance strategy for which he was severely criticized.[6] The untranslatable Gaelic is also explicitly placed in antithesis to what Horatio confesses is the typical Englishman's experience of Irish music, namely, "the false medium of comic airs, sung by some popular actor" on the English stage (*WIG*, 72).

But while the English stage fails entirely in conveying the music of Ireland, the novel has its own way of not caricaturing this music but dulling it, representing it only to silence it. In some sense, the novel is at a distinct disadvantage to live performance from the beginning; able only to report speech and song, it is always a transcription, a silent representation, and can never equal those moments in the theater when Robert Owenson sang aloud in Gaelic from the stage, both constituting a native Irish community and alienating the Anglo-Irish ascendancy. Horatio's obsessive use of the power of his gaze as an artist consistently succeeds in transforming Glorvina's live performances at the harp into static scenes of the picturesque, and his reproduction of her through the medium of the visual in effect silences her. Noting the harp as "an instrument singularly picturesque" (*WIG*, 98), he proceeds to capture Glorvina: "That beautifully pensive expression which touches the countenance of Glorvina, when breathing her native strains, I have most happily caught; and her costume, attitude, and harp, form as happy a combination of traits, as a single portrait perhaps ever presented" (*WIG*, 101). She becomes part of a visual composition; she is frozen in time, speechless, voiceless, part of a picturesque image. Moreover, just as Horatio obsessively works at his drawings, she begins to neglect her harp in favor of her pencil: "The pencil is never out of her hand; her harp lies silent, and her drawing-book is scarcely ever closed" (*WIG*, 86). The silent harp is the symbol of the ways in which Horatio obsessively translates the aural into the visual, and the ways in which Glorvina moves from being a live (Irish) performer to a model for picturesque portraits by an (English) artist. With the silencing of her harp, the traditional symbol of Irish nationalism,[7] Glorvina becomes the object and inspiration of the English hero's representational powers.[8] In this sense *The Wild Irish Girl* represents the triumph of the English male gaze; for Horatio, sight is everything, the source of all his power, the means to a new conquest of Ireland made possible by representation. In fact, the English narrator's reliance on sight lies in marked contrast to that of the blind Gaelic bard: "He never regretted the loss of sight, but used gayly [*sic*] to say, 'my eyes are only transplanted into my ears'" (*WIG*, 89, n. 3). The insistence on the English male gaze in Owenson's novel sidesteps the failure of the ear to comprehend the foreign tongue by translating everything Irish into the universal system of visual apprehension—that is, mastery through the eye/I of the English first-person narrator.

Moreover, the final validation of Glorvina as a suitable love object for the English hero occurs through the anglicization of her language—that is, through the distance she stands from the Irish language in any of its forms. This shows the dilemma of trying to escape the dialect of the stage Irishman by producing its opposite: the binary of Irish representation simply produces the other side of the caricatured dialect of the stage Irishman in the entirely anglicized speech of Glorvina. Horatio responds to his friend, the Englishman who functions as the final arbiter of the acceptability of Glorvina and Irishness, "You ask me if I am not disgusted with her brogue? If she had one, I doubt not but I should; but the accent to which we English apply that term, is here generally confined to the lower orders of society; and I certainly believe, that purer and more grammatical English is spoken generally through Ireland, than in any part of England whatever; for here you are never shocked by the barbarous and unintelligible dialect peculiar to each shire in England" (*WIG*, 132). The passage recycles one of the standard ripostes of the day, namely, that the Irish peasant spoke better English than regional Englishmen (caricatured in the Yorkshire clown of the London stage), thus making English—not Irish—the standard language by which speech is measured, in Ireland as well as England. So, instead of authenticating Irish speech patterns (along the lines of the Edgeworths' *Essay on Irish Bulls*), Horatio validates Glorvina by claiming perfect English for her: "Her English, grammatically correct, and elegantly pure, is spoken with an accent that could never denote her country" (*WIG*, 132). Sanitized of any trace of the brogue, her English bears no sign of Irish.

In these ways the untranslatability of the Irish language—and the Englishman's attempt to "master" "this wreck of ancient dialect" (*WIG*, 88)—is sidestepped in what amounts to a wholesale translation of all things Irish into English. I mean here that the untranslatability of Irish becomes the corollary of the basic narrative structure of the entire novel. Because the novel is told in English in the first person, we are continually reminded of the one-sidedness of the narrative, its peculiar distance and difference from the Irish world it attempts to "seize" and "capture," its valorization of its own language world, the world of English. The English hero explains that in the art lessons he gives the heroine he is "a pedagogue master": "I guide her hand," he says (*WIG*, 97), but in effect he controls not only the pencil with which she sketches but also the pencil with which he, in the course of the narrative, sketches the Irish heroine and everything Irish. So, the first-person narration locks the reader into the English perspective; Horatio's narration mediates Irishness, through his own English eyes and ears, for an English reader. In this sense the entire narrative of the novel is no more than the Englishman's entirely subjective sketch of Irish culture; the words of his narrative produce a "mimic copy" (*WIG*, 53) parallel to the copy he makes of her when he sketches her. Reducing everything to an "enchanting picture," a "finished . . . picture," the narrator admits the failure of his narration: "But how cold—how inanimate—how imperfect this description!" (*WIG*, 52–53). His translation of Glorvina, alive and singing at her harp, into a static image is a microcosm of what the narrative in general does; her voice cannot be heard, and we "see" and "hear" her only through his reportage, his narration, his English.[9] In this way the novel stands in stark contrast to Edgeworth's *Castle Rackrent*, where untranslatability is dealt with in another way, in allowing the first-person narrator to be a native Irish speaker: as Edgeworth explains in her preface, "To those who are totally unacquainted with Ireland, the following Memoirs will perhaps be scarcely intelligible. . . . The editor . . . had it once in contemplation to translate the language of Thady into plain English; but Thady's idiom is incapable of translation."[10]

The extent to which the text is an English translation, or complete absorption, of Irishness is demonstrated when the scene in which he sketches Glorvina shows her copying the picture he has made of her castle—that is, "copying . . . the imitation" (*WIG*, 97) the English artist has made of the Irish landscape. She reproduces her own immediate world not directly but through the copy that the English artist has made of it, copying his copy of Ireland, in a kind of allegory of the way in which the English (and perhaps even the Irish) know Ireland only through English eyes: "Ireland" circulates as an English fantasy. She even tells him, "You must guide my hand" (*WIG*, 97). In one of Edgeworth's Irish novels, an Englishwoman explains that the Irish attempt to recreate Ireland "for our reception, and for our English eyes."[11] Glorvina is enlisted—she enlists herself—in perpetuating the English picturesque tradition of copying the Irish landscape. In his search for genuine womanhood, earlier in the novel the hero dismisses "servile copies, sketched by the finger of art" (*WIG*, 65), but in such scenes Glorvina becomes a servile copy sketched by his artist's fingers, and even a servile copier of his copy of her own landscape.[12]

Like Virginia in *Belinda*, Glorvina is Rousseau's "child of Nature" (*WIG*, 151) in danger of becoming a slave of art, both as the artist's subject and the artist's pupil. In fact, Horatio's schooling of Glorvina in French novels and romances follows in the footsteps of Edgeworth's Clarence. Horatio gives her Rousseau's *Julie, or the New Heloise* (1761) and St. Pierre's *Paul and Virginia*, in what looks like the hero's direct critique of Edgeworth's *Belinda*, almost as if Horatio expects to succeed with Glorvina where Clarence failed with Virginia: "Let our English novels carry away the prize of morality from the romantic fictions of every other country; but you will find they rarely seize on the imagination through the medium of the heart; and as for their heroines, I confess that though they are the most perfect of beings, they are also the most stupid" (*WIG*, 144). In this way Horatio attempts a kind of seduction of the Irish heroine by enlisting her identification with the French heroines Julie and Virginia, and to aid in this complete identification he speaks to Glorvina in the exact words of Rousseau's St. Preux (*WIG*, 171). Rejoicing in the fact that "her days and nights are devoted to the sentimental sorcery of Rousseau" (*WIG*, 148–49)—the sorcery of books that *Belinda* warns against—"I perceived her lost over a book" (*WIG*, 144). In this way he attempts to remake the wild Irish girl into a heroine of French romance.[13] The master-pedagogue masters her not directly but through a triangular structure in which she is made to serve books and pictures at his direction. In all the ways I have noted, the Irish heroine seems caught in the nets of representation, always serving and performing for English eyes—a fact that became ironically true for the author herself, when she confessed about her reception in England: "I was treated . . . in character with the habits of a 'wild Irish girl.' So there I sat, the lioness of the night, exhibited and shown off."[14] The wild Irish girl has no function for Londoners other than to be exhibited, to be stared at, to function as a theatrical sideshow, in effect set beside the stage Irishman.

The marriage between Glorvina and Horatio in the end clearly signals England's Act of Union with Ireland, which was approvingly figured at the time as a marriage between two distinct races, but which was criticized in widely disseminated political prints that represented the Union as England's rape of Ireland, or at least as the sexual conquest of Hibernia; Maria Edgeworth, for example, wrote to her aunt, "There is a political print just come out, of a woman, meant for Hibernia, dressed in orange and green, and holding a pistol in her hand to oppose the Union."[15] Owenson's novel apparently ends with the conventional happy marriage between the two families, the two races, and the two religions, in a celebration of union/Union. But the successful climax of Owenson's novel is so overstated (in the words of Horatio's father) that the erasure of difference, rather than its cooperative coexistence, seems the goal: "Let the names of Inismore and M—— be inseparably blended, and the distinctions of English and Irish, of protestant and catholic, for ever buried" (*WIG*, 250). This ending is predicated on a series of highly symbolic reaffiliations that conclude the novel. In the end Horatio's father sees himself as Glorvina's "father" (*WIG*, 244, 247), while Glorvina's father sees Horatio as a "son," with Horatio acknowledging, "From your hands I seemed to have received a new existence" (*WIG*, 221). By remaking Horatio's father into Glorvina's father and Glorvina's father into Horatio's father, the conclusion seems to erase familial and ethnic difference, so that exogamy does not simply become endogamy—it threatens to become incest. In the enthusiasm for the happy union and climax, difference is simply eradicated.

The Irishwoman's instrumentality in this climax is clear. Orphaned at the end, and flanked by two powerful Englishmen, "sunk on her knees between the father and the son" (*WIG*, 239), betrothed to one and at the last minute suddenly given to the other, Glorvina becomes purely instrumental in the plots of the Englishmen. She has already been given away by her Irish father to the English father: "Take my child," the Prince had told Horatio's father, as he "placed the hand of his daughter in mine, confirming the gift" (*WIG*, 249). And then the English father turns over the hand of the Irishwoman to his English son. After all, the earl's goal all along has been based on ancestral guilt, and he has recognized the instrumentality of the Prince's daughter as a solution to his family's past crimes against Ireland: he has been motivated by the idea of "retributing the parent through the medium of the child" (*WIG*, 247). The foreign woman is typically instrumental at a number of levels in this novelistic tradition: she is the daughter of a father, the representative of an oppressed race, the beloved of a conquering race. In other words, her role is thoroughly symbolic; she is a means to an end, a "medium" or mediator, and as such typically loses her own individual identity.[16]

It is therefore fitting that the text ends by returning to the voice of the father, the English patriarch, who encloses the world of *The Wild Irish Girl* by writing the first and last letters. Here at the end, the letter is read aloud by another father figure, Father John, to the children Glorvina and Horatio—though the letter is addressed to Horatio alone, closing the Irish heroine out of the correspondence. The final performance of the novel, then, imagines not the voice of the wild Irish girl at her harp but rather the voice of the father, the voice of English patriarchal power. In short, the final performance of the novel is the authorization of the English father's voice in a letter to his English son. In closing the novel with the English father's voice, Owenson's novel is in marked contrast to those Irish tales of Edgeworth's that close with a letter written in Irish dialect, so that ethnic and linguistic differences are at least voiced and not translated into standard English.[17] At the end the English father in Owenson's novel, while giving Horatio instructions on how to play the role of *"English landholder"* among the Irish, warns that he is "not placed by despotism over a band of slaves" (*WIG*, 250) but forgets to warn the young man who has posed and functioned throughout his sojourn in Ireland as an artist that he should not make of the Irish people slaves of art. In a novel so overburdened with quotation, with footnotes, with allusion, with a variety of discursive and narrative modes, the wild Irish girl—literally veiled in the end (*WIG*, 238, 242, 249), as she was in our first glimpse of her—struggles to emerge from behind the veil of representation, so that in the end *The Wild Irish Girl* seems in effect to marry political and aesthetic conquest—that is, to underscore the mutually constitutive dangers of both forms of slavery.

With a traveling English hero and a beautiful, harp-playing heroine in the peripheries, *Waverley* directly responds to the questions raised by *The Wild Irish Girl*. But Scott's Highland heroine attempts to forestall and even prevent what occurs in *The Wild Irish Girl*, namely, the attempt at every point to incorporate minority culture, to catch it and seize it, to translate it and anglicize it. Flora consistently functions to suggest the ways in which Highland culture is closed to the English hero, especially through her successful resistance not simply to Waverley's romantic illusions about her but also to her brother Fergus's machinations to use her to snare Waverley for the Jacobite cause. She refuses to become the symbol for the easy reconciliation between England and Highland Scotland by rejecting an easy marriage with the Englishman that would either convert him to the Highland cause or subsume her in the hegemonic culture. In this way Flora guards the ethnic and cultural border rather than redrawing or erasing it.

These differences with *The Wild Irish Girl* are made all the more palpable by the way in which Scott does in fact follow the formula of the model. In *Waverley* once again the hero is English, and once again his encounter with a peripheral culture is mediated by his encounter with a beautiful, exotic woman. As in all these novels, he has been misled by books, by "that internal sorcery"[18] of the library that both Edgeworth and Owenson acknowledge. But Scott shrewdly alters this paradigm by having Waverley not so much prejudiced against the Highlands as mesmerized by romantic illusions of adventures in an exotic world, making him particularly susceptible to romanticizing rather than demonizing the other culture, but nonetheless incorporating it into his own private vision. The novel highlights the ways in which, even in his encounters with the two Scottish heroines (Flora and Rose), it is various texts that continue to mediate, define, and redefine ethnic difference for him. Finally, acknowledging Waverley's sentimental reading[19] and what I have called the dangers of private reading, I will analyze the various ways, some more legitimate than others, in which ethnicity is theatricalized in *Waverley*. While Scott was a critic of the stereotypical "Sawnies" regularly represented on the London stage, he brilliantly locates theatricality at the heart of ethnic culture and understands the varied theatrical ways in which insiders and outsiders attempt to perform, share, and reproduce ethnic culture. So thoroughly is theatricality at the center of his novel, I will suggest that while critics have understood Flora as a performing heroine,[20] it is in fact Waverley's role as a performing hero that takes us to the novel's deepest strategies and meanings.

Like Horatio's first glimpse of the Prince and his daughter at a Catholic mass, Waverley's first glimpse of Highland life situates him as an outsider and a spectator at a highly theatricalized communal event in the chapter entitled "A Highland Feast." He is defined from the beginning as an outsider, as "the English stranger," whose reaction to the screaming of the bagpipes, the "clang of the Celtic tongue," and the "Babel of noises" was so strong that he "dreaded his ears would never recover" (*W*, 96–97). He watches and listens as the family bard performs in a language he does not understand: the Celtic verses sought "to lament the dead, to apostrophize the absent, to exhort and entreat and animate those who were present" (*W*, 98). First, the verses act across time and space: they include those dead and alive, here and elsewhere, past and present, "young and old" (*W*, 103). Second, the verses have a direct and powerful effect on the members of the audience, even inciting them to a kind of participation, which further fuels the bard: "The ardour of the poet appeared to communicate itself to the audience . . . ; all bent forwards towards the reciter, many sprung up and waved their arms in ecstacy. . . . When the song ceased, there was a deep pause, while the aroused feelings of the poet and of the hearers gradually subsided"

(*W*, 98). The emphasis on the union of performer and audience, on the interaction between them, on the ecstasy shared among them, suggests the way in which the performance of the verses defines, shapes, and constitutes membership in this Highland community. The clan community is defined through interactive performance and knows itself by recognizing itself in the verses, in the family bard, in the fellow members of the audience. The English stranger witnesses a shared cultural experience that is open to its members but closed to outsiders. While Waverley seeks to have the performance unlocked for him by a commentator—that additional reader or spectator who can correctly read the text or performance—this scene locks the stranger out and proceeds without him. The scene is an important demonstration of how representation works inside an ethnic community. The performance of the verses by and for the ethnic community stands in striking contrast to the representation of ethnic identity staged by an ethnic insider specifically for an outsider.

This contrast is realized when this scene of communal performance is followed, two chapters later in "Highland Minstrelsy," by the set piece of Flora's performance for Waverley alone. In the earlier scene, the performance occurs in the original language for the Highland community; in the later scene, it occurs in a translation for a foreigner. Even Fergus, who later will understand how to use Flora and the romantic illusions of Waverley to enlist him in the Jacobite cause, makes fun of Waverley's interest here: "Captain Waverley is a worshipper of the Celtic muse, not the less so perhaps that he does not understand a word of her language" (*W*, 102). Through Waverley's encounter with Flora, Scott sets the limits of cross-ethnic identification and interrogates the kinds of romantic identification and projection that simply co-opt ethnic difference. Flora immediately establishes Waverley's position, reminding him of his outsider status: "You know how little these verses can possibly interest an English stranger, even if I could translate them" (*W*, 102–3). In this way the foreign woman meets the Englishman on the grounds of cultural difference, in a negotiation about cultural texts and artifacts, forms of representation. Flora provides the English hero not simply with a performance but with a series of clues on how to listen, how to read, how to appreciate, though she is consistently skeptical of his understanding. She provides, then, not only text but also commentary, in much the same way that Staël's Corinne introduces Lord Nelvil to the antiquities of Rome at the same time that she understands that his English heart will be closed in so many ways to these foreign objects. Moreover, Flora supplies the kind of critical commentary in person, in a theatrical performance, that Waverley lacked when in the privacy of his uncle's library he read of heroes and their adventures.

Before Flora agrees to recite the verses, she issues several warnings. She will be able to provide only "a rude English translation" (*W*, 104), only "my imperfect translation" (*W*, 106), and perhaps the sharpest warning of all: not only will the merit of the verses "evaporate in translation," they will—perhaps even more important—"be lost to those who do not sympathise with the feelings of the poet" (*W*, 103). So, even in translation Waverley is liable to be locked outside of this performance because he is not a member of the community and does not share its beliefs. The irony of this scene focuses on the misdirection of Waverley's sympathetic identification, toward the beauty of Flora rather than the Jacobite cause and Highland values encoded in the verses Flora sings. Flora's commentary keeps distancing Waverley from the text and the performance; in effect, she interrupts and complicates the simple reception of the song through her warning commentaries. If Glorvina willingly allows Horatio to be swept away with romantic illusions by her performance of Celtic verses in *The Wild Irish Girl*, Flora is a much chillier performer, with no interest in Waverley's romantic projections and with an understanding of what in fact is at stake in entering fully into the performance of the verses—namely, a cultural and political commitment that would radically alter his identity. All of these distancing devices—Waverley's outsider status; his ignorance of the language and customs of the Highlanders; Fergus's mockery of his enthusiasm; Flora's imperfect translation and her multiple warnings; the artificial, staged performance for a single listener—are signs that secure rather than breach the boundary between Highlander and Englishman, and remind us of the different performance that unites the Highland listeners earlier in "A Highland Feast."

While the effect of Flora's sung verses is incomplete in converting Waverley to the Highland cause—at least in part due to her critical warnings and her repeated rejection of his attentions—the effect of Flora's own written verses later in the novel moves Waverley a further step toward accepting the plaid. This is so precisely because her verses arrive without her commentary, without her warnings, and even without her knowledge. It is Fergus who sends Flora's lines of verse to Waverley; unable to persuade his sister to manipulate Waverley into joining their cause, Fergus nonetheless succeeds in using her by using her verses. Since Fergus's direct entreaties to Waverley seem to fail, he enlists the powers of representation to mediate the distance between Highlander and Englishman, without the aid of commentator or author. While Flora's verses lead to an important scene that demonstrates the dangers of Waverley's private reading, they first show that Flora herself has been the victim of sentimental and uncritical reading. Fergus has explained that "since she could spell an English book, she has been in love with the memory of the gallant Captain Wogan" (*W*, 133), so Flora herself has been interpellated through books to believe in sacrificing everything, including one's life, to the Jacobite cause. Hence, Flora has become the woman "who will never love mortal man" (*W*, 254). She is in love, like *Belinda*'s Virginia, with a phantom, a book's portrait; and while she does not pine away in indolence for her phantom lover like Virginia, she sacrifices all pleasures, and all potential lovers, for a ghost.

Reading about Captain Wogan inspires Flora herself to enter the realm of representation by writing verses about the fallen hero, and it is these that Fergus sends to Waverley. Waverley's sentimental reading of these verses in private recalls two earlier scenes. First, in a revision of the scene in which the power of verse activates the martial spirit of the Highlanders in "A Highland Feast," Fergus hopes to use Flora's verses to activate the same spirit in the English stranger—these are verses written in English, not by the family bard but by the Chief's beautiful sister, and so they can speak directly to Waverley. Second, in a revision of the scene in which Flora's song is accompanied by critical commentary and discussion, Flora's verses are read by Waverley without the benefit of her distancing commentary. So, theatrical, public performance in both of the earlier scenes is replaced here with private reading, allowing Waverley to indulge all his romantic illusions with no one to correct them.

Fergus's brilliant move to win Waverley through the powerful mediating force of Flora's verses has its desired effect: "Whatever might be the real merit of Flora Mac-Ivor's poetry, the enthusiasm which it intimated was well calculated to make a corresponding impression upon her lover. The lines were read—read again—then deposited in Waverley's bosom—then again drawn out, and read line by line, in a low and smothered voice, and with frequent pauses which prolonged the mental treat" (*W*, 148). The private act of reading allows Waverley (with no warnings from Flora) to make of the poem what he will, to read into it all the romance and adventure that he wishes. What he mistakes as a love poem to him actually is the reason she can never love him; in love with phantoms, with the ghostly past, no mortal lover will ever be her choice. By reading the verses aloud sotto voce, he enacts them, makes them his own by reciting them (instead of just reading them), a self-indulgent and narcissistic form of theatricality. At the same time, "this pantomime of affectionate enthusiasm" (*W*, 148) that he performs while reading is still a private act, not reaching an audience that can awaken him, interrogate him, correct him; instead, he is left to his private fantasies, performing his pantomime for himself. It is a fine demonstration of that "internal sorcery" of private reading—as opposed to public performance—against which the novel warns.

It therefore comes as no surprise that Scott, later in the novel, has the verses read a second time, this time in public, with a different meaning, and with Waverley as the audience, not the reader; in other words, the private letter and the verses it includes are triangulated by being opened to a second reader, who attempts to awaken Waverley from his illusory interpretation by providing a critical commentary. The letter and the verses are read by Major Melville as incriminating evidence: "I cannot but find some analogy between the enterprize I have mentioned and the exploit of Wogan, which the writer seems to expect you should imitate" (*W*, 158). The Major perfectly understands the process of identification (and Fergus's strategic use of it), recognizing that Wogan is being represented as a model for Waverley to copy—the Englishman who goes over to the Jacobite cause. In opening the private letter to a public reading, the Major discovers criminal writing and reading, not the private amours of the hero.

If Flora's brother uses her verse without her authorization and against her own purposes, she is given another opportunity to use verse to reorient Waverley away from herself and toward Rose. In addition, Waverley is given another opportunity, this time in public, to recite verses that will illuminate rather than obfuscate his relationship with Flora. I refer here to the scene in which Waverley, now wearing the plaid, reads Shakespeare aloud. In moving from the performing heroine (Flora singing Celtic verses) to the performing hero (Waverley reciting Shakespeare) Scott moves as well from the family bard of the Highlanders to the national bard of England, and from a homogenous Highland audience to a Scottish audience that is divided along geographic and ideological lines. In this scene, performance will define and constitute not a single Highland clan but significant divisions within Scotland itself. Even before Waverley's performance the battle lines are drawn when national identity is negotiated in literary terms through a debate over "whether the Gaelic or Italian language was most liquid and best adapted for poetry" (*W*, 255): the debate splits along regional and nationalist lines, with the Highland ladies choosing the former, the Lowland ladies the latter. Then, when the group is asked to choose between Fergus performing on the flute or Waverley reading Shakespeare, Lowland Rose casts the deciding vote for the latter, and Waverley's English pride is pricked by Highland Flora's vote when, in irritation, he utters his ironic understatement to himself, "Shakspeare [*sic*] is worth listening to" (*W*, 256). The audience is then divided again, this time in its appreciation of Waverley's reading: "All the company applauded with their hands, and many with their tears" (*W*, 256), Flora among the former and Rose among the latter. The emphasis once again falls on the effect of the performance on the audience (as a way of constituting and differentiating between communities) and on the ways in which aesthetic and political interests intersect and affect reception. After all, Rose's reaction to Shakespeare recalls Waverley's earlier instruction of her—that is, "Edward's readiness to comment, to recite, to explain difficult passages" in the "best English poets, of every description, and other works on belles lettres" (*W*, 65). So, just as Flora has been the Englishman's instructress in Celtic poetry, Waverley has been the Lowland lady's instructor in English poetry, in scenes organized around questions of literary and nationalist assimilation and response. In this way the English hero's encounters with both Rose and Flora have been organized around the performance, interpretation, and reception of texts or cultural artifacts.

While Rose contributes her tears to Waverley's public reading, Flora becomes a textual commentator again, this time in settling a dispute about the English bard's play. So, while her absence as a commentator on her own verses is stressed earlier, she seizes the opportunity here to comment on Shakespeare's verses. When a debate ensues about "the levity with which the hero transfers his affection from Rosalind to Juliet" (*W*, 256), Flora delivers a textual commentary that is at the same time a personal lesson for Waverley on how to read and how to love. Flora argues about Romeo (and Waverley), "His love is at first fixed upon a woman who could afford it no return" (*W*, 256). Quoting the line about Rosalind (and herself), "She hath forsworn to love," Flora argues it was in fact wise of Romeo to transfer his affections, and Waverley, listening attentively, learns the lesson—this time articulated in a text in English—and decides to "resign my suit" (*W*, 257). In this way, Waverley's performance does not simply showcase the Englishman's talent for English poetry but also serves as a form of instruction, with the essential aid of Flora's commentary.

Here again an act of reading, because it is made public, becomes the center of conversation, debate, and finally instruction. The highly successful performance of Waverley in reading aloud several scenes from Shakespeare settles the preceding debate between Flora and Rose about whether Waverley's best talents lie on the battlefield or in the library (Flora pictures him writing and reciting verses to his beautiful wife). The scene makes clear that Waverley ultimately belongs on the domestic hearth of Rose rather than on the battlefield of rebellion that Flora admires. So, just as Henry Crawford's performance of Shakespeare in *Mansfield Park* becomes further evidence of how he is unfit for the antitheatrical heroine in Austen's novel, Waverley's performance becomes evidence of how he is an unfit suitor for Flora and a fit one for Rose. And while in *Mansfield Park* (published in the same year as *Waverley*) the theatricals threaten to confuse and even criminalize sexual relations, here they simplify and enlighten those relations, by moving Waverley away from Flora and toward Rose. Finally, Waverley redefines his romantic object—the anglicized Lowland heroine rather than the exotic Highland Flora—through the object of English national idolatry, through the national bard of England (even though it takes a Highland lady to help him understand the text's relevance to his own situation). After all, in the words of Henry Crawford, Shakespeare is "part of an Englishman's constitution."[21]

Before *Waverley* concludes it is the hero's fate to give one more performance after his public recital of Shakespeare. When Waverley, in disguise as Frank Stanley, met the real Frank Stanley, the young English nephew of Colonel Talbot, "the young student was inquisitive about Waverley's campaigns, and the manners of the Highlands, and Edward was obliged to satisfy his curiosity by whistling a pibroch, dancing a strathspey, and singing a Highland song" (*W*, 293). In one sense, Waverley lays aside one disguise for another in this scene, as he lays aside the mask of Stanley and puts on the mask of the Highlander. Whereas before he wore the plaid and fought alongside the Highlanders as "an adopted son" (*W*, 325), here he is merely copying Highland ways in a deliberate performance given by an Englishman for an Englishman to quench English curiosity. Waverley, the disciple tutored by Flora in Highland song, becomes a receptacle of Highland tradition, and replaces Flora by becoming the purveyor of Highland manners to the young English student. Here whistling, dancing, and singing, popular cultural forms, are ripped from the context of the lived experience of the Highlanders and put on display as a form of education. While they signify in one way within the community, they signify differently outside the community; as forms of representation they solidify the community itself, while here they become the exchange between two Englishmen, one with experience of Highland life, the other without. In this scene Highland life becomes mediated through and for English eyes, with one saving grace—Waverley at least has had first-hand experience of the culture he is copying and performing. The structure of this scene copies the narrative structure of Owenson's novel, in which the traveling Englishman reports to the uninitiated and ignorant Englishman at home about the minority culture, but because Scott's novel is not a first-person narrative it is not limited to this one (English) perspective.

From another angle, this theatrical performance of Highland culture balances Waverley's earlier performance of English culture through Shakespeare, and thereby points to the deeply theatrical structure of the entire narrative of Waverley's adventures, in which the hero tries on, sometimes quite literally, every mask and every vantage point that the novel comprehends. In this sense the novel is organized entirely around the performing hero, and theatrical performance becomes the primary access to other cultures. Given his own hybrid nature, with a Roman Catholic mother, a Jacobite uncle, and a father who supports the Hanoverian government, Waverley is not simply an unstable and fantastic waverer. He is the possessor of a hybrid identity that in fact realizes itself—its selves—by performing a wide variety of roles. He wears the Hanoverian uniform just as he wears the Highland plaid, and he is mistaken for a relative of Fergus's during the latter's trial, and is even taken for the Chevalier (*W*, 152) at one point, and toward the end of the novel he poses as a "surveyor" (*W*, 303). Late in the novel Colonel Talbot explicitly points to what amounts to only the most recent of Waverley's performances: "This youngster, Edward Waverley, alias Williams, alias Captain Butler, must continue to pass by his fourth *alias* of Francis Stanley, my nephew" (*W*, 292). Beyond all the literal terrains that Waverley traverses, the theatrical functions as a special symbolic space that opens up more than one point of view and thereby produces a kind of multiple consciousness; role-playing, as in Adam Smith's theatrical model, is the surest path to sympathy with another. In this light Waverley's theatrical cross-dressing is not the kind of caricatured cross-dressing that dominated the London stage—the Englishman playing the Sawney for other Englishmen. In fact, I am arguing that the caricaturing of Scottish identity through the stage Sawney is deliberately replaced here by a series of theatrical performances by the hero that move toward embracing and legitimizing multiple ethnic and cultural points of view.

In fact Waverley wavers insofar as he is a mirror of the characters he meets in a double sense: he mirrors their individual identities just as he mirrors their own shape-changing. He cross-dresses in a novel in which ethnic and class cross-dressings are encountered everywhere: Donald Bean Lean as the peddler, David Gelatly as the Baron, Callum Beg as a Lowland country groom, and so on. Ethnic and class identities are performative, at least in part because in the 1740s in Britain identities were in fact hybrid, and political allegiances were constantly shifting. Characters surprisingly have more than one identity, more than one language: Donald Bean Lean "laid aside his Highland dress" (*W*, 80) for his French army uniform, and old Janet, apparently understanding only Gaelic, suddenly communicates in Lowland Scots (*W*, 182). Scottish identity is reproduced in *Waverley* in no single, monological voice or caricature, and it is in this sense that Scott's goal was "to describe these persons, not by a caricatured and exaggerated use of the national dialect" (*W*, 341). The extraordinary multi-plication of spoken languages (Gaelic, Lowland Scots, French, the Cumberland dialect)[22] and hybrid identities that Waverley encounters are meant to compli-cate the stage dialect that characterized the typical, one-note Sawney. And just as Waverley's mother is Catholic, we recall that Fergus and Flora's mother is French, and while Waverley wears both the costume of the Hanoverian and the Highlander, so does Fergus, who once was in the employ of King George. Waverley in this way becomes a mirror of the identities around him, just as he looks at himself in the mirror in the famous scene in which he sees himself as himself and as Fergus (who announces, "My short green coat . . . will fit him exactly" [*W*, 197]). There is in *Waverley*, then, a kind of interchangeability of identities, in part because history is simply the accident that makes of us dif-ferent actors, different performers, "in this great and perilous drama" (*W*, 136) of the 'Forty-Five and the continuing invention and evolution of Great Britain. It is in this sense that Waverley's servant can comment to him, after the execu-tions of Fergus and Evan at the end, "It's a great pity of Evan Dhu, who was a very weel-meaning good-natured man, to be a Hielandman" (*W*, 329). In this light the events of *Waverley* are seen as the consequences of no more than the accidents of birth and the accidents of history. Similarly, the narrator comments early on, "Had Fergus Mac-Ivor lived sixty years sooner than he did, he would, in all probability, have wanted the polished manner and knowledge of the world which he now possessed; and had he lived sixty years later, his ambition and love of rule would have lacked the fuel which his situation now afforded" (*W*, 91–92). To make the point another way, Waverley's ancestors fought for the Stuarts, and Fergus's descendants would most likely be loyal Britons.

The movement of the hero through the various geographic and linguistic zones in *Waverley* has a dizzying and disorienting effect on both hero and reader that in the end is at least comprehensive if not always comprehensible, intended for English eyes but not always understood by English eyes. Even Edgeworth, herself a brilliant user of native dialects, confessed: "The novelty of the High-land world . . . is all new to us. . . . We are sensible that there is a peculiar merit in the work which is in a measure lost upon us, the *dialects* of the Highlanders, and the Lowlanders, &c. But there is another and a higher merit with which we are as much struck and as much delighted as any true born Scotchman could be."[23] The reader of standard English feels both confusion as well as conversion, as if in the end a "true born Scotchman." In a world in which political allegiances and national definitions are in constant flux, Waverley becomes the conduit for a variety of points of view—ethnic, aesthetic, cultural, regional, political, and so on. His role, like that of the reader, is to see all sides, to live all sides; this is the only way that the novel can accomplish its goal—"It is the object of this history to do justice to all men" (*W*, 171), even if history itself often fails in accomplishing such justice. I mean here that athwart the happy ending of the novel falls the shadow of "the butchery" (*W*, 329) that condemns Fergus and Evan to death. Both the trial and the execution function as political theater:[24] in the Hanoverian theater of (in)justice, the courtroom, Evan Dhu's powerful words spoken in dialect elicit "a sort of laugh" from the self-satisfied but uncomprehending "audience" (*W*, 320), while during Fergus's final subjection to the spectacle of imprisonment and execution he understands his role as actor: "'This is well GOT UP for a closing scene,' said Fergus, smiling disdainfully as he gazed around upon the apparatus of terror" (*W*, 327). In these climactic scenes Scott revises the comedy of the stage Sawney into the spectacle of the tragic end of the Highlanders.

Coda: "These Weeping Ladies in the Boxes at the Theatre"

By insistently picturing ethnicity through the beautiful, exoticized female in performance—Glorvina and Flora singing their native verses or Mirah singing at the piano to an audience—this novelistic tradition consistently represents ethnic difference for an English spectator through a series of patently aestheticized and eroticized figures. We have here a strategy of winning the sympathy of the English reading public by substituting the sympathetic ethnic female for her stage precursor, the caricatured ethnic male. As a double for the English reader, the prejudiced English hero sheds his prejudices by learning of foreign customs and manners through a kind of beautiful foreign muse. But as I have shown both in my preceding chapter and in this one, these novels problematize this strategy of aestheticizing and eroticizing the female other by exploring the dilemma of cross-ethnic identification and the knotted interrelation of sympathy and mastery. Moreover, the collapse of an entire culture into a single vessel, the beautiful foreign woman, is also interrogated. The English hero in Staël's *Corinne, or Italy* (where the title aptly signals such a collapse) notes the problem himself, when he wonders whether he loves the great monuments of Italian culture only because he loves Corinne—that is, only because she has eroticized them for him: "But who knows whether it is not really the deep tenderness you are stirring up in my heart that makes me sensitive to everything I see."[25] Has the English hero fallen in love with these other cultures or simply with the foreign woman who represents them? The hero of *Daniel Deronda* poses essentially the same question—namely, is it only Mirah's beauty that stimulates his interest in the Jews? Deronda raises the issue for this entire tradition by questioning his own motives when he rescues Mirah as she is about to drown herself: he tries to reassure himself, "'I should not have forgotten the look of misery if she had been ugly and vulgar,' he said to himself," as if "to justify himself for feeling that sorrow was the more tragic when it befell delicate, childlike beauty. But there was no denying that the attractiveness of the image made it likelier to last."[26]

Deronda's self-questioning is part of a skeptical tradition that poses the dilemma of what one might call the vexed relationship between the aesthetics of sympathy and the ethics of social action. Edgeworth, for example, in following both Rousseau and Dugald Stewart, claims that the arts, in their aestheticization of suffering, can function as an impediment to genuine sympathy, as in her criticism of novel reading: "It diminishes, instead of increasing, the sensibility of the heart; a combination of romantic imagery is requisite to act upon the associations of sentimental people, and they are virtuous only when virtue is in perfectly good taste. . . . The imagination, which has been accustomed to this delicacy in fictitious narratives, revolts from the disgusting circumstances which attend real poverty, disease, and misery."[27] In this light, Lord Henry's remark in Wilde's *The Picture of Dorian Gray* is no simple or light-hearted witticism but the final moment of a deeply skeptical tradition about the legitimacy of sympathetic identification: "I can sympathize with everything, except suffering. . . . It is too ugly, too horrible, too distressing."[28] Such remarks invite the larger question, Can a work of art in any sense be said to contribute to social action? Can the sympathy we feel for suffering in art be translated into sympathy for the suffering of real people?

During the second half of the eighteenth century such questions were typically posed and answered in relation to the theater in what became a widely disseminated debate about theatricality and sympathetic identification. Rousseau set the terms of the debate for the entire post-Enlightenment tradition when, in his *Letter to M. d'Alembert on the Theatre*, he charged that the tears we shed in the theater simply make us self-satisfied and falsely absolve us of any real moral action: "In giving our tears to these fictions we have satisfied all the rights of humanity without having to give anything more of ourselves; whereas unfortunate people in person would require attention from us, relief, consolation, and work, which would involve us in their pains and would require at least the sacrifice of our indolence." Hence Rousseau's picture, taken from Plutarch, of the "tyrant . . . [who] hid himself at the theatre for fear of being seen groaning [in sympathy] with [the characters on stage], while he heard without emotion the cries of so many unfortunate victims slain daily by his orders." Where are the palpable social benefits, asks Rousseau, of the pity this man feels inside the theater? Rousseau goes on, in a modern setting, to castigate and dismiss "these weeping ladies in the boxes at the theatre, so proud of their tears."[29] By signaling the sympathetic effects of theatergoing, the figure of the weeping spectator and especially the weeping lady became a significant trope that was employed not only by the generation of novelists I am analyzing but also by a wide range of writers and even graphic artists, as in Thomas Rowlandson's 1807 engraving *Tragedy in London* (figure 8), in which an entire audience of spectators weeps at the tragedy on stage.

Clearly responding to Rousseau's *Letter*, Denis Diderot not only accepts but enforces the distinction between real life and theater, in some ways to appreciate how art heightens life and in fact opens a path to sympathy that real life often closes. In his celebrated *The Paradox of Acting* (1773), Diderot calls attention to "the difference between the tears raised by a tragedy of real life and those raised by a touching narrative," and then goes on to explain how "a really unhappy woman . . . may weep and fail to touch you," because of some oddity in her accent or "some trivial disfigurement in her,"[30] while a great actor in copying her grief will eliminate these elements and move you to tears. While Diderot takes up the trope of the weeping spectator within the context of the eighteenth-century's extended debate over whether or not the actor experiences the emotion he portrays, Edmund Burke locates the weeping spectator at the center of the political crisis over the French Revolution. Having reviewed Rousseau's *Letter* in the *Annual Register* for 1759, Burke uses the figure of the weeping spectator in *Reflections on the Revolution in France* (1790) to analyze and evaluate his own reaction to the revolution. Burke uses the image of himself weeping in the theater not to disqualify such an emotion but to capture how profound an effect the revolution has had on him—that is, how much more moving the "spectacle" of the revolution is than even such a spectacle as presented on the stage. In such a light the man of feeling, who regularly sheds tears at the theater, must in fact weep more deeply still at the revolution. Burke explains that if he were to fail to weep at the spectacle of the revolution, and only to weep at it on the stage, "people would think the tears that Garrick formerly, or that Siddons not long since, have extorted from me, were the tears of hypocrisy; I should know them to be the tears of folly"—in other words, they would be the tears of Rousseau's weeping lady, shed only in

Figure 8: *Tragedy in London*. Courtesy of Fine Arts Museums of San Francisco, Achenbach Foundation for Graphic Arts.

the theater and not for a tragedy in real life. For Burke, the genuinely sympathetic spectator at the theater is prepared to shed even greater tears at the tragic spectacle of the revolution, for "indeed the theatre is a better school of moral sentiments than churches."[31] Burke's figure of the weeping spectator, then, is a call to all those who shed tears at the theater—to the sentimental public of the Enlightenment—to share the common feeling of tragedy at the spectacle of the revolution. In *A Vindication of the Rights of Men* (1790) Mary Wollstonecraft immediately countered Burke by at once charging that "your tears are reserved . . . for the declamation of the theatre," quoting Rousseau's *Letter* on "the tears that are shed for fictitious sorrow"[32] as the context for her critique. Only a few months later Thomas Paine, following Rousseau's argument exactly, joined the fray in *The Rights of Man* (1791–92) by similarly attacking what he saw as the artificially theatrical reaction of Burke to the revolution: "He is not affected by the reality of distress touching his heart, but by the showy resemblance of it striking his imagination. . . . His hero or heroine must be a tragedy-victim expiring in show, and not the real prisoner of misery, sliding into death in the silence of a dungeon." For Paine, all of Burke's "theatrical exaggerations" are engineered "to produce a stage effect" that will result in "a weeping effect."[33] Such writers seize on Rousseau's figure of the weeping spectator at the theater and turn it into a trope that measures the depth, sincerity, and legitimacy of a spectator's feeling. Moreover, as a way of understanding the central political crisis of the time, the Burke-Wollstonecraft-Paine exchange demonstrates both the centrality of the actual experience of Georgian theatergoing as well as its immensely fluid figural use.

But it is Madame de Staël's location of this trope and the issue of theatricality in general at the heart of *Corinne, or Italy* that had the most direct impact on the British novelistic tradition I am analyzing. Profoundly influenced by Rousseau's *Letter*,[34] Staël anchors her novel about national differences in key scenes that demonstrate the sympathetic effects of theatricality on the English hero, Oswald Lord Nelvil: he is initially intrigued by a foreign woman at her performance in Italian in Rome, she wins him over by performing the English bard in an Italian translation, and she loses him at a performance on the London stage at which he sympathetically identifies with a weeping lady in the theater. Of special importance to my argument here are the ways in which Oswald's sympathetic identification in such key theatrical scenes directly influenced both *Waverley* and *Harrington*. Waverley's public reading of *Romeo and Juliet*, for example, borrows directly almost point by point the scene in *Corinne* in which a performance of the same play follows a debate over national literary differences where aesthetic tastes mirror national identities, so that a performance of Shakespeare is used both to establish national identities and to explore cross-national romance. Corinne's response to this debate is to perform her own translation of *Romeo and Juliet* in Italian, and in this way to bridge the (national) gap between herself and Oswald, for Staël makes use of the paradigmatic novelistic plot that begins with the English hero's prejudices: Oswald was "prejudiced against Italians and Italy from the start" (*C*, 17), and more generally, "the English are slaves to the customs and habits of their country" (*C*, 49). Corinne uses her insistence on the hybrid genius of Shakespeare to support the hybrid romance between herself and Oswald: setting Romeo and Juliet in Italy, "Shakespeare wrote the play with the southern imagination," so that, "translated into Italian, *Romeo and Juliet* seems to return to its native tongue" (*C*, 126). During the play Oswald so identifies with Corinne's performance that he periodically breaks down the line between theater and life, and identifies entirely with Romeo: in the scene in the burial vault, "Nelvil thought she was reaching her arms out to him as if to call for help, and he rose in a burst of frenzy" (*C*, 129), and seeing Corinne after the performance, "Oswald threw himself at Corinne's feet and spoke these words of Romeo's in English" (*C*, 130). Corinne, then, has wisely used the national bard of England, but in a translation in Italian, and Oswald's sympathetic identification with Romeo moves him to declare his love for the foreign woman, Corinne. Scott revises this scene by using the same play—which directly engages the central dilemma of both novels, lovers separated by a profound familial or national divide—not to bridge the gulf between Flora and Waverley (in the manner of *Corinne*) but rather to reassert the Englishness of the hero and to direct him to Rose. Moreover, Scott and British writers in general owe to Staël this association between the personal, the national, and the aesthetic, which she was proclaiming in a series of books praised by reviewers in Britain (who denominated her "beyond all comparison the first female writer of her age")[35] but also quite explicitly in *Corinne*: "Oswald and Corinne disagreed [over a series of works of art], but their differences here as in everything else had to do with differences of nations, climates, and religions" (*C*, 146). In fact, these differences finally become the basis of the tragic denouement, for Oswald can never fully get beyond his wish—"If only you had the same religion, the same country as I!" (*C*, 162).

The tragic realignment of Oswald away from Corinne, or Italy, and toward England, is staged at a celebrated performance of the Georgian stage. For this scene Staël brings Corinne to London, where she watches Oswald in the audience, reversing the initiating moment of their affair which brought him to Rome, where he watched her on the stage (and where, typically in these novels, the English hero's first glimpse of the foreign woman occurs in a theatrical setting). The narrator records the kinds of national and aesthetic discriminations that dominate *Corinne* and regularly surface in these novels by pinpointing the differences between English and French theatricality. To epitomize English theatricality (and to re-anglicize her hero), Staël has her characters attend the celebrated performance of Sarah Siddons in one of the triumphs of the Georgian stage, David Garrick's *Isabella* (1757), an adaptation of Thomas Southerne's *The Fatal Marriage* (1694). Used both by Burke and by Staël, the figure of Mrs. Siddons became during the Georgian period a touchstone in the debate over the effects of theatricality and the trope of the weeping spectator. The *London Chronicle* reported of Siddons's performance of *Isabella* at Drury Lane in 1782, "The best panegyric we can make upon this Lady's performance of the pathetic scenes, is to remark, there was scarce a dry eye in the whole house, and that two Ladies in the boxes actually fainted,"[36] while Scott recorded, when she performed in Edinburgh, that "she fairly cried herself sick at her own part," and spectators followed suit, so that "never was there such a night for laundresses."[37] Moreover, for late Georgian theatrical culture generally, Mrs. Siddons represented something especially English. William Hazlitt eulogized, "The homage she has received is greater than that which is paid to Queens. . . . She was the stateliest ornament of the public mind. She was . . . the idol of the people,"[38] while James Boaden recalled Siddons dressed up as Britannia in celebration of George III's recovery from illness in 1789.[39] So, for Burke, Siddons became a vehicle for distinguishing between English and French spectacle—in the first case, the ennobling tragic art of Mrs. Siddons on the stage, in the second, the "atrocious spectacle" of revolution in France. And for Staël, whose visit to England in 1793 occurred during the actress's reign in *Isabella*, Siddons was the quintessential model to argue for the genuine passion the English performer felt during the performance and against the "general rules" (*C*, 340) of the French theater, and therefore another means of moving the English hero back into the orbit of English cultural influence.

After establishing the power of Siddons's performance, this scene in *Corinne* turns entirely to a drama that is played out not on the stage but in the audience: "Corinne noticed all eyes turning toward . . . Lucile," Oswald's English love interest, and then "suddenly, in the box facing hers, she caught sight of Lord Nelvil whose gaze was fixed on Lucile . . . and he was absorbed in Lucile alone" (*C*, 340–41). So distressed at the scenes taking place on the stage, "Lucile was bathed in tears she tried to conceal by moving to the back of her box" (*C*, 341), while Oswald continues to watch her; when the play is finished he assists Lucile and her mother from the theater, as Corinne watches from a protected position, the hidden spectator throughout the scene, resuming her role as the foreign woman hidden from the English spectator and so once again positioned beyond his understanding. So, a counterscene of theatricality, not the English bard italianized in Rome but a celebrated production in London of a play adapted by Garrick and acted by Siddons, wins Oswald for an English (rather than Italian) bride. Moreover, and perhaps even more important, the scene relocates the hero's love interest from the actress on the stage (where he first sees Corinne, in Rome) to the weeping lady in the audience (Lucile, in London), recalling Oswald's persistent (English) objections to Corinne's public performance.

Edgeworth was fascinated by Staël for many years, regularly reading her works and responding to them in novels such as *Leonora* (1806) and *Helen*

(1834).[40] She read *Corinne* in 1808 and seemed almost embarrassed by how deeply it moved her: "I have read 'Corinne' with my father, and I like it better than he does. In one word, I am dazzled by the genius, provoked by the absurdities, and in admiration of the taste and critical judgment of Italian literature displayed through the whole work. . . . I almost broke my foolish heart over the end of the third volume, and my father acknowledges he never read anything more pathetic."[41] Edgeworth went on to adapt the scene of the weeping lady at the theater in *Corinne* for the chapter in *Harrington* in which hero and heroine attend a performance of Shakespeare. In both scenes the attention of the English hero moves from the action at an iconic performance on the Georgian stage to his absorption in a distraught female member of the audience who attempts to hide her emotion and whom he assists out of the theater and eventually marries. The critical turning point in both scenes occurs when the hero shares a sympathetic identification with the woman in the audience. But whereas in *Corinne* the exotic foreign woman merely watches such a scene (and remains hidden, obscured), only to realize that she has been left behind by the English hero, in *Harrington* it is the exotic foreign woman who absorbs the interest of the English hero, and moreover, moves him into the performative experience of seeing from her point of view a performance that itself enunciates the conditions of prejudice against the foreign other. In Staël's scene, then, the Englishness of the hero is crystallized (and consequently the exotic woman is obscured in the shadows), while in Edgeworth's reworking of the scene the context in which the English hero can broaden his understanding and sympathy beyond merely English attitudes is achieved (because the exotic woman is in some sense revealed, illuminated)—so that Harrington can in the course of the novel take heroic action to become "the champion of the Jews" (*H*, 128). (Staël had already demonstrated her English hero's enlightened sympathy when on his way to Rome he saves a community of Jews in the ghetto at Ancona from a fire, while others "begged Oswald to let the Jews burn" [*C*, 14]. As the "deliverer" and "benefactor" [*C*, 16] of the Jews, Oswald anticipated by a decade the British novel's celebrated Jewish champions, Edgeworth's Harrington and Scott's Ivanhoe.)

In these novels, the English hero consistently chooses for his bride the weeping lady at a theatrical performance. For Oswald, she is the woman who suffers in private, not on the public stage, and for Waverley, she is the woman of feeling, for when Waverley finishes his public recitation of Shakespeare he notes that Flora applauded with her hands while Rose applauded with her "tears," concluding about the latter, "She has more feeling too" (*W*, 256). For

Harrington, she is the woman who demonstrates the pain of Jewish suffering. The emphasis in all these novels is not on the original act of creation, or even on the performance itself, but rather on the act of reception, the way in which a theatrical performance moves the beholder. As Corinne guides Oswald through the masterworks of Italian art and architecture, she counsels him, "Let us consider the effect they produce" (*C*, 155). The theater facilitates studying reception because the consequences of performance are visible and palpable; they are frequently shared in common and communicable to other audience members. In this way the theater becomes a kind of laboratory, testing and measuring the effects of sympathetic identification on the audience. In these novels the English hero is put in the position of being able to evaluate the heroine's reaction to a theatrical performance, and he chooses the weeping lady. Even in Rowlandson's *Tragedy in London* (figure 8), in the midst of the satirically grotesque figures of the weeping audience he places just off center an attractive pair, a weeping lady attended by a gentleman who faces not the stage but her, entirely absorbed in her distress.

But perhaps most important of all, these scenes measure not simply or even primarily the emotion of the weeping lady but rather the effect she has on another spectator—that is, on the spectator who watches her and who is profoundly affected and even changed by watching her. This act of triangulation lies at the center of the revision that all these novels perform on Rousseau's figure of the weeping lady at the theater. Oswald's heart is softened not by the event on the stage but by the real woman suffering in the audience, just as Harrington is moved finally not by the drama on the stage but by the real woman suffering in the audience. And Staël adds an even further layer of spectatorship: Corrine watches Oswald watching the weeping lady (who watches the play), and in so doing Corinne is moved to understand that she must begin to relinquish Oswald to Lucile.

I close with Heinrich Heine's powerful use of the trope of the weeping lady, making clear how the dynamic of the triangulation of sympathetic identification became central to concepts of theatricality during this period. Like Staël, when Heine was in England his frequent visits to the theater made a profound impression on him, which he recorded in various texts. In *Shakespeare's Maidens and Women* (1838), for example, he recalls his visits in 1827 to "Drury Lane, where I so often saw Shakespeare's historical dramas played, and where Kean moved my soul so mightily."[42] Heine explains how well known the works of Shakespeare are in England ("not only by the cultivated, but by the people" [*HH*, 1.257]), how Shakespeare is known there not just as a poet but also as a writer of history, and how "the Germans have comprehended Shakespeare better than the English" (*HH*, 1:267), in a claim similar to Corinne's about her Italian *Romeo and Juliet*, in attempts by both writers to make Shakespeare the property of the world, not just England. For my purposes, Heine's shaping of his entire text around the sympathetic effects produced by *The Merchant of Venice* is especially pertinent. In his section on Portia, Heine ends with an extended fantasy about searching in present-day Venice for Shylock, hearing "a voice in which tears flowed as they were never wept from eyes. There was a sobbing which might have moved a stone to pity. . . . And this voice seemed to be well known to me—as if I had heard it long long ago, when it wailed just as despairingly, 'Jessica, my child!'" (*HH*, 1.401). The analysis of Portia ends—indeed, the entirety of *Shakespeare's Maidens and Women* ends—by directing attention away from the heroine and not simply toward the pathos of Shylock but toward the impression this figure must make on any human spectator, and more—"a sobbing which might have moved a stone to pity." With such a figure Heine almost dares the spectator to look on Shylock's grief and not take pity, not weep—that is, once again theater becomes the testing ground of the spectator's sympathy, and one's humanity depends on the act of sympathetic identification.

But Heine does not simply have to imagine or conjure such a spectator, for he has seen one with his own eyes. Heine shows us a weeping spectator in a description that bears an uncanny resemblance to the scenario that Edgeworth has given us in *Harrington*: both episodes focus on a woman deeply pained at a performance of *The Merchant of Venice*. Heine recalls, "When I saw this piece played in Drury Lane there stood behind me in the box a pale British beauty who, at the end of the fourth act, wept passionately, and many times cried out, 'The poor man is wronged!' It was a countenance of noblest Grecian cut, and the eyes were large and black. I have never been able to forget them, those great black eyes which wept for Shylock!" (*HH*, 1.377). Like Edgeworth, Heine moves the central theatrical moment from the stage proper to the audience, and unlike Rousseau he locates the potentially curative aspect of the theatrical experience not in the weeping lady but in the profound effect her sympathetic identification has on another spectator. It is important to recognize, then, that both Edgeworth and Heine (like Staël) triangulate Rousseau's scene of the weeping lady by adding a second spectator. This second spectator functions at least in part to de-aestheticize the sympathetic experience precisely insofar as he identifies not with the art object but with a real human being, embodied in a female spectator in pain.

Finally, it is certainly a special irony that Heine, a converted Jew, is potentially re-Judaized through the pain a British woman feels at a production of *The Merchant of Venice*, seeing anew through her eyes, through the eyes of the weeping lady.

New Scenes for Old Farces

IN THE OPENING decades of the nineteenth century and even through the Victorian period, the plays I have discussed in the course of this book, while largely unknown today, continued to live an important life. In these concluding pages I wish to suggest the multiple ways in which Georgian comedies and farces survived after their initial productions, and the effects of this survival. This will mean briefly following the afterlife of these plays, first, as they continued to be performed well beyond their initial productions; second, as they were collected and recollected by critics, biographers, and historians who began the work of compiling and writing Georgian theatrical history; and finally, as they functioned to inhabit and to motivate the novel in a productive interaction between stage and novel throughout the nineteenth century.

While the stage continued to represent a variety of ethnic minorities through the Victorian period, often repeating the kinds of strategies popular on the Georgian stage,[1] the figure of the stage Jew achieved special prominence in a variety of nineteenth-century discourses, especially in novels of the 1890s. After all, the figure of Shylock, produced by the national poet of England and perennially present on the English stage, continued to weigh on the national consciousness and to produce more and more debate, making the stage Jew an issue that simply would not go away. So, throughout the nineteenth century the history of staging the Jew (especially in the characters of Shylock and Sheva) continued to signal important features of English culture, to chart important shifts in public sentiment on the Jewish Question, and to ground important debates on the intersection of Jewish and English identities. Moreover, the figure of the Jew remained at the center of questions of English national identity for other reasons. As I have shown elsewhere, the question of Jewish toleration at the turn of the nineteenth century became a crucial way of defining, evaluating, and contrasting different national identities—England versus France versus Spain—so that the Jewish Question became a central key to defining the English national character in a broadly international context.[2] Finally, the rise of anti-Semitism in England as well as Europe and Russia in the last quarter of the nineteenth century acutely reopened the issue of the Jewish Question in defining English national identity, especially when particular social and political conditions in England raised for some the specter of a specific Jewish threat against England and English values.

Plays from the 1770s, such as *The West Indian*, *The Duenna*, and *The Fashionable Lover*, and even *Love à la Mode*, first produced in 1759, remained part of the regular repertory in the opening decades of the nineteenth century. This meant, for example, that while Cumberland's and Dibdin's sympathetic Jews of the 1790s were part of a liberalizing Enlightenment attitude that was carried over into the novels of Edgeworth and Scott, neither the stage nor the novel closed the book on prejudice against Jews. I have already discussed the kind of backlash that Cumberland suffered at the hands of Cobbett and others, but perhaps of even more importance were the ways in which stage revivals were used to undermine the sentimental Jews of Cumberland and Dibdin. In the opening decades of the nineteenth century their benevolent Jews played in the same season, and even on alternate nights, with revivals and double bills that featured conventional stage Jews. For example, in 1808 audiences could have seen *Love à la Mode* on November 8 and 11 and *The Jew and the Doctor* on November 10, and in several seasons (such as 1801–2 and 1803–4) audiences could have seen both *The Jew* as well as revivals of *The Duenna* and *The Merchant of Venice*, while the power of *Love à la Mode*'s anti-Jewish caricature found support by being paired not only with *Merchant* but also with *The Duenna* in the opening decades of the nineteenth century. It is therefore important to realize that Cumberland's and Dibdin's Jews did not banish from the stage these earlier, anti-Semitic portraits: on different nights audiences were treated to benevolent Sheva and vengeful Shylock or generous Abednego and cunning little Isaac, demonstrating the kind of cultural schizophrenia that I have suggested was the hallmark of Enlightenment and post-Enlightenment British culture.

In fact, revivals could function deliberately to counteract more recent and more liberal plays. For example, a critic for the *Monthly Mirror* in May 1808 clearly viewed a revival of Cumberland's *Fashionable Lover* as a tool to argue against the playwright's later philo-Semitic conversion in *The Jew*: "In Colin, we see Mr. Cumberland's first attempt at anomalous character—from a benevolent Scot, it was but a stride to a benevolent Jew. Of the Jews, whom a great politician once, in our presence, with more truth than elegance, called 'lice on the body politic,' Mr. Cumberland then seemed to entertain a different opinion from that, which he has lately maintained on the stage. . . . We only say, that he *seems* to have changed his opinion, for we verily believe, (as we hold him to be sane,) that notwithstanding his Jews, who go about doing good, his *sow's ears* of which he makes *silk purses*, he thinks in strict conformity with the politician above" (p. 401). Dismissing Cumberland's benevolent Scot, the reviewer turns his response to the revival of *The Fashionable Lover* on the nefarious Jew Napthali, as if the stage in 1808 were reinstating this character from Cumberland's 1772 comedy in order to embarrass and put to rout Cumberland's sympathetic Sheva of the 1790s. While I have already analyzed the ways in which Cumberland's Sheva initiated an explicit public debate in the press about Shylock and more generally about the Jews in England, here I am suggesting that even the scheduling of the theatrical repertory could be seen as a way of entering and extending that debate. In short, stage revivals and theater reviews became the occasion for (re)staging the debate over Jewish identity, and a revival from earlier decades could function to undermine a more recent attempt at liberal toleration.

Many of the comedies and farces that I have discussed were performed even during the Victorian period. *Love à la Mode, Love Laughs at Locksmiths, Rochester; or, King Charles the Second's Merry Days, The Belle's Stratagem, The West Indian, The Jew and the Doctor, The Young Quaker,* and *The Irishman in London* all had Victorian productions.[3] But even before these productions became increasingly infrequent, other means were being developed to keep alive these plays and every aspect of their history. For example, the *Monthly Mirror* began the immense undertaking of publishing the history of the Georgian theater, acknowledging the cultural and social importance of this history as well as the ephemeral nature of all live performance. The journal announced in its February 1799 issue that it would begin a series entitled "History of the Stage, from the commencement of Garrick's management [in 1747]." The series became an extraordinary archive of fact and anecdote, and took the form of a daily calendar for Drury Lane and Covent Garden in which every performance was listed, with the names of the performers and the parts they played, as well as footnotes that ran on for pages, describing the characteristics of different performers and their performance strategies, the reception of the plays by audiences, and so on. In addition, a series of stage histories (typically containing an annual register of plays) began to appear from the 1760s onward, the most important being John Genest's *Some Account of the English Stage, from the Restoration in 1660 to 1830* (1832), a remarkable work in ten volumes that recorded dates of performances and cast lists as well as critical opinions.[4] Finally, these plays were preserved by a vast publication enterprise that began in the mid-eighteenth century and became especially active in the opening decades of the nineteenth century. Individual copies of many of these plays were published regularly and inexpensively, and were second in popularity only to fiction at the circulating libraries;[5] *The Jew*, for example, was reissued almost yearly in the period between 1794 and 1808, and intermittently in the 1820s. Beginning in the 1770s and 1780s grand anthologies of plays also began to appear, sometimes edited by popular playwrights themselves (such as Elizabeth Inchbald and Thomas Dibdin) and sometimes including valuable editorial commentaries;[6] even Walter Scott got into the act, with a five-volume edition of *The Modern British Drama* (1811).

The popular impression these plays made on the public meant that they could be recirculated in a variety of modes, reborn time and again in various recognizable guises over the following decades. For example, an 1828 engraving entitled *New Scene for The Old Farce of The Jew and The Doctor* (figure 9) used Thomas Dibdin's 1798 farce to reimagine his generous Jew as the famous Jewish financier, Nathan Meyer Rothschild (dressed as an old-clothes man), trying to bribe the Duke of Wellington in what was a political controversy in the late 1820s. The title of the print suggests the general reusability of such plays, their extended and fluid currency. And in fact Dibdin's farce did surface in a variety of venues. Maria Edgeworth, for example, was delighted with a private performance of *The Jew and the Doctor* at Castle Forbes in 1805,[7] and the farce continued to be played publicly at least as late as 1839 when it was performed at Drury Lane.[8] Moreover, it had been published by Inchbald in her seven-volume *Collection of farces and other afterpieces, which are acted at the Theatres Royal, Drury-Lane, Covent-Garden, and Hay-Market* (1809), along with a number of other plays I have discussed, such as *Love à la Mode, The Irishman in London, The Register-Office,* and *The Apprentice.* It is this collection that Charles Dickens read over and over again as a child,[9] and it was *The Jew and the Doctor* that he wrote to Mark Lemon about in 1847 when they were looking for a "new farce" to produce.[10] Ultimately, Dickens did in fact put to good use the old farce he read as a child when he created the benevolent Jew Riah in *Our Mutual Friend* (1864–65)—like Abednego, Riah is a benevo-

Figure 9: *New Scene for The Old Farce of The Jew and The Doctor.* Courtesy of the Library of the Jewish Theological Seminary.

lent Jew who shelters and protects a helpless Christian girl.[11] In sum, these are the kinds of intersections among various forms of popular culture—stage farce, graphic print, private theatrical, anthology, and novel—that allow us to see how, over a period of more than half a century, new scenes were made from old farces.

As these plays began to be less frequently performed, they became the object of scrutiny for critics and historians. One of the central topics that emerged in the reassessment of the Georgian stage undertaken during the Victorian period was the history of the stage Jew, taken up both by non-Jews and by an increasing number of Jewish intellectuals who began to enter the public sphere in order to write Anglo-Jewish history. For example, James Picciotto, the author who rightly claimed to be the first Jewish writer to give a full historical account of the Jews in England in a series of sketches first published in the *Jewish Chronicle* and then collected in book form in 1875,[12] returned to the Shylock/Sheva debate that was so prominent in the 1790s and immediately thereafter. Picciotto had a double agenda here, to assess not only the importance of Cumberland amid the growing spirit of toleration in the 1790s but also the lasting social and political influence of Cumberland's benevolent Jew in a world that still was not secure from anti-Semitism. When praising Cumberland's attempt "to raise and defend an unjustly vilified race," Picciotto reported that "while audiences flock to hiss at the cruelty and avarice of Shylock, the existence of the beneficent Sheva is scarcely known to the present generation." According to Picciotto, by the 1870s Sheva was a kind of relic about whom he could say only, "Still doubtless some good was effected by Cumberland's *Jew* at the period of its production."[13]

In the midst of his assessment Picciotto returned to what became a recurrent focus for the nineteenth century, namely, the role of Shylock in English culture and history, and specifically the romantic reinterpretation of Shylock: "Much ingenuity has been exercised in endeavouring to prove that William Shakespeare, in drawing the character of Shylock, desired secretly to justify the Jews. . . . He depicted a Jew in conformity with the small knowledge or prejudices of his audience."[14] Frederick Hawkins's "Shylock and Other Stage Jews," which appeared in *The Theatre* on November 1, 1879, represents the kind of special pleading for Shylock from an apparently philo-Semitic perspective that had become common in England from the period of Edmund Kean and William Hazlitt onward. Extending into the Victorian period the kind of debate that we saw *The Jew* initiate in the 1790s, Hawkins immediately links the history of the stage Jew with the history of the Jews in England and English national identity. For the philo-Semitic critic this meant prefacing an analysis of this stage history with what was frequently a list of the persecutions the Jews had suffered in England: "The persecutions to which the scattered Children of the Promise were subjected in this country during the twelfth and thirteenth centuries may be said to form one of the darkest chapters of our history" (p. 191). The opening pages of the essay record these persecutions in some detail, in part to prepare the ground for the major argument, namely, that *The Merchant of Venice* "was intended as a *plea for toleration towards the Jews*" (p. 193)—in other words, Shakespeare's play flowed athwart the mainstream of English anti-Semitism.

Hawkins makes his argument by focusing on the various interpretations of the stage Jew in the long eighteenth century, finally measuring the distance England has come from the early modern period by noting about Cumberland's *The Jew*, "Had such a piece been represented at the time of the production of *The Merchant of Venice* the theatre would have been sacked" (p. 197). Hawkins explains that Cumberland's play "must have had a salutary effect, if only as tending to disabuse the public mind of the impression that the

Jews were strangers to virtue in any form, and so preparing the public for one of the most remarkable impersonations ever witnessed on the stage" (p. 198)—namely, Kean's Shylock. Hawkins, who published a biography of Kean in 1869, demonstrates the importance of Georgian stage history by rightly suggesting that it was Cumberland's play that contributed to the sympathetic reading of Shylock that Kean presented, and in Kean's hands *The Merchant of Venice* "doubtless added strength to the movement which resulted in the removal of Jewish disabilities" (p. 198).

The line of influence that Hawkins draws from Cumberland's Sheva to Kean's Shylock is closer to the historical truth than the argument of recent scholars who claim that either Hazlitt's defense of Kean's sympathetic portrayal of Shylock or an essay by Richard Hole that rewrites Shylock's character from a Jewish perspective turned the tide on interpretations of Shylock.[15] The Georgian stage at the turn of the nineteenth century incited what I have demonstrated was a public debate about Shylock, Sheva, and the history of the Jews, and the plays of Cumberland and Dibdin contributed to a changing view of how to perform a more tolerant version of the Jew on the stage in general and in *The Merchant of Venice* in particular. Sheva put pressure on Shylock, and that pressure was manifest everywhere, from Kean's humane performance to Hazlitt's eventual embracing in 1816 of Kean's sympathetic interpretation. Hazlitt himself had already implied the kind of historical linkage I am suggesting: "Shakespear's malignant has outlived Mr Cumberland's benevolent Jew. In proportion as Shylock has ceased to be a popular bugbear . . . he becomes a half-favourite with the philosophical part of the audience, who are disposed to think that Jewish revenge is at least as good as Christian injuries."[16] I would add that Hazlitt's conclusion, "Shakespear could not easily divest his characters of their entire humanity: his Jew is more than half a Christian,"[17] repeats the kind of commentary that was common about Sheva in the Georgian period—namely, that he was a Christian at heart, not a Jew—and in this way subverts (if unintentionally) the basis of Jewish identity by enacting a subtle form of conversion. In fact, during the Georgian period the Jew with a Christian heart became a common trope, as did the black with a white one.[18]

Jewish critics and historians through the end of the Victorian period were consistent in their skepticism about a sympathetic Shylock and continued to understand theater history as an index to social and political history. In the November 13, 1891, Jubilee Supplement celebrating the fiftieth anniversary of the *Jewish Chronicle,* in the midst of articles about the most important

Jewish questions by the most important Jewish intellectuals of the time, an article by Israel Abrahams entitled "Jews and the Theatre" encapsulated the kind of attention to Jews and theatricality that had become a preoccupation in the late nineteenth century. Abrahams measures what amounts to not only a failure of progress but also a kind of regression when he records that, in the wake of the reemergence of anti-Semitism in the later nineteenth century, "I read the other day the statement in the leading Viennese journal that if 'Nathan the Wise' had been written now it would have been hissed off the stage"—a remark that allows him to bring the question closer to home: "'Nathan the Wise' is the favourite role of some of the greatest modern actors on the Continent, and it is scarcely creditable that . . . this play . . . has never been produced on the English stage" (p. 22). While praising Lessing, Abrahams confesses, "In England we have been less fortunate. . . . Shylock has so completely dominated the English stage that, no great dramatist since Shakespeare has attempted to introduce Jewish characters" (p. 22). Abrahams then records the importance of both Cumberland and Dibdin, remarking that "'The Jew,' despite its weakness as a work of Art, made a considerable sensation. It was frequently played in England; it was translated into almost every language of Europe, and was often performed in continental cities" (pp. 22–23). Still, the final verdict in the 1890s is wholly negative: "From the very earliest times we [Jews] have had to submit to raillery on the stage. . . . And the Jews could not regard the stage, with much affection while this lasted. While this *lasted*! Has it ever ceased? No!" (p. 22).

So, as the history of the stage and the history of the Jews were being written in tandem during the Victorian period, writers continued to argue over the seminal Georgian period, and especially the roles that Shylock, Sheva, and a post-Sheva Shylock played on the stage and in the national consciousness. But while such acts of critical retrieval and reassessment were taking place, the staging of Jewish identity was in fact undergoing significant changes through the interaction between novel and stage. While in my previous two chapters I explored the ways in which the stage fueled certain developments in the early nineteenth-century novel, it is equally true that this new tradition of novels in turn influenced the stage. An important development on the nineteenth-century stage, the introduction of the stage Jewess, was due at least in part to the extraordinary success of Rebecca in Scott's *Ivanhoe*, which as I have already explained appeared in multiple stage adaptations, many of which chose to showcase the Jewish characters in response to the theater audience's appetite for ethnic spectacle. But adaptations of Scott's

Ivanhoe were not the only vehicles in which a sympathetic Jewish heroine appeared on the stage, finally breaking the spell of the absence of Jewish female stage characters (except for Shakespeare's Jessica and characters in biblical dramas). The novelistic tradition that I explored in the preceding two chapters made the idea of cross-ethnic and cross-national romance popular, and the stage quickly followed by representing this theme tragically through the sentimental Jewess. While the Georgian stage had been dominated by a long line of Jewish male characters, during the Victorian period Jewish heroines were imported and adapted for the London stage, two in particular making notable successes. First, numerous adaptations of Eugene Scribe's and Fromental Halévy's opera *La Juive* (Paris, 1835) played in London from 1835 onward, most famously James Robinson Planche's *The Jewess; or, The Council of Constance*, which enjoyed London productions in 1835, 1842, 1851, 1859, and 1863. Second, several adaptations of Salomon Mosenthal's *Deborah* (Budapest, 1849) were performed in London in the 1860s as well as later in the century, the most famous being Augustin Daly's *Leah the Forsaken*, productions of which opened in London in 1863, 1872, and 1897, while an 1892 adaptation matched the Jewish stage heroine with the celebrated Jewish actress Sarah Bernhardt.[19] The emergent liberalizing attitude toward the Jews on the stage in the late Georgian period was remembered and recorded by Victorian writers as a bridge to a play like *Leah*: "The purpose of the dramatist in this play [*Leah*] . . . is akin to that of Lessing's *Nathan der Weise* and Cumberland's *Jew*," and again, "Cumberland's play of 'The Jew' supplies the moral, and the Book of Deuteronomy much of the language of 'Leah.'"[20] Meanwhile these imported plays portrayed the kinds of illiberal attitudes Jews faced elsewhere as a spur to English toleration.

The sentimental stage Jewess in turn influenced the novel, in what continued to be a form of cross-fertilization between the two forms. George Henry Lewes recorded his and George Eliot's experience at the theater in 1864 at a production of *Leah the Forsaken*: "In the evening we went to the Adelphi, having a private box sent us, to see Miss Bateman as Leah. While wondering at the badness of the piece, I thought of writing one for [the actress] Helen Faucit and amused myself with sketching a plot. . . . In the morning I suggested to Polly that *she* should do the piece. She rather liked the suggestion."[21] However bad they thought *Leah*, Eliot's increasing interest in the Jews in the 1860s must have made her a sympathetic spectator, and in fact *Leah the Forsaken's* depiction of virulent anti-Semitism, the play's portraits of the suffering but nonetheless heroic Jewish maiden and the cowardly crypto-Jew, and its central theme of cross-religious and cross-ethnic romance worked their way into Eliot's verse drama *The Spanish Gypsy* (1868) and novel *Daniel Deronda* (1876). The "forsaken" Jewish maiden of the play's title even became a central paradigm for the two heroines in *Deronda*, but whereas *Leah* (like *Ivanhoe*) imagines the Jewish heroine forsaken in the end, Eliot's novel in a powerful act of revision gives the Jewish maiden a husband and leaves Gwendolen, the Christian heroine, "forsaken."[22]

These kinds of exchanges between stage and novel occurred frequently and regularly during the Victorian period, from direct adaptations of novels for the stage (stage adaptations of Charles Dickens's *Oliver Twist* [1838], for example, were produced before the last installment of the novel was published) to less apparent uses of plays in such novels as *Our Mutual Friend* and *Daniel Deronda*. But it was in the 1890s that this interaction between novel and stage on the question of Jewish identity occurred most powerfully, responding to the rise of English anti-Semitism that began during the period of Benjamin Disraeli's premiership in the 1870s and culminated in a crisis in the 1880s and 1890s when waves of Jewish immigrants escaping pogroms settled in England.[23] Newspapers, magazines, books, and parliamentary reports recorded the horrors of the pogroms as well as what many saw as a Jewish takeover of England, or as W. H. Wilkins put it, *The Alien Invasion* (1892): "If we wish to perpetuate that healthy, sturdy stock which has made England what she is, we must prevent the strain from being defiled by this ceaseless pouring in of the unclean and unhealthy of other lands."[24] As one contemporary observer claimed about the renewed importance of the Jewish Question in the 1880s, while "the manifold changes which have taken place during the past half century in the civil, political, and social status of the Jews of Europe would alone have sufficed to attract . . . public attention," their recent persecution in Germany and Russia, as well as the attack on them in the English press, has meant that "a more public interest has been aroused which has already had the effect of elevating the Jews of modern times to a higher and exceptional importance."[25]

Perhaps the most popular and most telling exchange between novel and stage in the Victorian period that reflects the Jewish threat to English values occurred when the huge success of George du Maurier's novel *Trilby* led to a sensational stage play in the following year. Herbert Beerbohm Tree, who was eventually to play a number of Jewish roles (such as Shylock and Fagin), not only starred as Svengali but also increased the focus on the Jewish character so much that *Punch* ran a review entitled "The Marvellous Feat of Tree-ilby

Svengalivanised." In keeping with the stage's emphasis on the Jewish characters of nineteenth-century novels (such as Scott's Rebecca and Dickens's Fagin), *Trilby* was turned into a vehicle for Svengali, "on whom all eyes are fixed, and in whom the interest is centred," and in keeping with the ways in which performers and authors of Jewish characters were typically seen as Judaized, Svengali "so dominates the story, that the author of his being will be remembered as GEORGE JEW MAURIER." The novel and play produced an unusually powerful Jewish male character to compete with the sentimental stage Jewess, taking his place alongside the two other dominant male Jewish figures on the Victorian stage—"He is Shylock and Fagin, Mephistophelessized"[26]—and suggesting the ways in which the representation of Jewish identity was perennially susceptible to anti-Semitic demonization.

Moreover, the popular success of *Trilby* reveals how those questions that the Georgian theater raised were reinvented in the 1890s. Du Maurier's theatrical emphasis on delineating the various voices of the novel's characters as well as their visual features in his famous drawings that accompany the text served the novel's goal of representing the kinds of ethnic and national types that had been the staples of the Georgian stage. Set in the 1850s when a number of Georgian plays were still being performed in London, *Trilby* becomes a kind of multiethnic spectacle, including such characters as Sandy the Scot, "with a pleasing Scotch accent,"[27] and Taffy the Yorkshireman, who "with a very good imitation of the Yorkshire brogue, sang a Somersetshire" song (*T*, 116), recalling the popular Yorkshire clown of the Georgian stage. Meanwhile Svengali is pictured with all the stereotypical conventions of the Jew—"shabby and dirty," with "sallow face," "a beard of burnt-up black" (*T*, 11), and "bold, black, beady Jew's eyes" (*T*, 44)—and he speaks the kind of lisping stage dialect that was invented for the Georgian stage. What was new was the striking hybridity of the characters: Trilby, born of an Irish father and Highland mother, speaks English "with an accent half Scotch and certain French intonations" (*T*, 13), while Svengali speaks "German-Hebrew-French" (*T*, 47) with a pronounced lisp.

Despite the cosmopolitan and ethnically hybrid nature of the cast of characters, there is a flattening out of British ethnic diversity in order to stage a kind of mythic battle between Englishness and Jewishness. The three British male protagonists, all smitten with Trilby, are introduced to the reader as "Englishmen" (*T*, 4) and appeal to her because of their Englishness: "They were English, and she loved to hear her mother-tongue and speak it" (*T*, 60). Even Trilby's Irish-Scottish parentage is subsumed and translated into Englishness when she becomes the object of all the men's desire: "her beautiful white English bosom" (*T*, 121) is posed against the "filthy black Hebrew sweep" Svengali (*T*, 48). And Svengali has those features that are "so offensive to the normal Englishman" (*T*, 11), "so disliked by his English friends" (*T*, 47). For this reason the paradigmatic courtship competition for the heroine involves winning her by nothing short of a nationalist (re)conversion, reclaiming her from her French ways and warding off the Jew's seductive threats: "So they lent her books—English books: Dickens, Thackeray, Walter Scott. . . . She grew more English every day; and that was a good thing" (*T*, 64). By defining the Jew against all these "English" characters, the novel has the same effect as those Georgian multiethnic spectacles that attempted to solidify the bonds of the English, Scots, and Irish as "Britons" (*T*, 110) in opposition to the Jew as the real outsider. But whereas the Georgian theater typically showed the Jewish interloper cast out, in *Trilby* he wins the English heroine and makes her "his wife, slave, and pupil" (*T*, 245). A grotesque lover as always, the Jew nonetheless finally becomes a successful lover on the stage, as *Punch* recorded on November 16, 1895, when it showed Tree as Svengali compelling Trilby's love in *Mr. Tree Svengalivanting. "You must learn to love me!"* (figure 10). The Jew's power to triumph over his English competitors and to steal from them the English heroine is completed when, in a kind of conversion, he reproduces Trilby as La Svengali, the female version of the foreign Jew, the entirely Judaized English heroine.

Finally, Svengali's ultimate power is expressed not simply by his enslavement of the English heroine but also, and perhaps more important for the kind of theatrical history I am recording here, by the power he exerts in the theater. *Trilby* goes so far as to situate Svengali in a position that radically alters the conventional, long-standing role of the caricatured Jew on the stage. Du Maurier consistently locates Svengali in theatrical situations that allow him to control his audience and manipulate his British counterparts, thereby supplementing and in many ways superseding his conventional role as the caricatured stage Jew. In short, in *Trilby* the Jew becomes not the product but rather the agent of theatrical invention. From the beginning Svengali reduces all who hear him to tears by his passionate piano playing, and eventually he produces tears in his audience when he controls Trilby's voice to produce the kinds of beautiful sounds that she is unable to produce on her own—a music that in fact goes beyond words, beyond the Babel of language, and most important, beyond the mongrel dialect the Jew speaks. In this way Trilby becomes the instrument by which the Jew transcends his own Jewishness and

Mr. Tree Svengalivanting. "You must learn to love me!"

Figure 10: *Mr. Tree Svengalivanting. "You must learn to love me!"*

subjugates the audience to his power. "This revelation of what the human voice could achieve" (*T*, 214–15), especially clear in the "song without words" (*T*, 218), is engineered by the Jew whose modern history is marked by what the Georgian stage invented and described as "the damned Jew's dialect." So *Trilby* imagines the Jew transforming "the harsh, hoarse, weak raven's croak he used to speak with" (*T*, 42), his "very thin and mean and harsh [voice, which] . . . often broke into a disagreeable falsetto" (*T*, 11), into an "apotheosis of voice" (*T*, 213). In this way *Trilby* marks a fantasized ending to what the Georgian period saw as the Jew's "circumcised," or mutilated, tongue.

Du Maurier's picture of the Jew's will to power through music derives from Richard Wagner's "Judaism in Music" (1850), which argued that the repellent outward appearance of the Jew and especially his "outlandish and unpleasant . . . voice-sounds," "a creaking, squeaking, buzzing snuffle," have left open to the Jew only one avenue of aesthetic production—namely, music: "The Jew . . . has nevertheless been able in the widest-spread of modern art-varieties, to wit in Music, to reach the rulership of public taste." In fact, Wagner's description of "the be-Jewing of modern art"[28] became a staple of representations of Jewish identity in the 1890s, and *Trilby* is not the only novel that pictured the Jew liberated from his position as the caricatured stage Jew and newly in charge of theatrical performance in one way or another. In Oscar Wilde's *The Picture of Dorian Gray*, for example, there is "the fat Jew manager"[29] whose theater has "a dreadful orchestra, presided over by a young Hebrew" (*DG*, 50), but it is in this theater that Dorian finds the actress Sybil Vane. Anticipating the three Englishmen in *Trilby*, Dorian argues that he, Basil, and Lord Henry "must get her out of the Jew's hands. She is bound to him" (*DG*, 55). In both novels, then, the Jew, no longer a caricature on the stage, works a kind of theatrical magic himself, by being in charge of an English female performer whom the English protagonists attempt to rescue from the Jew. Wilde ironizes this situation by making the "hideous Jew," with "greasy ringlets" and "soiled shirt" (*DG*, 50), the purveyor of "'The Bard,' as he insisted on calling [Shakespeare]" (*DG*, 52), the symbol of English theater and of Englishness itself. Du Maurier's and Wilde's Jews, while still carrying a conventional set of caricatured markers, nonetheless function as rulers of public taste (to use Wagner's terms), or at least as controllers of the theatrical arena, and thereby revise the conventional role of the stage Jew, the passive figure of caricature on the stage.

In Henry James's *The Tragic Muse* (1890), the story of the actress Miriam Rooth, who is "more than half a Jewess,"[30] functions as another example of the novel's powerful revision of the conventional stage Jew in the 1890s. Here the Jew's role on the stage is not as a one-dimensional, stereotypical caricature but as a multidimensional actress, the purveyor of "a hundred [characters]" (*TM*, 139). The plot focuses on how the Jewish performer must be transformed to function successfully on the English stage and thereby to enthrall English audiences. She is compared to Mrs. Siddons, the subject of Joshua Reynolds's famous painting *The Tragic Muse* (1784); hence the heroine's nickname and James's title, as well as the novel's profound investment in Georgian theater history. Both Miriam and her English coach (and eventual suitor) Peter Sherringham aim toward bringing back what Wilde's Lord Henry (satirically) calls "the palmy days of the British Drama" (*DG*, 49) and what James's Peter (reverentially) calls the days of "Garrick or Mrs. Siddons or John Kemble or Edmund Kean" (*TM*, 136), the most celebrated actors of the Georgian stage. James had special access to this world of the Georgian theater through his close friend Fanny Kemble (herself an actress, but more important, the niece of Mrs. Siddons), whom he knew from the early 1870s through her death in 1893. She accompanied James to the theater and was full of anecdotes of the stage, and perhaps most important of all, "She made us touch Mrs. Siddons, and whom does Mrs. Siddons not make us touch."[31] Fanny Kemble was particularly on James's mind during the writing of *The Tragic Muse*, which initiated the period between 1890 and 1895 during which James was chiefly devoted to writing plays and attempting to make a career in the theater.

Like *Trilby*, *The Tragic Muse* enacts a battle over the national identity of the cosmopolitan heroine. Like the heroine of *Trilby*, Miriam is of mixed parentage, the daughter of a German-Jewish stockbroker and an English-woman. In James's novel, the battle over the female performer centers on whether Miriam should perform in French or its alternative, "the language of Shakespeare" (*TM*, 92), and there is the same attempt to anglicize her. The neophyte Jewish actress is "loud and coarse," and told that she must "find her voice" (*TM*, 94–95) if she is to be a great actress. At first she is capable only of "close, rude, audacious mimicry" (*TM*, 128), not unlike the talk of "parrots," the "mimicked speech"[32] that Wagner claims is the Jew's attempt to speak the native language of his adopted country. When Peter complains that "purity of speech, on our stage, doesn't exist," that the London theater is given over to "abominable dialects and individual tricks," and that he wants to rees-tablish "a positive beauty to utterance," Miriam volunteers but is told: "But you're not English. . . . You're a Jewess—I'm sure of that" (*TM*, 134–35). Peter tutors her in Milton and Wordsworth (just as the Englishmen give Trilby books by Thackeray and Dickens), and Miriam takes as her goal "speaking divine English" (*TM*, 135), but "he continued to object to the girl's English, with its foreign patches" (*TM*, 149): "He made her stick to her English and read Shakespeare aloud to him" (*TM*, 148). In the end *The Tragic Muse* gives us not Shakespeare's Shylock, the stage Jew, but Miriam, the Jewish stage actress, shining in Shakespeare's plays, even in the roles that Mrs. Siddons made famous (such as Constance and Juliet). Again anticipating Svengali's production of a kind of heavenly melody through Trilby, *The Tragic Muse* ends when "Miriam's Juliet was . . . expressed in the truest divine music that had ever poured from tragic lips" (*TM*, 486). In such ways the theater becomes transformed into a site in which the Jewish performer transcends that specific liability that marked Jews both on stage and off—namely, the Jewish jargon—turning garbled words into heavenly music.

While there is a significant difference between the outright anti-Semitism of the portrait of Svengali and the much more sympathetic, nuanced portrait of Miriam, they share the features that increasingly were seen to constitute both the Jew and the performer in the late Victorian period. Jonas Barish has argued that the traditional association between Jews and actors from the early modern period onward was based on the connection between "the wandering Jew" and "the vagabond mountebank."[33] James's portrait of Miriam employs these associations: she and her mother are termed "wanderers" and "exile[s]" (*TM*, 98) and "vagabonds" (*TM*, 415), and the novel in general remarks that "the great current of the age" is marked by "the adoration of the mime," "the preponderance of the mountebank" (*TM*, 104). Such associations were unusually prevalent in the late nineteenth century, so much so that Friedrich Nietzsche simply collapsed the categories of actor and Jew in the 1880s: "As for the *Jews*, the people who possess the art of adaptability par excellence, . . . one might see them virtually as a world-historical arrangement for the production of actors, a veritable breeding ground for actors. And it really is high time to ask: What good actor today is *not*—a Jew?"[34]

The prevalent conjunction and confusion of actors with Jews began to be almost automatic in the late nineteenth century, even by Jewish writers. Lucien Wolf, one of the pioneers of Anglo-Jewish historiography, published an essay in the *Jewish Chronicle* in 1893 in which he attempts to restore the Georgian history not of Gentiles posing as Jews (that is, the history of the stage Jew, which he says has been "done to death") but of Jewish performers themselves, especially the group that was known collectively as "Astley's Jews." In an act of historical retrieval, Wolf recalls the actor-singer and theater manager Jacob De Castro's performing in Sheridan's *Duenna* and singing "'Sheva's Creed,' to a house packed to the ceiling with his Jewish admirers," as well as Daniel Mendoza's "sparring displays on the stage." Wolf's attempt to rescue such fragments of Jewish theatrical history functions at least in part to record "that flexible mimicry which has preserved the Jewish people through their long outlawry. . . . The Hebrew has been the classic mime of the world's history, and the Jewish actor is the final product of the procrustean bed of the Hebrew Diaspora."[35]

But it was only one short step from understanding the Jewish victim or survivor as performer to characterizing the Jewish performer as world dominator, as a novel like *Trilby* suggests. So it may come as no surprise to find Herbert Beerbohm Tree, who himself was rumored to be Jewish, claiming before the Maccabaean Society in 1892, "Our art owes to your great race its most distinguished exponents. It has given us Kean and the Kembles, Rachel, and Sarah Bernhardt, not to mention many others. Indeed, just as, in social affairs, one is apt to say 'Cherchez la femme,' so nowadays, when a great art work is presented to the public, one exclaims, 'Cherchez le Juif.'" In Tree's sweeping association, the great Georgian tradition of English actors becomes a Jewish tradition, and Tree goes on to identify those characteristics that put Jews in their current position of "dominating the world."[36] The "be-jewing of modern art" was, in short, code for Jewish world domination. In this context we can see that one of the hallmarks of the late Victorian period was the reconfiguration of the relationship between Jews and the theater, replacing the Jew's theatrical powerlessness as the butt of jokes and the useful tool of Gentile culture with the apotheosis of the Jew's theatrical power, not simply as the quintessential wearer of masks but finally as the agent and master (not the victim and servant) of theatrical illusion.

In this chapter I have outlined the ways in which Georgian plays were kept alive over the course of the nineteenth century, from stage revivals to acts of collection and recollection to the incorporation and transmutation of plays into different forms of popular culture such as the graphic print and the novel. I have focused on significant nineteenth-century innovations in the staging of Jewish identity that recapitulated and reinvented the Georgian stage's central questions about theater and nation, about stage Jews and English identity, but as I suggested in Chapter 1, considerably more research is needed on the ways in which British theatrical culture represented a variety of ethnic, religious, provincial, and colonial minorities, both in Georgian London and beyond.[37] In these final pages, I have emphasized the ways in which novels in the 1890s, while working within and against a stage tradition that was established during the Georgian period, responded to an increasingly prevalent view of the Jew's theatrical power during a period of acute anti-Semitism. This has led me to argue that novels in the 1890s took over and profoundly revised the relationship between Jews and the theater, just as earlier the theater had rewritten the conventional stage Jew as a sentimental comic hero and even deconstructed the culture's entire practice of staging Jewish identity through the trope of the cross-dressing Gentile, while the early nineteenth-century novel critiqued and rewrote the ethnic caricatures of the stage—all signal moments of historical change in the theatricalization of ethnic identity in Britain. In order to emphasize the importance of the retrieval of Georgian theater history, I have suggested in this chapter the uses to which Victorian writers put this history, especially in analyzing the performance history of the stage Jew, most notably as a means of (re)formulating the relationship between the Jewish Question and English national identity. I hope that my own retrieval of Georgian theatrical history in the course of this book has revealed not only the complex ways in which ethnic and national identities were constructed, disseminated, questioned, and demystified but also the importance of this history for understanding how the theatricalization of ethnic identity functioned both on and beyond the arena of the Georgian stage.

NOTES

CHAPTER I. "FAMILY QUARRELS"

1. Thomas Dibdin, *The Reminiscences of Thomas Dibdin*, 2 vols. (London: Henry Coburn, 1827), 1.341.

2. Quoted from a review in the *Oracle*, in Dibdin, *Reminiscences*, 1.347.

3. Kevin Whelan, "The Green Atlantic: Radical Reciprocities Between Ireland and America in the Long Eighteenth Century," in *A New Imperial History: Culture, Identity, and Modernity in Britain and the Empire, 1660–1840*, ed. Kathleen Wilson (Cambridge: Cambridge University Press, 2004), goes on to argue that this "incorporating" policy represented a "newly aggressive, exclusive British nationalism" that was "metropolitan, militant, imperial, xenophobic" (p. 217). H. J. Hanham, *Scottish Nationalism* (Cambridge, Mass.: Harvard University Press, 1969), explains that anti-unionists argued that if a union was necessary, "it should have been a federal not an incorporating union" (p. 66).

4. Allan I. Macinnes, *Clanship, Commerce and the House of Stuart, 1603–1788* (East Lothian: Tuckwell Press, 1996), argues that "the immediate aftermath of the 'Forty-Five was marked by systematic state terrorism, characterised by a genocidal intent that verged on ethnic cleansing" (p. 211). Colin Kidd, "Ethnicity in the British Atlantic World, 1688–1830," in *A New Imperial History*, ed. Wilson, claims that such an argument "involves a considerable measure of exaggeration" (p. 273). Also see Thomas William Heyck, *The Peoples of the British Isles: A New History from 1688 to 1870* (Belmont: Wadsworth, 1992), who records that "Lord Chesterfield . . . urged a policy of genocide . . .—the chiefs were to be captured and the peasantry massacred" (p. 129). Also see S. J. Connolly, "Varieties of Britishness: Ireland, Scotland and Wales in the Hanoverian State," in *Uniting the Kingdom? The Making of British History*, ed. Alexander Grant and Keith J. Stringer (London: Routledge, 1995), who views as "something close to genocide" the call for "a complete embargo on grain exports into the Highlands as a means of extirpating rebellion there once and for all" (p. 194). John Prebble, *Culloden* (1961; rpt. Harmondsworth: Penguin, 1966), sees the battle of Culloden as marking "an end to Gaeldom" (p. xiii). See Victor Kiernan, "The British Isles: Celt and Saxon," in *The National Question in Europe in Historical Context*, ed. Mikulas Teich and Roy Porter (Cambridge: Cambridge University Press, 1993), on the English transformation of the Celts (p. 1).

5. M. Dorothy George, *London Life in the XVIII Century* (London, 1925), pp. 117–19.

6. See Connolly, "Varieties of Britishness," in *Uniting the Kingdom?* ed. Grant and Stringer, p. 204, and Whelan, "The Green Atlantic," in *A New Imperial History*, ed. Wilson, p. 231.

7. See Frank Felsenstein, *Anti-Semitic Stereotypes: A Paradigm of Otherness in English Popular Culture, 1660–1830* (Baltimore: Johns Hopkins University Press, 1995), pp. 190–91.

8. Francis Place, quoted in R. Leslie-Melville, *The Life and Work of Sir John Fielding* (London: Lincoln Williams, 1934), p. 266.

9. Horace Walpole, letter to Lady Ossory, December 14, 1771, *The Yale Edition of Horace Walpole's Correspondence*, ed. W. S. Lewis, 48 vols. (New Haven: Yale University Press, 1937–93), 32.68.

10. See William Cobbett, *Cobbett's Weekly Political Register* 69 (June 5, 1830), where he goes on to proclaim: "I have pelted them many a time with snow-balls, or rotten apples, or clods of dirt; and I thought I was doing my duty" (pp. 732–33).

11. John Brewer, "The Misfortunes of Lord Bute," *The Historical Journal* 16, no. 1 (March 1973): 3–43, p. 19.

12. Prebble, *Culloden*, p. 227.

13. *The London Stage, 1660–1800*, part III (1729–1747), ed. Arthur H. Scouten, 2 vols. (Carbondale: Southern Illinois University Press, 1961), records "An Occasional Song on the Defeat of the Rebels by Beard" for April 25, 1746, at Covent Garden (2.1236).

14. See Paul Monod, "Pierre's White Hat: Theatre, Jacobitism and Popular Protest in London, 1689–1760," in *By Force or by Default? The Revolution of 1688–1689*, ed. Eveline Cruickshanks (Edinburgh: J. Donald, 1989), pp. 159–89.

15. John Jackson, *The history of the Scottish stage, from its first establishment to the present time* (Edinburgh, 1793), p. 374.

16. Richard Cumberland, *The Observer* (1785), no. 38, rpt. in *The British Essayists*, ed. A. Chalmers (Boston: Little, Brown, 1866), 38 vols., 32.266.

17. See, for example, the review of Isaac Brandon's *Kais, or Love in the Deserts*, in *Satirist, or Monthly Meteor* 2 (April 1808), in which the reviewer refers to the author as "'cunning little Isaac'" (p. 199).

18. [Walter Scott,] review of *Memoirs of the Life of John Philip Kemble, Esquire, Including a History of the Stage from the Time of Garrick to the Present Period*, by James Boaden, *Quarterly Review* 34 (June 1826): 196–248, pp. 200–201.

19. Leigh Hunt, "Enjoyments of the Theatre," in *Leigh Hunt's Dramatic Criticism, 1808–1831*, ed. Lawrence Huston Houtchens and Carolyn Washburn Houtchens (New York: Columbia University Press, 1949), p. 252.

20. Marc Baer, *Theatre and Disorder in Late Georgian London* (Oxford: Clarendon Press, 1992), p. 193.

21. See, for example, Sir St. Vincent Troubridge, "Theatre Riots in London," pp. 84–97, in *Studies in English Theatre History* (London, 1952). For a more recent account, see Gillian Russell's excellent analysis of the military's role in "riotous assemblies" in *The*

Theatres of War: Performance, Politics, and Society, 1793–1815 (Oxford: Clarendon Press, 1995), pp. 106–21.

22. Francis Congreve, *Authentic Memoirs of the Late Mr. Charles Macklin, Comedian* (London: J. Barker, 1798), pp. 39–40.

23. See "introduction" in *The Plays of George Colman the Elder*, ed. Kalman A. Burnim (New York: Garland, 1983), 6 vols., 1.xix–xx.

24. See William Cooke, *Memoirs of Charles Macklin, Comedian* (1804; rpt. New York: Benjamin Blom, 1972), p. 298; William W. Appleton, *Charles Macklin: An Actor's Life* (Cambridge, Mass.: Harvard University Press, 1960), p. 214.

25. "Theatre," *Universal Magazine of Knowledge and Pleasure* (December 1802), p. 456.

26. Scott, review of *Memoirs*, p. 200.

27. Jürgen Habermas, *The Structural Transformation of the Public Sphere: An Inquiry into a Category of Bourgeois Society*, trans. Thomas Burger (Cambridge, Mass.: MIT Press, 1993), argues that in the early eighteenth century the press began to function as an organ of the public and hence as "the fourth estate" (p. 60). Also see J. A. W. Gunn, *Beyond Liberty and Property: The Process of Self-Recognition in Eighteenth-Century Political Thought* (Kingston: McGill-Queen's University Press, 1983), on the press (p. 90) and on the people (pp. 79–88) as "the fourth estate."

28. Theophilus Cibber, *Two Dissertations on the Theatres* (1756), quoted in Harry William Pedicord, *The Theatrical Public in the Time of Garrick* (New York: Columbia University Press, 1954), p. 20. Colman's epilogue to Hugh Kelly's *Clementina* (1771), quoted in Allardyce Nicoll, *A History of Late Eighteenth-Century Drama, 1750–1800* (Cambridge: Cambridge University Press, 1927), p. 13.

29. Arthur Murphy, *The Life of David Garrick* (1801; rpt. New York: Benjamin Blom, 1969), 2 vols., 2.201.

30. Maria Edgeworth, *Harrington*, in *Tales and Novels*, 10 vols. (New York: AMS Press), 9:56: "As a veteran wit described it, 'There were at this time four estates in the English Constitution, kings, lords, commons, and the theatre.'"

31. John Tomlinson, *Cultural Imperialism: A Critical Introduction* (Baltimore: Johns Hopkins University Press, 1991), p. 84.

32. Peter Stallybrass and Allon White, *The Politics and Poetics of Transgression* (Ithaca: Cornell University Press, 1986), pp. 80 and 82.

33. Thomas Whincop, *Scanderbeg: or, love and liberty* (London, 1747), p. 237.

34. David Garrick, *The Farmer's Return from London*, in *The Plays of David Garrick*, ed. Henry William Pedicord and Fredrick Louis Bergmann (Carbondale: Southern Illinois University Press, 1980), 7 vols., 1.250. This interlude was performed at the patent theaters in 1762, 1766, 1774, 1779, and 1781.

35. Epilogue (1789) by M. P. Andrews to Frederic Reynolds's *The Dramatist*, quoted in Nicoll, *Late Eighteenth-Century Drama*, p. 10.

36. Walpole, letter to Lady Ossory, July 1, 1789, *Correspondence*, 34:51.

37. *The Complete Works of William Hazlitt*, ed. P. P. Howe (London: J. M. Dent, 1930–34), 21 vols., 18.297.

38. Quoted in Todd Endelman, *The Jews of Georgian England, 1714–1830: Tradition and Change in a Liberal Society* (Philadelphia: Jewish Publication Society of America, 1979), p. 126.

39. James Boaden, *Memoirs of the Life of John Philip Kemble, Esq.* (London, 1825), 2 vols., 2.334.

40. Boaden, *Memoirs*, 1.397.

41. M. J. Landa, *The Jew in the Drama* (1926; rpt. New York: Ktav, 1969), p. 175.

42. Requested to write the prologue for the revival, Charles Bucke reported that "the Jews . . . took so much offence at the representation—particularly as it occurred during the week of Passover,—that, for the whole of the remaining season, it was more difficult to recognize a JEW in the house, than even a WOMAN OF FASHION" (Preface, *The Italians; or The Fatal Accusation: A Tragedy with a Preface* [London: G. and W. B. Whittaker, 1819], n. p.).

43. Robert Southey, *Letters from England: By Don Manuel Alvarez Espriella* (London: Longman, Hurst, Rees and Orme, 1807), 3 vols., 3.175.

44. Richard Cumberland, *The Memoirs of Richard Cumberland*, ed. Richard J. Dircks, 2 vols. in 1 (1807; rpt. New York: AMS Press, 2002), 1.167.

45. Quoted in Wylie Sypher, *Guinea's Captive Kings: British Anti-Slavery Literature of the XVIIIth Century* (Chapel Hill: University of North Carolina Press, 1942), p. 117.

46. Diary of Richard Cross [September 8, 1753], quoted in Pedicord, *Theatrical Public*, pp. 42–43.

47. James L. Lynch, *Box, Pit, and Gallery: Stage and Society in Johnson's London* (Berkeley: University of California Press, 1953), p. 261.

48. Charles Macklin, *Love à la Mode*, in *Four Comedies by Charles Macklin*, ed. J. O. Bartley (London: Sedgwick and Jackson, 1968), p. 46.

49. Walpole, letter to Horace Mann, June 14, 1780, *Correspondence*, 25.62.

50. *The Letters of Junius*, ed. John Cannon (Oxford: Clarendon Press, 1978), pp. 20–21.

51. John Tobin, *The Faro Table; or, The Guardians* (London: John Murray, 1816), p. 49.

52. George Colman the Elder, *The Oxonian in Town*, reprinted in *Plays of George Colman the Elder*, ed. Burnim, Advertisement and p. 2.

53. Quoted in Matthew J. Kinservik, *Disciplining Satire: The Censorship of Satiric Comedy on the Eighteenth-Century London Stage* (Lewisburg, Pa.: Bucknell University Press, 2002), p. 194.

54. "Preface" to Richard Brinsley Sheridan, *The Rivals*, in *The Dramatic Works of Richard Brinsley Sheridan*, 2 vols., ed. Cecil Price (Oxford: Clarendon Press, 1973), 1.71.

55. Charles Beech Hogan, *The London Stage, 1776–1800: A Critical Introduction* (Carbondale: Southern Illinois University Press, 1968), pp. clxxvii–clxxviii. Charles Harold Gray, *Theatrical Criticism in London to 1795* (1931; rpt. New York: Benjamin Blom, 1964), passim.

56. See L. W. Conolly, *The Censorship of English Drama, 1737–1824* (San Marino: Huntington Library, 1976), pp. 95 and 174–80.

57. Hugh Kearney, *The British Isles: A History of Four Nations* (Cambridge: Cambridge University Press, 1989), p. 174.

58. E. A. Wrigley, "A Simple Model of London's Importance in Changing English Society and Economy, 1650–1750," in *Past and Present*, no. 37 (July 1967), 44–70, pp. 63 and 49.

59. Quoted in George, *London Life*, p. 111.

60. Sypher, *Guinea's Captive Kings*, p. 87. In my next chapter I explain how the Scots and Irish worried that their children would remain in England after being educated there.

61. On Newton's prints see David Alexander, *Richard Newton and English Caricature in the 1790s* (Manchester: Whitworth Art Gallery and University of Manchester, 1998), p. 123 and plates 22–23, and Michael Duffy, *The Englishman and the Foreigner* (Cambridge: Chadwyck-Healey, 1986), pp. 18 and 293. See Herbert M. Atherton, *Political Prints in the Age of Hogarth: A Study of Ideographic Representations of Politics* (Oxford: Clarendon Press, 1974), on prints showing the Scots as invaders of England, pp. 211–14.

62. Leslie-Melville, *Life and Work of Sir John Fielding*, p. 265.

63. Endelman, *Jews of Georgian England*, p. 173. Also see Harold Pollins, *Economic History of the Jews in England* (London: Associated University Press, 1982), pp. 48 and 65.

64. George, *London Life*, pp. 134–38.

65. Kearney, *British Isles*, p. 8. He goes on to include, but only "in the closing decades of the nineteenth century," "an influx of Jewish refugees."

66. Paul Langford, *A Polite and Commercial People: England, 1727–1783* (Oxford: Oxford University Press, 1992), p. 327.

67. James Horn, "British Diaspora: Emigration from Britain, 1680–1818," in *The Eighteenth Century*, vol. 2 of *The Oxford History of the British Empire*, ed. P. J. Marshall (Oxford: Oxford University Press, 1998), p. 31.

68. Alexander Murdoch, *British History, 1660–1832: National Identity and Local Culture* (New York: St. Martin's Press, 1998), p. 85. Whelan, "The Green Atlantic," in *A New Imperial History*, ed. Wilson: "As many as 60,000 Irish left in the 1790s" and arrived in America with "a strong sense of ethnic allegiance," pp. 224–25. Horn, "British Diaspora," in *The Eighteenth Century*, ed. Marshall, p. 46.

69. "To the Printer," *Gazetteer and New Daily Advertiser*, December 28, 1765, and "Postscript. To the Printer," *London Chronicle*, April 7, 1767.

70. *Public Advertiser*, January 1, 3, 4, 6, 9, 1787.

71. Neil McKendrick, John Brewer, and J. H. Plumb, *The Birth of a Consumer Society: The Commercialization of Eighteenth-Century England* (Bloomington: Indiana University Press, 1982), pp. 275–80. Also see David Worrall, *Harlequin Empire: Race, Ethnicity and the Drama of the Popular Enlightenment* (London: Pickering and Chatto, 2007), on theater building in the provinces and on the immense numbers of people who attended the

theater (in London around 1818 "a nightly figure of 10,000 persons witnessing some form of dramatic entertainment seems a conservative estimate"), p. 19.

72. Iain Macintosh and Geoffrey Ashton, *The Georgian Playhouse: Actors, Artists, Audiences and Architecture, 1730–1830* [catalogue of an exhibit held at the] Hayward Gallery, London, 21 August to 12 October 1975 (London: Arts Council of Great Britain, 1975), n.p.

73. See, for example, Jean-Christophe Agnew, *Worlds Apart: The Market and the Theater in Anglo-American Thought, 1550–1750* (Cambridge: Cambridge University Press, 1986): "London's theater had lost most of its nerve and much of its audience by the middle of the [eighteenth] century" (p. 161).

74. Richard Sennett, *The Fall of Public Man* (New York: W. W. Norton, 1974), pp. 38, 17, 42, and 52 (where Sennett cites Daniel Defoe's *A Tour Through the Whole Island of Great Britain* [1724] for "the exception of 'the Irish horde'").

75. Agnew, *Worlds Apart*, pp. 13, 159–60.

76. E. P. Thompson, "Patrician Society, Plebeian Culture," in *Journal of Social History* 7 (Summer 1974): 382–405 (quote on p. 396). See John Brewer, "Theater and Counter-Theater in Georgian Politics: The Mock Elections at Garrat," in *Radical History Review* 22 (Winter 1979–80): 7–40, for a rare early study of the interplay between the London stage and the theatricality of everyday life.

77. Jeffrey N. Cox, volume 5 of *Slavery, Abolition, and Emancipation: Writings in the British Romantic Period* (London: Pickering and Chatto, 1999), 8 vols., ed. Peter J. Kitson and Debbie Lee, 5:vii–xxvi; Felicity A. Nussbaum, *The Limits of the Human: Fictions of Anomaly, Race, and Gender in the Long Eighteenth Century* (Cambridge: Cambridge University Press, 2003), especially chapter 8; Virginia Mason Vaughan, *Performing Blackness on English Stages, 1500–1800* (Cambridge: Cambridge University Press, 2005); Roxann Wheeler, *The Complexion of Race: Categories of Difference in Eighteenth-Century British Culture* (Philadelphia: University of Pennsylvania Press, 2000). Also see David Worrall, *The Politics of Romantic Theatricality, 1787–1832: The Road to the Stage* (Palgrave Macmillan, 2007), pp. 68–106, for a different view of blackface on the eighteenth-century stage. Betsy Bolton, *Women, Nationalism and the Romantic Stage: Theatre and Politics in Britain, 1780–1800* (Cambridge: Cambridge University Press, 2001), especially part III ("Mixed Drama, Imperial Farce"), and Daniel O'Quinn, *Staging Governance: Theatrical Imperialism in London, 1770–1800* (Baltimore: Johns Hopkins University Press, 2005).

78. Julie A. Carlson, *In the Theatre of Romanticism: Coleridge, Nationalism, Women* (Cambridge: Cambridge University Press, 1994), p. 3; Russell, *Theatres of War*, p. 16.

79. See O'Quinn, *Staging Governance*, on "the relative lack of scholarship on oratory, theatre, and other forms of performance" (p. 351), and Bolton, *Women, Nationalism and the Romantic Stage*, on "theatre, ignored by historians and critics alike as a degraded form" (p. 4). Russell, *Theatres of War*, has complained of "the hitherto narrowly empirical and apolitical biases within theatre history" (p. 15), and Jane Moody, *Illegitimate Theatre in London, 1770–1840* (Cambridge: Cambridge University Press, 2000), sets out "to revise

our assumptions about the supposedly apolitical character of late Georgian performance" and "the theatre's virtual absence from Romantic scholarship" (pp. 2–3).

80. Edward D. Coleman, *The Jew in English Drama: An Annotated Bibliography* (New York: New York Public Library, 1943); J. O. Bartley, *Teague, Shenkin and Sawney: Being an Historical Study of the Earliest Irish, Welsh and Scottish Characters in English Plays* (Cork: Cork University Press, 1954); G. C. Duggan, *The Stage Irishman: A History of the Irish Play and Stage Characters from the Earliest Times* (New York: Benjamin Blom, 1969); Landa, *The Jew in the Drama*. Also see H. R. S. Van Der Veen, *Jewish Characters in Eighteenth-Century English Fiction and Drama* (1935; rpt. Ktav, 1973), and Edgar Rosenberg's prefatory essay attached to this reprint, "Tabloid Jews and Fungoid Scribblers." For a more recent and richly analytical approach, see Joseph Th. Leerssen, *Mere Irish and Fior-Ghael: Studies in the Idea of Irish Nationality, Its Development and Literary Expression Prior to the Nineteenth Century* (Amsterdam: John Benjamins, 1986).

81. Wheeler, *Complexion of Race*, p. 11.

82. See O'Quinn's claims in *Staging Governance* that there occurred "the resignification of whiteness on the stage in the late 1780s" and "the transformation in audience-performance relations in the illegitimate theatre" in the 1790s (p. 31).

83. Moody, *Illegitimate Theatre*, pp. 54–55, 242.

84. J. G. A. Pocock, "British History: A Plea for a New Subject," *Journal of Modern History*, 47 (December 1975): 603, 616. Michael Ragussis, "Jews and Other 'Outlandish Englishmen': Ethnic Performance and the Invention of British Identity Under the Georges," *Critical Inquiry* 26 (Summer 2000): 793–96.

85. Earlier studies, such as Sybil Rosenfeld's *Strolling Players and Drama in the Provinces, 1660–1765* (Cambridge, 1939) and La Tourette Stockwell's *Dublin Theatres and Theatre Customs: 1637–1820* (1938; rpt. New York: B. Blom, 1968), have been supplemented in a slow and fragmentary manner: John E. Cunningham, *Theatre Royal: The History of the Theatre Royal Birmingham* (Oxford: George Ronald, 1950); Arnold Hare, *The Georgian Theatre in Wessex* (London: Phoenix House, 1958); J. L. Hodgkinson and Rex Pogson, *The Early Manchester Theatre* (London: Anthony Blond, 1960); Kathleen Barker, *The Theatre Royal, Bristol, 1766–1966* (London: Society for Theatre Research, 1974); *Theatre Royal Bath: A Calendar of Performances at the Orchard Street Theatre, 1750–1805*, ed. Arnold Hare (Bath: Kingsmead Press, 1977); *The Yorkshire Stage, 1766–1803: A Calendar of Plays*, ed. Linda Fitzsimmons and Arthur W. McDonald (Metuchen, N. J.: Scarecrow Press, 1989). More recent important analytical studies include Errol Hill, *The Jamaican Stage, 1655–1900: Profile of a Colonial Theatre* (Amherst: University of Massachusetts Press, 1992); Christopher J. Wheatley, *"Beneath Ierne's Banners": Irish Protestant Drama of the Restoration and Eighteenth Century* (Notre Dame: University of Notre Dame Press, 1999); Helen M. Burke, *Riotous Performance: The Struggle for Hegemony in the Irish Theatre, 1712–1784* (Notre Dame: University of Notre Dame Press, 2003); Kathleen Wilson, "The Black Widow: Gender, Race and Performance in England and America," in *The Island Race: Englishness, Empire and Gender in the Eighteenth Century* (London: Routledge, 2003).

86. David Cannadine, "British History as a 'New Subject': Politics, Perspectives and

Prospects," in *Uniting the Kingdom?* ed. Grant and Stringer, is the best overall guide to the importance of the "new British history" (p. 22) and the challenges made to the "four-nations" approach (pp. 24–26). See S. J. Connolly, R. A. Houston, and R. J. Morris, "Identity, Conflict and Economic Change: Themes and Issues," in their anthology *Conflict, Identity and Economic Development: Ireland and Scotland, 1600–1939* (Preston, UK: Carnegie, 1995), on the idea that "the national framework needed to be supplemented by a regional perspective" (p. 4). See Kearney, *British Isles*, on the limits of "nation-based history" (p. 2), and Murdoch, *British History*, who argues that "the idea of Britain . . . transcended traditional 'four-nations' national, political and cultural identities in favour of a new imperial identity" (p. 87). Also see *Strangers Within the Realm: Cultural Margins of the First British Empire*, ed. Bernard Bailyn and Philip D. Morgan (Chapel Hill: University of North Carolina Press, 1991), which attempts to be "transnational in spirit, pluralist and multicultural in approach" and "to embrace, some, at least, of the diverse ethnic experiences of the first British Empire" (p. 30).

87. Thomas Dibdin, *The School for Prejudice* (London: T. N. Longman and O. Rees, 1801), p. 50.

88. *The true-born Scot: inscribed to John Earl of Bute* (London: Printed for the author, and sold by E. Sumpter, 1764), pp. 10 and 16.

89. Dana Rabin, "The Jew Bill of 1753: Masculinity, Virility, and the Nation," *Eighteenth-Century Studies* 39, no. 2 (2006) (quote on p. 165).

90. See Frank Felsenstein and Sharon Mintz, *The Jew as Other: A Century of English Caricature, 1730–1830* (New York: Library of the Jewish Theological Seminary of America, 1995), p. 37, for the print *Randall, the Irish Lad and Belasco, the Jew Champion* (1817), and p. 40, for *The Comical Gills* (1820).

91. John Ford, *Prizefighting: The Age of Regency Boximania* (Newton Abbot: David and Charles, 1971), p. 36.

92. [Edward Long,] *The History of Jamaica* (1774; rpt. New York: Arno Press, 1972), 3 vols., 2.460.

93. John Wilkes, *The North Briton*, no. 34, Jan. 22, 1763, 2 vols. (Dublin: John Mitchell and James Williams, 1764), 2.196.

94. J. G. A. Pocock, "Conclusion: Contingency, Identity, Sovereignty," in *Uniting the Kingdom?* p. 300.

95. J. G. A. Pocock, "England," in *National Consciousness, History, and Political Culture in Early-Modern Europe*, ed. Orest Ranum (Baltimore: Johns Hopkins University Press, 1975), p. 100. Kathleen Wilson, *The Sense of the People: Politics, Culture and Imperialism in England, 1715–1785* (Cambridge: Cambridge University Press, 1995), pp. 334 and 174. In *The Island Race*, Wilson stresses the performative nature of English identity (p. 17), an idea at the center of my article "Jews and Other 'Outlandish Englishmen'" and my chapter 2 here. Murray G. H. Pittock, *Celtic Identity and the British Image* (Manchester: Manchester University Press, 1999), has demonstrated "the insistent ethnicization of the Celt in the British imagination," arguing more generally that "ethnic identities are used

as presumptions of inferiority in the language of established and powerful states everywhere" (pp. 6–7).

96. Linda Colley, "Britishness and Otherness: An Argument," *Nations and Nationalisms: France, Britain, Ireland and the Eighteenth-Century Context*, ed. Michael O'Dea and Kevin Whelan (Oxford: Oxford University Press, 1995), pp. 63–64. Raphael Samuel has argued that Colley's focus on the united nation of Britons "passes lightly over matters where explosive contradictions are more apparent," and he imagines a history that "focuses on the tenacity of our island ethnicities, and allows more conceptual space for schisms and secessions" ("Four Nations History," in *Island Stories: Unravelling Britain*, ed. Alison Light [London: Verso, 1998], p. 31). At the extreme other end of the spectrum, some historians have gone so far as to announce that "British history starts only when the Scotch and Irish became English speakers, in other words, a variant of Englishmen" (A. J. P. Taylor, "Comments," *Journal of Modern History* 47 [December 1975]: 622–26, p. 623) or that history writing needs "more kings and queens" and less of "this nonexistent history of ethnic entities" (G. R. Elton, quoted in David Cannadine, "British History: Past, Present—And Future?" *Past and Present*, no. 116 [August 1987]: 169–91, p. 188). For the most comprehensive and far-ranging critique of Colley, see J. C. D. Clark, "Protestantism, Nationalism, and National Identity, 1660–1832," *Historical Journal* 43, no. 1 (March 2000): 259–65.

97. E. P. Thompson, "Which Britons?" in *Persons and Polemics* (London: Merlin Press, 1994), p. 323.

98. Colin Kidd, *Subverting Scotland's Past: Scottish Whig Historians and the Creation of an Anglo-British Identity, 1689–c. 1830* (Cambridge: Cambridge University Press, 1993).

99. Kidd, "Ethnicity," in *New Imperial History*, ed. Wilson, pp. 276 and 273.

100. See Wheeler, *The Complexion of Race*, on the broad variety of discourses that develop over the course of the eighteenth century, and when and how they can be said to develop a racialist ideology.

101. *The Universal Songster; or, Museum of Mirth* (London: George Routledge, n.d.), 3 vols., 3.289–91.

102. *The new British universal jester, or the wit's companion* (London [1788]), pp. 11–21, 31–32, 45–49 passim.

103. For example, Nicholas Canny quotes an early English colonist as responding to the conquered Irish by planning to "overspread and incorporate them into ourselves, and so by an oneness take away the foundation of difference" ("Identity Formation in Ireland: The Emergence of the Anglo-Irish," in *Colonial Identity in the Atlantic World, 1500–1800*, ed. Nicholas Canny and Anthony Pagden [Princeton: Princeton University Press, 1987], p. 200).

104. See George, *London Life*, on burning a "Taffy" and a "Paddy" in effigy (p. 118), and Wilson, *Sense of the People*, on the ways in which crowds in a number of localities burned effigies of Bute (p. 213). I note the burning of Jewish effigies in Chapter 4.

105. Tamara L. Hunt, *Defining John Bull: Political Caricature and National Identity in*

Late Georgian England (Burlington, Vt.: Ashgate, 2003), p. 28. Brewer, "The Misfortunes of Lord Bute," p. 7.

106. See my Chapter 4 on the public's reaction to the vivisection of the Jews' bodies, and Prebble, *Culloden*, p. 269.

107. Atherton, *Political Prints*, p. 226.

108. Felsenstein, *Anti-Semitic Stereotypes*, pp. 146 and 193.

109. Atherton, *Political Prints*, p. 217.

110. See Pittock, *Celtic Identity*, pp. 26–28, for the ways in which Scots were portrayed "as lice-ridden cannibals with insatiable and disorderly sexual appetites" (p. 27).

111. In Atherton, *Political Prints*, see *The Whipping Post* (1762) (p. 96, plate 113), as well as graphic prints in general that emphasized Bute's "sexual prowess and physical endowments" and the way in which Bute's broomstick, bagpipes, and staff were used with obvious sexual meanings (pp. 219–22). See the two-part *The Colonies Reduced* and *Its Companion* (1768) in Wilson, *Sense of the People*, who makes the connection between Bute, foreignness, effeminacy, and sexual perversion (pp. 223–24).

112. Prebble, *Culloden*, p. 228.

113. John Douglas, *A Serious Defence of Some Late Measures of the Administration; Particularly with regard to the Introduction and Establishment of Foreign Troops* (London: J. Morgan, 1756), pp. 17, 22.

114. Horace Walpole, letter to Lady Ossory, December 15, 1787, *Correspondence* 33.587–88.

115. *Letters of Junius*, p. 163.

116. [Long,] *History of Jamaica*, 2.262.

117. Walpole, *Correspondence*, 20.178, n. 18.

118. Prebble, *Culloden*, p. 278, and Maureen Wall, *The Penal Laws, 1691–1760: Church and State from the Treaty of Limerick to the Accession of George III* (Dundalk, Ireland: Dundalgan Press, 1961), p. 26.

119. See Kathleen Wilson's brilliant historical narrative that begins with the insight that "the crisis of the '45 produced and legitimized a politics of identity" (p. 167), and then goes on to record how an increasing English patriotic fervor led to a consistent period of xenophobia aimed at both external and internal outsiders (*Sense of the People*, pp. 165–264 passim). This is the time period in which the theater exploded with new forms and strategies for portraying ethnic difference; hence my focus on the period from the 1750s through the opening decades of the nineteenth century.

CHAPTER 2. "CUTTING OFF TONGUES"

1. *In and Out of Tune*, n.p., Larpent Collection, manuscript no. 1541, Henry E. Huntington Library and Art Gallery. This operatic farce is usually attributed to Andrew Cherry but sometimes to Dennis Lawler, both of whom seem to have had a hand in writing it. It was first performed on January 3, 1808, at Drury Lane.

2. John Bernard, *Retrospections of the Stage* (London: Henry Colburn and Richard Bentley, 1830), p. 118.

3. Quoted from *St James Chronicle*, October 26, 1773, in William W. Appleton, *Charles Macklin: An Actor's Life* (Cambridge, Mass.: Harvard University Press, 1960), p. 180. The remark became famous and circulated for many years; see, for example, *The Olio, or, Museum of Entertainment* (London: Joseph Shackell, 1831), 6 vols., 6.90.

4. Charles Macklin, *Love à la Mode*, in *Four Comedies by Charles Macklin*, ed. J. O. Bartley (London: Sidgwick and Jackson, 1968), pp. 50, 56; hereafter abbreviated *LM*.

5. Anon., *Mordecai's Beard*, n.p., Larpent Collection, manuscript no. 865, Henry E. Huntington Library and Art Gallery.

6. Roger Fiske, *English Theatre Music in the Eighteenth Century*, 2nd ed. (1973; Oxford: Oxford University Press, 1986), p. 214.

7. Moses Mendez, *The Double Disappointment; A Farce* (London, 1760), pp. 8 and 37.

8. Gerald Berkeley Hertz, *British Imperialism in the Eighteenth Century* (London: Archibald Constable, 1908), pp. 101–2.

9. Thomas Sheridan, *Captain O'Blunder: or, The Brave Irishman* (London, 1771), pp. 9–10.

10. J. Reed, *The Register-Office* (Dublin, 1761), pp. 33, 41, 41, 28. This play was performed in 1761, 1764, 1767–79, and 1781.

11. A Lady, *The South Briton* (London, 1774), p. 56; hereafter in this paragraph page numbers appear in parentheses.

12. See chapter 5, "Bedtricksters," in Virginia Mason Vaughan, *Performing Blackness on English Stages, 1500–1800* (Cambridge: Cambridge University Press, 2005). Vaughan makes no mention of *The Cozeners*.

13. Samuel Foote, *The Cozeners* (London: Lowndes and Bladon, 1795), p. 65. This play was performed in 1774, 1775, 1776, and 1792.

14. George Farquhar, *The Beaux Stratagem*, in *The Works of George Farquhar*, ed. Shirley Strum Kenny (Oxford: Clarendon Press, 1988), 2 vols., 2.191, 219. This play was performed every year between 1707 and 1800.

15. James Boswell, *Life of Johnson*, ed. R. W. Chapman (Oxford: Oxford University Press, 1991), pp. 276–77; hereafter abbreviated *LJ*.

16. Andrew Erskine, in a letter to Boswell (February 16, 1764), in *Boswell in Holland, 1763–64*, ed. Frederick A. Pottle (Melbourne: William Heinemann, 1952), p. 172.

17. Michael Hechter, *Internal Colonialism: The Celtic Fringe in British National Development, 1536–1966* (Berkeley: University of California Press, 1977). Also see Victor Edward Durkacz, *The Decline of the Celtic Languages: A Study of Linguistic and Cultural Conflict in Scotland, Wales, and Ireland from the Reformation to the Twentieth Century* (Edinburgh: John Donald, 1983), on the ways in which the charity school movement in the eighteenth century attempted "the extirpation of the Gaelic language" (p. 63), which included not allowing children in the Highlands to speak Gaelic at school and moving them to the Lowlands in order to alienate them from their native culture and language.

18. Christopher Hill, *Reformation to Industrial Revolution: A Social and Economic History of Britain, 1530–1780* (London: Weidenfeld and Nicolson, 1967), pp. 15 and 28.

19. John Allingham, *Transformation; or, Love and Law* (Baltimore, 1814), p. 7 (discussed at length in chapter 4).

20. Henry Carey, *The Honest Yorkshire-man* (London, 1763), p. 23.

21. Horace Walpole, letter to Richard Bentley, December 24, 1754, *The Yale Edition of Horace Walpole's Correspondence*, ed. W. S. Lewis, 48 vols. (New Haven: Yale University Press, 1937–83), 35.200.

22. Thomas Sheridan, *A Course of Lectures on Elocution* (1762; rpt. Menston: Scolar Press, 1968), pp. 206 and 30.

23. See Thomas Sheridan, *An Oration, Pronounced before a Numerous Body of the Nobility and Gentry* (Dublin, 1757), p. 4. See Wilbur Samuel Howell, *Eighteenth-Century British Logic and Rhetoric* (Princeton: Princeton University Press, 1971), on Sheridan's ideas and influence, pp. 156–58, 218–42.

24. David Hume, letter to John Home, 28 July 1767, *The Letters of David Hume*, ed. J. Y. T. Greig (Oxford: Clarendon Press, 1932), 2 vols., 2.154.

25. Samuel Foote, *The Minor*, in *Plays by Samuel Foote and Arthur Murphy*, ed. George Taylor (Cambridge: Cambridge University Press, 1984), pp. 49–50. This play was performed every year between 1760 and 1780, and then intermittently through the 1790s.

26. Richard Cumberland, *The Fashionable Lover* (London: W. Griffin, 1772), p. 61. This play was performed in 1772, 1773, 1774, 1775, 1778, 1786, and 1795, and it continued to be popular through the opening decades of the nineteenth century.

27. *The Universal Songster; or, Museum of Mirth*, 3 vols. (London: George Routledge, n.d.), 3.290–91.

28. John O'Keeffe, *The Irish Mimic; or, Blunders at Brighton*, in *The Plays of John O'Keeffe*, 4 vols., ed. Frederick M. Link (New York: Garland, 1981), 4.36, 4.13, and 4.12. This play was performed every year between 1795 and 1800.

29. David Hume, "Of National Characters," in *Essays and Treatises on Several Subjects* (1753–54), *The Philosophical Works*, 4 vols., ed. Thomas Hill Green and Thomas Hodge Grose (Darmstadt: Scientia Verlag Aalen, 1964), 3.252.

30. [Edward Long,] *The History of Jamaica* (1774; rpt. New York: Arno, 1972), 2 vols., 2:475–85.

31. Arthur Murphy, *The Apprentice*, in *The Plays of Arthur Murphy*, ed. Richard B. Schwartz (New York: Garland, 1979), 2 vols., 2.40 and 2.38. This play was performed almost every year between 1756 and 1800.

32. Reed, *The Register-Office*, p. 33.

33. George Colman the Elder, *New Brooms! An Occasional Prelude*, in *The Plays of George Colman the Elder*, 6 vols., ed. Kalman A. Burnim (New York: Garland, 1983), 4.15.

34. Quoted in Marc Baer, *Theatre and Disorder in Late Georgian London* (Oxford: Clarendon Press, 1992), pp. 210–11.

35. *Daniel Cast into the Den of Lions, or True Blue Will Never Stain* (1763), reproduced

and discussed in Vincent Carretta, *George III and the Satirists from Hogarth to Byron* (Athens: University of Georgia Press, 1990), pp. 101–3.

36. Hume, letter to Gilbert Elliot, July 2, 1757, 1.255; letter to John Wilkes, October 16, 1754, 1.205; letter to Gilbert Elliot, September 22, 1764, 1.470; letter to William Straham, October 25, 1769, 2.209, in *Letters*, ed. Greig.

37. Sheridan, *A Course of Lectures on Elocution*, pp. 261–62.

38. Horace Walpole, *Memoirs of the Reign of King George the Third* (London: Lawrence and Bullen, 1894), 4 vols., 1.3–4.

39. On the many satirical prints that pointed to the foreignness of the first two Georges (for slighting England for Germany) and George III (for slighting England for Scotland), see Carretta, *George III*.

40. Thomas Sheridan, preface to *A General Dictionary of the English Language*, 2 vols. (1780; rpt. Menston: Scolar Press, 1967), 1. n. p.

41. See Appleton, *Charles Macklin*, pp. 120–21.

42. Francis Aspry Congreve, *Authentic Memoirs of the Late Mr. Charles Macklin, Comedian* (London, 1798), p. 40.

43. L. W. Conolly, *The Censorship of English Drama, 1737–1824* (San Marino: Huntington Library, 1976), p. 21.

44. Congreve, *Authentic Memoirs*, p. 40.

45. James Thomas Kirkman, *Memoirs of the Life of Charles Macklin* (London, 1799), 2 vols., 1.62–69.

46. William Cooke, *Memoirs of Charles Macklin, Comedian* (1804; rpt. New York: Benjamin Blom, 1972), pp. 223–25.

47. George Colman the Elder, *The Oxonian in Town*, in *Plays of George Colman the Elder*, 2.4. The play was performed in 1767, 1768, 1769, 1770, and 1772.

48. Macklin, *Four Comedies*, pp. 85 and 93–94; hereafter *The True-born Irishman* will be abbreviated *TBI*.

49. Paul Goring marks the limitations of this triumph by recalling that the play, while a success in Dublin, had only one performance in London (" 'John Bull, pit, box, and gallery, said No!': Charles Macklin and the Limits of Ethnic Resistance on the Eighteenth-Century London Stage," *Representations* 79 (Summer 2002): 61–88, pp. 65–66.

50. John Barrell, *English Literature in History, 1730–80: An Equal, Wide Survey* (London: Hutchinson, 1983), and Olivia Smith, *The Politics of Language, 1791–1819* (Oxford: Clarendon Press, 1984).

51. Barrell, *English Literature*, pp. 148, 157, 163.

52. Katie Trumpener, *Bardic Nationalism: The Romantic Novel and the British Empire* (Princeton: Princeton University Press, 1997), pp. 86–92, and Janet Sorensen, *The Grammar of Empire in Eighteenth-Century British Writing* (Cambridge: Cambridge University Press, 2000), pp. 21–23 and 99.

53. J. C. D. Clark, *Samuel Johnson: Literature, Religion and English Cultural Politics from the Restoration to Romanticism* (Cambridge: Cambridge University Press, 1994), p. 75.

54. P. J. Marshall, "A Nation Defined by Empire, 1755–1776," in *Uniting the Kingdom? The Making of British History*, ed. Alexander Grant and Keith J. Stringer (London: Routledge, 1995), p. 216.

55. Linda Colley, "Whose Nation? Class and National Consciousness in Britain, 1750–1830," *Past and Present* (November 1986), 113: 97–117, p. 102.

56. [Peter Lock,] *An Exmoor scolding, in the propriety and decency of Exmoor language, between two sisters* (Exeter, [1788]), pp. 5 and 3.

57. *Boswell: The Ominous Years, 1774–1776*, ed. Charles Ryskamp and Frederick A. Pottle (New York: McGraw-Hill, 1963), pp. 124–25.

58. Beattie's remarks are quoted in Ernest Campbell Mossner, *The Life of David Hume*, 2nd ed. (Oxford: Clarendon Press, 1980), p. 374; "To the Printer," *Gazetteer and New Daily Advertiser*, January 15, 1766.

59. Bernard, *Retrospections of the Stage*, 2.126.

60. George Colman the Elder, *Oxonian in Town*, in *The Plays of George Colman the Elder*, 2.9.

61. A passage that appeared in the *Morning Chronicle* after the opening of the play, quoted in Richard Little Purdy, introduction to Richard Sheridan's *The Rivals* (Oxford: Clarendon Press, 1935), pp. xvi–xvii.

62. See the entry on Lawrence Clinch in Philip H. Highfill, Jr., Kalman A. Burnim, and Edward A. Langhans, *A Biographical Dictionary of Actors, Actresses, Musicians, Dancers, Managers and Other Stage Personnel in London, 1660–1800* (Carbondale: Southern Illinois University Press, 1973), 16 vols., 3.334–35.

63. *A Scotsman's Remarks on the Farce of "Love à la Mode"* (London, 1760), pp. 10–11.

64. Cooke, *Memoirs of Charles Macklin*, pp. 273–74.

65. Cooke, *Memoirs of Charles Macklin*, p. 270.

66. "To the Editor of the Irish Magazine," signed "Clio," *Irish magazine, and monthly asylum for neglected biography* (December 1809), p. 536.

67. Richard Cumberland, prologue to *The West Indian*, in *Plays of Richard Cumberland*, 6 vols., ed. Roberta F. S. Borkat (New York: Garland, 1982), 1.n.p.

68. Sheridan, *Course of Lectures*, p. 33.

69. Reprinted in *The Performers and Their Plays*, ed. Shirley Strum Kenny (New York: Garland, 1982), p. 33. Kenny explains that the epilogue appeared in a periodical in 1762 and "must have been recited at the 6 May 1762 performance" at Drury Lane.

70. John O'Keeffe, *Recollections of the Life of John O'Keeffe* (1826; rpt. New York: Benjamin Blom, 1969), 2 vols., 1.335.

71. O'Keeffe, *Recollections*, 2.310.

72. Michael Ragussis, *Figures of Conversion: "The Jewish Question" and English National Identity* (Durham: Duke University Press, 1995), pp. 83–84.

73. Anon., *The Fair Refugee or The Rival Jews*, Larpent Collection, manuscript no. 651, Henry E. Huntington Library and Art Gallery, p. 32; hereafter abbreviated *FR*. This play was performed at the Haymarket on February 10, 1785.

74. Frank Felsenstein, *Anti-Semitic Stereotypes: A Paradigm of Otherness in English Popular Culture, 1660–1830* (Baltimore: Johns Hopkins University Press, 1995), p. 208.

75. *Scourge, or, Literary, theatrical, and miscellaneous magazine* 7 (June 1814), p. 516.

76. Charles Lamb, "Imperfect Sympathies" (*Elia*, 1823), in *The Works of Charles and Mary Lamb*, 5 vols., ed. E. V. Lucas (New York: AMS Press, 1968), 2.62.

77. "To the Editor of the Irish Magazine," signed "Clio," *Irish magazine, and monthly asylum for neglected biography* (December 1809), p. 536.

78. W. Clark Russell, *Representative Actors: A Collection of Criticisms, Anecdotes, Personal Descriptions, Etc.* (London, n.d.), p. 306.

CHAPTER 3. "CHEELD O' COMMERCE"

1. Quoted by Nicholas Cronk, in his introduction to Voltaire, *Letters Concerning the English Nation* (1733; rpt. Oxford: Oxford University Press, 1994), p. xiii.

2. Joseph Addison and Richard Steele, *The Spectator*, no. 69, May 19, 1711, in *The Spectator*, ed. Donald F. Bond, 5 vols. (Oxford: Clarendon Press, 1965), 1.292–93.

3. Addison and Steele, *The Spectator*, no. 69, May 19, 1711, 1.294.

4. Addison and Steele, *The Spectator*, no. 69, May 19, 1711, 1.295.

5. J. G. A. Pocock, *Virtue, Commerce, and History: Essays on Political Thought and History, Chiefly in the Eighteenth Century* (Cambridge: Cambridge University Press, 1985), pp. 108–9.

6. Pocock, *Virtue, Commerce, and History*, pp. 195–96.

7. Voltaire, *Voltaire's Notebooks*, ed. Theodore Besterman (Geneva: Institut et Musée Voltaire, 1952), 2 vols., continuously paginated, p. 43.

8. Baron de Montesquieu, *The Spirit of the Laws*, trans. Thomas Nugent, 2 vols. in 1 (New York: Hafner, 1949), 1.321 and 1.316.

9. Addison and Steele, *The Spectator*, no. 69, May 19, 1711, 1.296.

10. Voltaire, *Letters concerning the English Nation*, p. 43.

11. Quoted in J. Rumney, "Anglo-Jewry as Seen Through Foreign Eyes (1730–1830)," *Transactions of the Jewish Historical Society of England* 13 (1932–35): 329.

12. Montesquieu, *Spirit of the Laws*, 1.364–65.

13. Addison and Steele, *The Spectator*, no. 495, September 27, 1712, 4:255.

14. Addison and Steele, *The Spectator*, no. 1, March 1, 1711, 1.4.

15. *The Connoisseur*, in *The British Essayists*, ed. James Ferguson (London: Barnard and Farley, 1819), 45 vols., no. 1, January 31, 1754, 30.1–2. In a clearly satiric reference to Addison and *The Spectator*, the connoisseur writes, "I am a Scotchman at Forrest's, a Frenchman at Slaughter's, and at the Cocoa-Tree I am—an Englishman" (no. 1, January 31, 1754, 30.6).

16. *Jackson's Oxford Journal*, no. 12 (1753): 3, quoted by R. J. Robson, *The Oxfordshire Election of 1754* (Oxford, 1949), p. 89.

17. Thomas W. Perry, *Public Opinion, Propaganda, and Politics in Eighteenth-Century*

England: A Study of the Jew Bill of 1753 (Cambridge, Mass.: Harvard University Press, 1961), has recently (and successfully, in my view) been challenged by Frank Felsenstein, *Anti-Semitic Stereotypes: A Paradigm of Otherness in English Popular Culture, 1660–1830* (Baltimore: Johns Hopkins University Press, 1995), and James Shapiro, *Shakespeare and the Jews* (New York: Columbia University Press, 1996), for underestimating the level of anti-Semitism in the clamor over the "Jew Bill."

18. *The Gentleman's Magazine*, October 1753, 23.484. Reprinted from *Gray's Inn Journal*, October 27, 1753.

19. *A Scotsman's Remarks on the Farce of "Love à la Mode"* (London, 1760), pp. 6–8.

20. Miles Peter Andrews, *Dissipation* (London: T. Becket, 1781), p. 17. This play was performed at Drury Lane frequently in 1781, twice in 1782, and once in 1783.

21. Richard Cumberland, *The Memoirs of Richard Cumberland*, ed. Richard J. Dircks (1807; rpt. New York: AMS Press, 2002), 2 vols., 2.143.

22. Richard Cumberland, *The Fashionable Lover* (London: W. Griffin, 1772), p. 37.

23. *The Merchant of Venice* was performed at the patent theaters every year from 1741 to 1761, 1764 to 1765, 1767 to 1790, 1792 to 1793, and 1795 to 1800.

24. Charles Macklin, *Love à la Mode*, in *Four Comedies by Charles Macklin*, ed. J. O. Bartley (London: Sidgwick and Jackson, 1968), p. 53; hereafter abbreviated *LM*.

25. Daniel Defoe, *The True-Born Englishman. A Satyr*, in *Selected Poetry and Prose of Daniel Defoe*, ed. Michael F. Shugrue (New York: Holt, Rinehart and Winston, 1968), p. 48.

26. *The Case of the Jews Considered, With Regard to Trade, Commerce, Manufacturies and Religion, &c.*, by a Christian (London, 1753), p. 10.

27. [Thomas Baker], *An Act at Oxford* (London: Bernard Lintott, 1704), p. 9. The play was performed at Drury Lane in 1705 under the title *Hampstead Heath*.

28. Addison and Steele, *The Spectator*, no. 380, May 16, 1712, 3.428.

29. *The Connoisseur*, no. 38, October 17, 1754, 30.203, in *The British Essayists*, ed. Ferguson.

30. Thomas Brown, *The fourth and last volume of the works of Mr. Thomas Brown*, 8th ed. (London, 1744), pp. 186–87.

31. *The Fair Refugee or The Rival Jews*, Larpent Collection, manuscript no. 651, Henry E. Huntington Library and Art Gallery, p. 32; hereafter abbreviated *FR*.

32. [Henry Fielding], *Miss Lucy in Town, A Sequel to The Virgin Unmasqued* (London: A. Millar, 1742), p. 16; hereafter abbreviated *MLT*. The play was performed frequently in 1742 and was revived in 1770.

33. Mrs. Holford, *Neither's the Man* (London: G. Sael, n.d.), p. 10; hereafter abbreviated *NM*.

34. John O'Keeffe, *The Young Quaker* (London: John Cumberland, n.d.), pp. 39–40. After its premiere in 1783, this play was performed almost yearly during the remainder of the century, and continued to be performed regularly well into the nineteenth century.

35. Roger Fiske, *English Theatre Music in the Eighteenth Century*, 2nd ed. (1973; Oxford:

Oxford University Press, 1986), p. 414. The play premiered in 1775 and was performed every year (except 1799) for the remainder of the century and well beyond.

36. *The Duenna*, in *The Dramatic Works of Richard Brinsley Sheridan*, 2 vols., ed. Cecil Price (Oxford: Clarendon Press, 1973), 1.254–55; hereafter vol. 1 is abbreviated *D*.

37. Todd M. Endelman, *The Jews of Georgian England, 1714–1830: Tradition and Change in a Liberal Society* (Philadelphia: Jewish Publication Society of America, 5739/1979), p. 266.

38. *In and Out of Tune*, Larpent Collection, manuscript no. 1541, Henry E. Huntington Library and Art Gallery, n.p.

39. Anon., *The Israelites; or, The Pampered Nabob*, reproduced in H. R. S. Van der Veen, *Jewish Characters in Eighteenth-Century English Fiction and Drama* (1935; rpt. New York: Ktav, 1973), p. 358. Once ascribed to Tobias Smollett, this play was performed at Covent Garden in 1785.

40. *A Scotsman's Remarks*, p. 10.

41. Cumberland, *The Fashionable Lover*, p. 6; hereafter abbreviated *FL*. The play was performed in 1772, 1773, 1774, 1775, 1778, 1786, and 1795.

42. Horace Walpole, letter to Lady Ossory, August 4, 1783, *The Yale Edition of Horace Walpole's Correspondence*, ed. W. S. Lewis, 48 vols. (New Haven: Yale University Press, 1937–83), 33.410–11.

43. Beating the Jew on stage became a common practice: in O'Keeffe's *The Young Quaker* the Jewish seducer is beaten and kicked around in the third act and is simply pushed off the stage in the fourth act, while the Irish servant in *The Fair Refugee*, on hearing that a rich Jew may come courting, remarks: "A Jew! Ooh! Let him take care we don't catch him here, or by my faith he'll stand a nasty chance of undergoing a good beating" (*FR*, 43).

44. Quoted from *Whitehall Evening Post* in Stanley Thomas Williams, *Richard Cumberland: His Life and Dramatic Works* (New Haven: Yale University Press, 1917), p. 96.

45. Richard Cumberland, *The Jew* (London: Longman, Hurst, Rees, and Orme, n.d.), p. 40; hereafter abbreviated *J*. This play was performed every year from 1794 through 1800; it continued to be popular at Drury Lane during the first decade of the nineteenth century and then was occasionally performed there through the 1820s.

46. Thomas Dibdin, *The Reminiscences of Thomas Dibdin* (London: Henry Colburn, 1827), 2 vols., 1.210.

47. Thomas Dibdin, *The Jew and the Doctor* (London: T. N. Longman and O. Rees, 1800), p. 2; hereafter abbreviated *JD*. This farce was performed frequently at Covent Garden in 1798 and continued to be popular at Covent Garden and the Haymarket in 1799 and 1800; it played intermittently over the next decade, being performed as late as 1839 at Drury Lane.

48. *The Israelites*, in Van der Veen, *Jewish Characters*, p. 370.

49. Thomas Dibdin, *The School for Prejudice* (London: T. N. Longman and O. Rees, 1801), p. 82; hereafter abbreviatd *SP*. This play was performed at Covent Garden in the

1800–1801, 1801–2, 1806–7, and 1807–8 seasons, at the Haymarket in 1805, and as late as 1814 at both Drury Lane and Covent Garden.

50. George Colman the Younger, *New Hay at the Old Market* (London: T. Cadell and W. Davies, 1795), p. 11. This prelude played frequently at the Haymarket in 1795, and then in 1796 twice at Drury Lane and once at the Haymarket.

51. Review of the second edition of *The Jew, Analytical Review*, vol. 18, December 1794, p. 437.

52. Review of the second edition of *The Jew, The Monthly Review*, vol. 16, February 1795, pp. 153–54.

53. "Jewish Predominance," signed "Ethnicus," in *Cobbett's Political Register*, September 6, 1806, pp. 404–5.

54. "Decay of the Drama," *Cobbett's Political Register*, June 12, 1830, p. 770.

55. R. E. Raspe, preface to his translation of Gotthold Lessing's *Nathan the Wise* (London: J. Fielding, 1781).

56. William Taylor, preface to his translation of Gotthold Lessing's *Nathan the Wise* (London: R. Philips, 1805).

57. "Observations and Strictures on the Characters of Shylock and Sheva," *The Monthly Visitor, and Entertaining Pocket Companion*, vol. 1, January 1797, pp. 49–55.

58. Review of the third edition of *The Jew, The British Critic*, vol. 6, July 1795, p. 11.

59. Review in *The Lady's Magazine*, quoted in Williams, *Richard Cumberland*, p. 236.

60. D—G, the anonymous author of the prefatory remarks to French's Standard Drama edition of *The Jew* (no. 425), quoted in Louis I. Newman, *Richard Cumberland: Critic and Friend of the Jews* (New York: Bloch, 1919), p. 40.

CHAPTER 4. "CIRCUMCISED GENTILES," ON STAGE AND OFF

1. Allardyce Nicoll, *A History of English Drama, 1660–1900* (Cambridge: Cambridge University Press, 1952), 6 vols., 3.19–21; James J. Lynch, *Box, Pit, and Gallery: Stage and Society in Johnson's London* (Berkeley: University of California Press, 1953), p. 226.

2. A reviewer for the *London Chronicle*, quoted by Lynch, *Box, Pit, and Gallery*, p. 226.

3. Arthur Murphy, *The Apprentice*, in *The Plays of Arthur Murphy*, ed. Richard B. Schwartz, 4 vols. (New York: Garland, 1979), 2.15.

4. Terry Castle, *Masquerade and Civilization: The Carnivalesque in Eighteenth-Century English Culture and Fiction* (Stanford, Calif.: Stanford University Press, 1986), p. 50.

5. *General Evening Post* (from Thursday, April 30, to Saturday, May 2, 1772).

6. *Gazetteer and New Daily Advertiser* (Saturday, June 21, 1777).

7. *General Evening Post* (from Saturday, May 2, to Tuesday, May 5, 1772).

8. *Morning Chronicle and London Advertiser* (Saturday, May 9, 1772).

9. *Morning Post and Daily Advertiser* (Saturday, June 21, 1777).

10. Joseph Addison and Richard Steele, *The Spectator*, ed. Donald F. Bond, 5 vols. (Oxford: Clarendon Press, 1965), no. 14, March 16, 1711, 1.63.

11. Maria Edgeworth, *Harrington*, in *Tales and Novels*, 10 vols. (New York: AMS Press, 1967), 9.10.

12. Jane Austen, *Mansfield Park*, ed. James Kinsley (Oxford: Oxford University Press, 1998), p. 111.

13. *The Spectator*, no. 1, March 1, 1711, 1.4.

14. For an excellent and detailed analysis of the Old Price riots, see Marc Baer, *Theatre and Disorder in Late Georgian London* (Oxford: Clarendon Press, 1992).

15. See *The Covent Garden Journal*, 2 vols. (London: J. J. Stockdale, 1810), 1.184, 1.182, 1.183, 1.190, 1.189, 1.196.

16. *The Covent Garden Journal*, 1.232.

17. *The Covent Garden Journal*, 1.187.

18. *Jackson's Oxford Journal*, December 28, 1753.

19. See *Hogarth's Graphic Works*, compiled and with a commentary by Ronald Paulson (New Haven: Yale University Press, 1965), 2 vols., 1.229.

20. Thomas W. Perry, *Public Opinion, Propaganda, and Politics in Eighteenth-Century England: A Study of the Jew Bill of 1753* (Cambridge, Mass.: Harvard University Press, 1962), pp. 74–75.

21. *The Covent Garden Journal*, 2.522. See Baer, *Theatre and Disorder*, p. 216.

22. *The Covent Garden Journal*, 1.213.

23. See Charles Lamb, "Imperfect Sympathies" (*Elia*, 1823), in *The Works of Charles and Mary Lamb*, ed. E. V. Lucas (New York: AMS Press, 1968), 5 vols., 2.62.

24. On these new developments in Anglo-Jewish culture, see the excellent study by Todd M. Endelman, *The Jews of Georgian England, 1714–1830* (Philadelphia: Jewish Publication Society of America, 5738/1979); on Gordon, Brothers, and the culture of conversion, see Michael Ragussis, *Figures of Conversion: "The Jewish Question" and English National Identity* (Durham: Duke University Press, 1995).

25. *Morning Chronicle and London Advertiser*, Tuesday, September 1, 1772.

26. *Morning Chronicle and London Advertiser*, Friday, February 27, 1798.

27. *Morning Chronicle and London Advertiser*, Saturday, May 9, 1772.

28. *The Connoisseur*, no. 1, Thursday, January 31, 1754, in James Ferguson, *The British Essayists* (London: Barnard and Farley, 1819), 45 vols., 30.1–2.

29. For a more comprehensive study (and reproduction) of these satirical prints, see Israel Solomons, "Satirical and Political Prints on the Jews' Naturalization Bill, 1753," *Transactions of the Jewish Historical Society of England* 6 (1912): 205–33. Also see the excellent analysis of some of these prints, and the anxiety over circumcision, in Frank Felsenstein, *Anti-Semitic Stereotypes: A Paradigm of Otherness in English Popular Culture, 1660–1830* (Baltimore: Johns Hopkins University Press, 1995), pp. 139–46 and 192–200.

30. *The Protester, on Behalf of the People*, "by Issachar Barebone, one of the People," 21.122.

31. *The Protester, on Behalf of the People*, 10.58.

32. See Endelman, *The Jews of Georgian England*, p. 11.

33. See Felsenstein, *Anti-Semitic Stereotypes*, pp. 207–9.

34. Page numbers in parentheses refer to George Colman the Younger, *Love Laughs at Locksmiths: A Musical Farce*, in *Lacy's Acting Edition of Plays* (London: Thomas Hailes Lacy, n.d.), vol. 94. This farce played frequently at the Haymarket in 1803 and after that played there intermittently, even as late as the 1820s, while playing at Covent Garden in the 1808–9 and 1814–15 seasons, and surfacing at the Grecian as late as 1847.

35. Page numbers in parentheses refer to Andrew Franklin, *The Wandering Jew; or, Love's Masquerade* (London: George Cawthorn, 1797). This play had eleven performances at Drury Lane in 1797 and three in 1798.

36. Page numbers in parentheses refer to Theodore Edward Hook, *The Invisible Girl* (London: C. and R. Baldwin, 1806). This play premiered at Drury Lane in 1806.

37. Page numbers in parentheses refer to William Thomas Moncrieff, *Rochester; or, King Charles the Second's Merry Days* (London: John Lowndes, 1819). This play premiered at the Olympic Theatre in 1818, and it continued to be revived during the Victorian period at Sadler's Wells in 1839, at the Olympic in 1842, at the Victoria in 1843, and at the Grecian in 1856.

38. Page numbers in parentheses refer to [John Allingham], *Transformation; or, Love and Law* (Baltimore: J. Robinson, 1814). This afterpiece premiered at the Lyceum in 1810, and was performed at least a dozen times that season.

39. Hannah Cowley, *The Belle's Stratagem* (London: Longman, Hurst, Rees, and Orme, n.d.), p. 44. This play was performed almost every year between 1780 and 1800, and it continued to be performed regularly through the opening decades of the nineteenth century.

40. Richard Brinsley Sheridan, *The School for Scandal*, in *The Dramatic Works of Richard Brinsley Sheridan*, 2 vols., ed. Cecil Price (Oxford: Clarendon Press, 1973), 1.389.

41. See Charles Beecher Hogan, *The London Stage, 1776–1800: A Critical Introduction* (Carbondale: Southern Illinois University Press, 1968), pp. clxxi–clxxii.

42. Other plays that used the trope of the cross-dressing Gentile include: Thomas Baker, *An Act at Oxford*; Aaron Hill, *The Walking Statue; or, the Devil in the Wine Cellar* (which was first performed in 1709 at Drury Lane but continued to be performed there through the 1730s and played at Covent Garden in 1745); James Kenney, *Ella Rosenberg* (1807), a rare example of a melodrama using the trope; Archibald McLaren, *The Tricks of London; or, Honesty the Best Policy* (published 1812); Joanna Baillie, *The Siege* (published 1812); Frederick Fox Cooper, *Hercules, King of Clubs* (which played at the Strand in 1836 and at Sadler's Wells in 1837, and which apparently copied from *The Walking Statue* a hero disguised as a Jew and a servant disguised as a statue).

CHAPTER 5. NOVEL PERFORMANCES AND "THE SLAVES OF ART"

1. See Katie Trumpener, *Bardic Nationalism: The Romantic Novel and the British Empire* (Princeton: Princeton University Press, 1997), for a brilliant analysis of the national tale and the historical novel. See Michael Ragussis, *Figures of Conversion: "The Jewish*

Question" and English National Identity (Durham: Duke University Press, 1995), for the ways in which the figure of the Jew functioned in scenes of conversion in the nineteenth-century British novel.

2. Edgar Johnson, *Sir Walter Scott: The Great Unknown* (New York: Macmillan, 1970), 2 vols., 1.322–26.

3. [Walter Scott], review of *Memoirs of the Life of John Philip Kemble, Esquire, Including a History of the Stage from the Time of Garrick to the Present Period*, by John Boaden, *Quarterly Review* 34 (June 1826): 196–248, p. 201.

4. Walter Scott, *The Lives of the Novelists* (1825; rpt. London: J. M. Dent, 1910), pp. 124–25, 132.

5. Richard Cumberland, *The Memoirs of Richard Cumberland*, ed. Richard J. Dircks, 2 vols. in 1 (1807; rpt. New York: AMS Press, 2002), 1.195.

6. Scott, *Lives of the Novelists*, p. 290.

7. *Lady Morgan's Memoirs: Autobiography, Diaries and Correspondence* (London: Wm. H. Allen, 1862), 2 vols., 1.59.

8. *Lady Morgan's Memoirs*, 1.61.

9. *Lady Morgan's Memoirs*, 1.41.

10. See Owenson's pamphlet defending the Irish stage, signed "S.O.," *A Few Reflections, Occasioned By the Perusal of a Work, Entitled, "Familiar Epistles, to Fredrick J-S, Esq., on the Present State of the Irish Stage"* (Dublin, 1804).

11. Henry Adelbert White, *Sir Walter Scott's Novels on the Stage* (New Haven: Yale University Press 1927), pp. 102–23.

12. See Thomas Dibdin, *Humphrey Clinker: A Farce* (London: John Cumberland, n.d.), pp. 26–27. The farce was first performed in 1818 at the Royal Circus, and later at Sadler's Wells Theatre in 1828.

13. Quoted from a letter to Fanny Robinson, September 15, 1783, in Marilyn Butler, *Maria Edgeworth: A Literary Biography* (Oxford: Clarendon Press, 1972), p. 151.

14. Mrs. Edgeworth, [Harriet Butler, and Lucy Robinson,] *Memoir of Maria Edgeworth*, with a selection from her letters, 3 vols. (privately printed, 1867), 1.170.

15. *The Life and Letters of Maria Edgeworth*, ed. Augustus J. C. Hare (Boston: Houghton Mifflin, 1895), 2 vols., 2.392–93.

16. Butler, *Maria Edgeworth*, p. 277.

17. [Jeffrey, Francis], review of *Tales of Fashionable Life*, *Edinburgh Review* 14, no. 28 (July 1809): 375–88, p. 380.

18. Maria Edgeworth, *The Absentee*, ed. W. J. McCormick and Kim Walker (Oxford: Oxford University Press, 1988), p. 51.

19. Edgeworth, *The Absentee*, p. 107.

20. Maria Edgeworth, *Belinda*, ed. Kathryn J. Kirkpatrick (Oxford: Oxford University Press, 1994), p. 3; hereafter abbreviated *B*.

21. See Owenson's preface to the 1835 edition of *O'Donnel*, where she explains, "'O'Donnel' was the first of a series of National Tales," *Colburn's Modern Novelists* (London, 1836), p. vii.

22. Sir Walter Scott, *Waverley; or, 'Tis Sixty Years Since*, ed. Claire Lamont (Oxford: Oxford University Press, 1998), pp. 3–4.

23. Jean-Jacques Rousseau, *Julie, or the New Heloise*, trans. Philip Stewart and Jean Vaché, in *The Collected Writings of Rousseau* (Hanover, N.H.: University Press of New England, 1997), p. 3.

24. Quoted in John Tinnon Taylor, *Early Opposition to the English Novel: The Popular Reaction from 1760 to 1830* (New York: King's Crown Press, 1943), p. 49.

25. Jean-Jacques Rousseau, *Letter to M. d'Alembert on the Theatre*, trans. Allan Bloom, in *Politics and the Arts* (Ithaca: Cornell University Press, 1960), pp. 16–17.

26. Quoted in Wylie Sypher, *Guinea's Captive Kings: British Anti-Slavery Literature of the XVIIIth Century* (Chapel Hill: University of North Carolina Press, 1942), p. 178.

27. Richard Cumberland, *The Fashionable Lover* (London: W. Griffin, 1772), pp. 44 and 52.

28. *In and Out of Tune*, Larpent Collection (LA #1541), Henry E. Huntington Library and Art Gallery, n.p.

29. Maria Edgeworth, *Harrington*, vol. 9 of *Tales and Novels* (New York: AMS Press, 1967), p. 3; hereafter abbreviated *H*.

30. Quoted in Taylor, *Early Opposition*, p. 69, from *Eclectic Review* (June 1812), p. 606.

31. Adam Smith, *The Theory of Moral Sentiments*, ed. D. D. Raphael and A. L. Macfie, in *The Glasgow Edition of the Works and Correspondence of Adam Smith* (Indianapolis: Liberty Fund, 1982), 6 vols., 1.9–10.

32. From the preface to a story written in 1779, quoted in Butler, *Maria Edgeworth*, p. 64.

33. Maria Edgeworth, *Ormond*, ed. Claire Connolly (London: Penguin, 2000), p. 62.

34. Maria and R. L. Edgeworth, *Practical Education* (1801; rpt. Poole: Woodstock Books, 1996), 3 vols., 2.91, 2.2.

35. See Earl Wasserman, "The Sympathetic Imagination in Eighteenth-Century Theories of Acting," *Journal of English and Germanic Philology*, 46, no. 3 (July 1947): 264–72.

36. Letter to Miss Ruxton, December 26, 1814, *Memoir of Maria Edgeworth*, 1.310.

37. Letter to Mrs. Stark, September 6, 1834, *Memoir of Maria Edgeworth*, 3.152.

38. Maria Edgeworth, *Castle Rackrent*, ed. George Watson (Oxford: Oxford University Press, 1995), p. 4.

39. See *The Education of the Heart: The Correspondence of Rachel Mordecai Lazarus and Maria Edgeworth*, ed. Edgar E. MacDonald (Chapel Hill: University of North Carolina Press, 1977).

CHAPTER 6. "FOR OUR ENGLISH EYES"

1. On cross-ethnic and cross-racial romantic plots as the foundation for hybrid national cultures, see Michael Ragussis, *Figures of Conversion: "The Jewish Question" and English National Identity* (Durham: Duke University Press, 1995), especially chapters 3 and 4, and Katie Trumpener, *Bardic Nationalism: The Romantic Novel and the British Empire* (Princeton: Princeton University Press, 1997), especially chapter 3.

2. See James Buzard, "Translation and Tourism: Scott's *Waverley* and the Rendering of Culture," in *Yale Journal of Criticism* 8, no. 2 (Fall 1995): 31–59, on Edward Waverley as a kind of ethnographer (pp. 38–40).

3. Sydney Owenson, *The Wild Irish Girl: A National Tale*, ed. Kathryn Kirkpatrick (Oxford: Oxford University Press, 1999), p. 13; hereafter abbreviated *WIG*.

4. See Joep Leerssen, *Remembrance and Imagination: Patterns in the Historical and Literary Representation of Ireland in the Nineteenth Century* (Cork: Cork University Press, 1996), pp. 33–35, for Leerssen's explanation of how the "paradoxical dissociation of the Irish author from his/her Irish subject matter" (p. 34) is realized in these novelists' use of a first-person English narrator.

5. Mary Campbell, *Lady Morgan: The Life and Times of Sydney Owenson* (London: Pandora, 1988), p. 94.

6. Helen M. Burke, *Riotous Performance: The Struggle for Hegemony in the Irish Theater, 1712–1784* (Notre Dame: University of Notre Dame Press, 2003), p. 264.

7. See the fine discussion of the harp as a symbol of cultural and political nationalism (even adopted by the United Irishmen as their badge) in late eighteenth-century Ireland in Trumpener, *Bardic Nationalism*, pp. 4–11.

8. See Ina Ferris, *Romantic National Tale and the Question of Ireland* (Cambridge: Cambridge University Press, 2002), for a different reading, arguing that the hero is jolted "out of the controlling spectatorship of the detached gaze into the proximity and implication of response" (p. 59) because of the novel's validation of sound over sight (pp. 62–63).

9. On the issue of translation in the national tale, see Ina Ferris, "Translation from the Borders: Encounter and Recalcitrance in *Waverley* and *Clan-Albin*," *Eighteenth-Century Fiction* 9, no. 2 (January 1997): 203–22, in which she explains that "the genre is marked by a dense textuality and tends to thematize the problem of translation itself, so blocking any sense of transparent access to the represented culture" (pp. 208–9). Also see Leerssen, who argues that "Ireland as a representadum, as subject-matter, does not speak in its own voice but is spoken for" (*Remembrance*, p. 35).

10. Maria Edgeworth, *Castle Rackrent*, ed. George Watson (Oxford: Oxford University Press, 1995), p. 4.

11. Maria Edgeworth, *The Absentee*, ed. W. J. McCormick and Kim Walker (Oxford: Oxford University Press, 1988), p. 104.

12. What Ian Duncan, in *Modern Romance and Transformations of the Novel: The Gothic, Scott, Dickens* (Cambridge: Cambridge University Press, 1992), claims about Wa-

verley's tour of Scotland seems perhaps even truer of what I am claiming about Horatio's aestheticization and commodification of Glorvina for his English reader: "Tourism means visiting a scene, moving across it, above all *being in it without belonging to it*. A historical relationship to a place is replaced with an aesthetic and commodified one" (p. 89).

13. For a different view of the role of Rousseau's novel in Owenson's novel, see Nicola Watson, *Revolution and the Form of the British Novel, 1790–1825: Intercepted Letters, Interrupted Seductions* (Oxford: Clarendon Press, 1994), pp. 112–15.

14. Quoted in Campbell, *Lady Morgan*, p. 87.

15. See Nicholas Robinson, "Marriage Against Inclination: The Union and Caricature," in *Acts of Union: The Causes, Contexts and Consequences of the Act of Union*, ed. Daire Keogh and Kevin Whelan (Dublin: Four Courts Press, 2001), pp. 145–58, for prints that picture the violated Hibernia carried off as a prize by William Pitt the Younger and laying charges against Pitt for rape. In other prints she is shown as the weeping and reluctant partner of the Union, submitting against her will to union with John Bull. Also see *The Life and Letters of Maria Edgeworth*, ed. Augustus J. C. Hare (Boston: Houghton Mifflin, 1895), 2 vols., 1.68.

16. See the excellent discussion of the way in which "the marriage plot in these novels functions as an imperial family plot as well, constructing Ireland as a complementary but ever unequal partner in the family of Great Britain," in Mary Jean Corbett, *Allegories of Union in Irish and English Writing, 1790–1870: Politics, History, and the Family from Edgeworth to Arnold* (Cambridge: Cambridge University Press, 2000), p. 53. See Ragussis, *Figures of Conversion*, for an explanation of the ways in which the racialized daughter functioned in symbolic plots of nation-building (especially chapters 3 and 4).

17. The letter at the end of *The Absentee*, for example, is quoted in its entirety by Francis Jeffrey in his review of the novel, and he ends with: "She . . . makes us know and love the Irish nation far better than any other writer" (*Edinburgh Review* 20, no. 39 [July 1812], p. 126).

18. Sir Walter Scott, *Waverley; or, 'Tis Sixty Years Since*, ed. Claire Lamont (Oxford: Oxford University Press, 1998), p. 17; hereafter abbreviated as *W*.

19. See Watson's fine analysis of Waverley's misreading in *Revolution*, pp. 128–35.

20. On the idea of the performing heroine, see Ellen Moers, *Literary Women* (1963; rpt. London: Women's Press, 1986), chapter 9, "Performing Heroinism: The Myth of Corinne"; Ferris, *Romantic National Tale*, p. 77.

21. Jane Austen, *Mansfield Park*, ed. James Kinsely (Oxford: Oxford University Press, 1998), p. 306.

22. See Emma Letley, *From Galt to Douglas Brown: Nineteenth-Century Fiction and Scots Language* (Edinburgh: Scottish Academic Press, 1988), p. 13.

23. Maria Edgeworth, Letter to the Author of Waverley, October 23, 1814, in Mrs. Edgeworth [Harriet Butler, and Lucy Robinson], *Memoir of Maria Edgeworth*, with a selection from her letters, 3 vols. (privately printed, 1867), 1.305.

24. See historian Daniel Szechi's explanation of the theatricality of Jacobites' dying

declarations in "The Jacobite Theatre of Death," *The Jacobite Challenge*, ed. Eveline Cruickshanks and Jeremy Black (Edinburgh: John Donald, 1988), pp. 57–73.

25. Madame de Staël, *Corinne, or Italy*, trans. Avriel H. Goldberger (New Brunswick: Rutgers University Press, 1991), p. 87; hereafter abbreviated *C*. While technically a Scot, Oswald, Lord Nelvil is consistently rendered as representing English values.

26. George Eliot, *Daniel Deronda*, ed. Barbara Hardy (London: Penguin, 1986), p. 228.

27. Maria and R. L. Edgeworth, *Practical Education* (1801; rpt. Poole: Woodstock Books, 1996), 3 vols., 2.107.

28. Oscar Wilde, *The Picture of Dorian Gray*, ed. Isobel Murray (Oxford: Oxford University Press, 1981), p. 39.

29. Jean-Jacques Rousseau, *Letter to M. d'Alembert on the Theatre*, trans. Allan Bloom, in *Politics and the Arts* (Ithaca: Cornell University Press, 1960), p. 25.

30. Denis Diderot, *The Paradox of Acting*, trans. W. H. Pollock, in *The Paradox of Acting and Masks or Faces?* (New York: Hill and Wang, 1957), pp. 20 and 23.

31. Edmund Burke, *Reflections on the Revolution in France*, ed. L. G. Mitchell (Oxford: Oxford University Press, 1993), p. 81.

32. Mary Wollstonecraft, *A Vindication of the Rights of Men, A Vindication of the Rights of Woman, An Historical and Moral View of the French Revolution*, ed. Janet Todd (Oxford: Oxford University Press, 1999), p. 14.

33. Thomas Paine, *The Rights of Man, Common Sense, and Other Political Writings*, ed. Mark Philip (Oxford: Oxford University Press, 1998), pp. 102, 110, 110, and 100.

34. "The Discourse of Rousseau which has most struck me, is that against the establishment of public spectacles at Geneva," Baroness de Staël, *Letters on the Works and Character of J. J. Rousseau* (London, 1789), p. 13. This work appeared originally in French in 1788.

35. *Edinburgh Review* 21, no. 41 (February 1813): 1–2. Translations of Staël's work into English appeared quickly and regularly, and her work was reviewed regularly in the major periodicals. As Edgeworth wrote about Staël's arrival in England in 1813, "The Edinburgh review of her book has well prepared all the world for her" (ed. Hare, *Life and Letters*, 1.218).

36. "Theatrical Intelligence," *London Chronicle*, October 10–12, 1782, p. 355.

37. Quoted in Edgar Johnson, *Sir Walter Scott: The Great Unknown*, 2 vols. (New York: Macmillan, 1970), 1.324.

38. William Hazlitt, *The Selected Writings of William Hazlitt*, ed. Duncan Wu, 9 vols. (London: Pickering and Chatto, 1998), 3.144.

39. James Boaden, *Memoirs of Mrs. Siddons*, 2nd ed., 2 vols. (London: Henry Colburn and Richard Bentley, 1831), 2.277–78.

40. In *The Novels and Selected Works of Maria Edgeworth* (London: Pickering and Chatto, 1999), 12 vols., see the introductions to volume 3 (ed. Marilyn Butler and Susan Manly, pp. ix–xii) and volume 9 (ed. Susan Manly and Cliona OGallchoir, p. ix).

41. Edgeworth, Letter to Miss Ruxton (April 1808), in ed. Hare, *Life and Letters*, 1.164–65.

42. Heinrich Heine, *Shakespeare's Maidens and Women*, in *The Works of Heinrich Heine*, 8 vols., ed. Charles Godfrey Leland (London: William Heinemann, 1892), 1.258; hereafter abbreviated *HH*.

EPILOGUE

1. Irish playwrights, for instance, continued the work of deconstructing the stage Irishman even while reproducing other ethnic and national caricatures. See Richard Allen Cave's excellent essay "Staging the Irishman," in *Acts of Supremacy: The British Empire and the Stage, 1790–1930*, ed. J. S. Bratton (Manchester: Manchester University Press, 1991).

2. Michael Ragussis, *Figures of Conversion: "The Jewish Question" and English National Identity* (Durham: Duke University Press, 1995), especially chapters 3 and 4.

3. See Donald Mullin, *Victorian Plays: A Record of Significant Productions on the London Stage, 1837–1901* (New York: Greenwood Press, 1987).

4. See Jacky Bratton, *New Readings in Theatre History* (Cambridge: Cambridge University Press, 2003), for a fine account of theater historiography in the Georgian and Victorian periods.

5. Neil McKendrick, John Brewer, and J. H. Plumb, *The Birth of a Consumer Society: The Commercialization of Eighteenth-Century England* (Bloomington: Indiana University Press, 1982), p. 272.

6. The many multivolume editions that were produced include *Bell's British Theatre* (1776–1797); *Sharpe's British Theatre* (1804–1805); Mrs. Inchbald's *The British Theatre* (1800–1815); Thomas Dibdin's *The London Theatre* (1815–1825); *Cumberland's British Theater* (1826–1863).

7. Elisabeth Inglis-Jones, *The Great Maria: A Portrait of Maria Edgeworth* (London: Faber and Faber, 1959), p. 86.

8. Toby Lelyveld, in *Shylock on the Stage* (London: Routledge and Kegan Paul, 1961), claims that *The Jew and the Doctor* was a "stage favorite in the '40s" (p. 58).

9. John Forster, *The Life of Charles Dickens* (London: J. M. Dent, 1929), 2 vols., 1.11.

10. *The Letters of Charles Dickens*, 12 vols., ed. Madeline House and Graham Storey (Oxford: Clarendon Press, 1965–2002), 5.114.

11. Harry Stone, "Dickens and the Jews," *Victorian Studies* 2 (March 1959): 223-253, notes Dickens's use of Dibdin's farce in *Our Mutual Friend* (p. 247).

12. James Picciotto, *Sketches of Anglo-Jewish History*, rev. and ed. Israel Finestein (London: Soncino Press, 1956), p. xiv.

13. Picciotto, *Sketches*, p. 230.

14. Picciotto, *Sketches*, p. 229.

15. See Jonathan Bate, *Shakespearean Constitutions: Politics, Theatre, Criticism, 1730–1830* (Oxford: Clarendon Press, 1989), p. 181, and Richard Hole, "An Apology for the

Character and Conduct of Shylock," *Essays by a Society of Gentlemen, at Exeter*, 2 vols. (Exeter, 1796).

16. William Hazlitt, *Characters of Shakespear's Plays* (1817), in *The Selected Writings of William Hazlitt*, ed. Duncan Wu, 9 vols. (London: Pickering and Chatto, 1998), 1.228.

17. William Hazlitt, *A View of the English Stage* (1818), in *Selected Writings*, 3.128.

18. See John Tobin, *The Faro Table; or, The Guardians* (London: John Murray, 1816): "I am not the only one who wears the heart of a Christian under the habit of a Jew" (p. 49). Also see William Macready, *The Irishman in London; or, The Happy African* (New York: Longworth, 1809): "If her face was but as white as her heart, she'd be a wife for a pope" (p. 31). [Edward Long], *The History of Jamaica*, 2 vols. (New York: Arno Press, 1972), reports that Francis Williams "defined himself 'a *white* man acting under a black *skin*'" (2.478).

19. Mullin, *Victorian Plays*, p. 197. See Edward D. Coleman, *The Jew in English Drama: An Annotated Bibliography* (1943; rpt. New York: New York Public Library and Ktav, 1968), pp. 94–95, for various adaptations of *Deborah* using a variety of titles through the 1890s. On Bernhardt as Leah, see Janis Bergman-Carton, "Negotiating the Categories: Sarah Bernhardt and the Possibilities of Jewishness," *Art Journal* 55, no. 2 (Summer 1996): 60–63.

20. "Dr. Mosenthal," *Theatre* 1, no. 5 (February 1877), p. 53; "Some Recent Dramatic Successes," *Bentley's Miscellany* 55 (January 1864), p. 71.

21. George Henry Lewes's Journal, London, February 8, 1864, reprinted in *The George Eliot Letters*, ed. Gordon S. Haight, 9 vols. (New Haven: Yale University Press, 1954–78), 4.132.

22. George Eliot, *Daniel Deronda*, p. 877. Mirah is haunted by the idea of being forsaken (pp. 231, 253, 264), but once she is rescued by Deronda she recognizes, "I was not forsaken" (p. 264), while Gwendolen uses the term to describe herself (pp. 258 and 839).

23. Colin Holmes, *Anti-Semitism in British Society, 1876–1939* (New York: Holmes and Meier, 1979), remains the best general guide to the topic.

24. W. H. Wilkins, *The Alien Invasion* (London: Methuen, 1892), p. 102. Also see W. Cunningham, *Alien Immigrants to England* (1897), and Arnold White, *The Problems of a Great City* (1886).

25. Charles Kensington Salaman, *Jews as They Are* (London: Simpkin, Marchall, 1882), p. 3.

26. *Punch*, November 16, 1895, p. 232. See George Taylor, "Svengali: Mesmerist and Aesthete," in *British Theatre in the 1890s: Essays on Drama and the Stage* (Cambridge: Cambridge University Press, 1993), ed. Richard Foulkes, p. 108, and Shearer West, "The Construction of Racial Type: Caricature, Ethnography, and Jewish Physiognomy in Fin-de-Siècle Melodrama," *Nineteenth Century Theatre* 21, no. 1 (Summer 1993): 27–29.

27. George du Maurier, *Trilby* (Oxford: Oxford University Press, 1998), p. 5; hereafter abbreviated *T.*

28. These quotations are from *Richard Wagner's Prose Works*, trans. William Ashton Ellis (London: Kegan Paul, Trench, Trubner, 1894), 8 vols., 3.85, 3.87, and 3.82, respectively.

29. Oscar Wilde, *The Picture of Dorian Gray*, ed. Isobel Murray (Oxford: Oxford University Press, 1981), p. 80; hereafter abbreviated *DG*.

30. Henry James, *The Tragic Muse*, ed. Philip Horne (London: Penguin, 1995), p. 49; hereafter abbreviated *TM*.

31. Henry James, "Frances Anne Kemble," in *Essays in London and Elsewhere* (London: James R. Osgood, McIlvaine, 1893), p. 89.

32. *Richard Wagner's Prose Works*, 3.89.

33. Jonas Barish, *The Antitheatrical Prejudice* (Berkeley: University of California Press, 1985), p. 465.

34. Friedrich Nietzsche, *The Gay Science*, trans. Walter Kaufmann (New York: Random House, 1974), p. 317.

35. Lucien Wolf, "Astley's Jews," *Jewish Chronicle*, May 26, 1893, p. 13.

36. "Mr. Beerbohm-Tree on the Drama," *The Era*, November 19, 1892. There is no evidence that either Kean or the Kembles were Jewish, but Kean's sympathetic portrayal of Shylock opened him to the accusation (Lelyveld, *Shylock on the Stage*, p. 53), while John Philip Kemble's hiring of Jewish pugilists during the Old Price riots of 1809 secured his representation as a Jew (see my chapter 4). Meanwhile, Tree begins the speech I quote by evading the question of whether or not he is Jewish. In *Thoughts and After-Thoughts* (New York: Funk and Wagnall, 1913), Tree claimed that "the Jews . . . are perhaps the most dominant race in the world to-day" (p. 29), and that "most good actors have either Irish or Jewish blood" (p. 102).

37. For example, provincial and colonial theaters produced many of the plays under discussion in this book: Errol Hill, *The Jamaican Stage, 1655–1900: Profile of a Colonial Theatre* (Amherst: University of Massachusetts Press, 1992), records productions of such plays as *Leah* and *The Jewess* as well as *The Jew* and *The Jew and the Doctor* (pp. 80, 88, 109–11); and *Theatre Royal Bath: A Calendar of Performances at the Orchard Street Theatre, 1750–1805*, ed. Arnold Hare (Bath: Kingsmead Press, 1977), records productions of such plays as *Love à la Mode, Love Laughs at Locksmiths, The Oxonian in Town, Transformation, The Walking Statue, The Wandering Jew, The West Indian*, and *The Young Quaker*; *The Yorkshire Stage, 1766–1803: A Calendar of Plays*, ed. Linda Fitzsimmons and Arthur W. McDonald (Metuchen, N.J.: Scarecrow Press, 1989), records productions of such plays as *Love à la Mode, Dissipation, Family Quarrels, The Honest Yorkshireman, The Jew and the Doctor*, and *The Fashionable Lover*. But we have almost no analysis of the nature of the performances and the reactions of audiences.

INDEX

ACKNOWLEDGMENTS

This book bears my name as sole author, but it was produced with the assistance of many people and institutions. Generous grants from the National Endowment for the Humanities, the American Council of Learned Societies, and Georgetown University provided me with extended and uninterrupted periods of time without which this book never could have been written. Librarians and curators at the Library of Congress, the Library of the Jewish Theological Seminary, the Harvard Theatre Collection (Houghton Library), the New York Public Library, the Huntington Library, and the Folger Shakespeare Library aided me in doing the archival research that forms the basis of this book. And my time spent working with the staff of the University of Pennsylvania Press, most notably with the Senior Humanities Editor Jerome Singerman, has been unusually happy. Over the years I benefited, while still rethinking the argument of this book, from congenial and stimulating audiences at Princeton, Johns Hopkins, Harvard, and the University of California at Los Angeles. I owe a special debt of thanks to colleagues and friends Patrick O'Malley, John Glavin, Paul Betz, Lindsay Kaplan, Donna Even-Kesef, Jill Hollingsworth, and Gerry Mara, who helped me in numerous ways.

My last acknowledgment is of the first importance: Susan Lanser and I have been engaged in an enduring collaboration that has lasted over the course of our adult lives, so I thank her for what has been a lifetime of support and exchange, personal and professional.

Earlier versions of portions of this book appeared in *Critical Inquiry* 26 (Summer 2000) and *The Jews and British Romanticism: Politics, Religion, Culture*, ed. Sheila A. Spector (New York: Palgrave Macmillan, 2005).